"A key factor in improving the competitive position of the United States in the global economy will be the broader use of intelligence in the private sector. By explaining how businesses can use intelligence techniques legally and ethically, Larry Kahaner's *Competitive Intelligence* makes an important contribution to our nation's future economic strength"
— U.S. Representative Anthony C. Beilenson, Former Chairman,
Permanent Select Committee on Intelligence

"Conversational, highly accessible. . . . The smart snooper's bible."
— *Publishers Weekly*

"Anyone who reads this book and is not convinced of the critical importance of competitive intelligence should not occupy a position of importance in the modern business world. . . . Required reading for everyone who has ever said: 'Nothing goes on in this industry that I don't already know about.' . . . Aimed at general business readers, telling them who does what and how well they do it—naming names. And therein lies its strength."
— *Competitive Intelligence Review*

"Politicians on both sides of the aisle have long used competitive intelligence as a key to winning elections. Now, Larry Kahaner has provided business leaders with a primer on how to use the same techniques. *Competitive Intelligence* is a book no 'war room' should be without."
— Howard Paster, Chairman and CEO, Hill and Knowlton and
Former Assistant to President Clinton

"You need to know what competitors know and what they know you know. You need to know what's in *Competitive Intelligence*."
— Barry Nalebuff, Yale School of Management and author
of *Co-Opetition*

"Kahaner's book should be required reading at America's business schools. Without question the single best book for helping managers and executives appreciate the critical importance of CI for corporate survival and success."
— William C. Boni, Associate Director, Amgen

"This book provides a detailed method to win over business competitors using information collected through legal and ethical means. . . . Information

is the strongest weapon in the global economic competition, and national prosperity depends upon the use of competitive intelligence as an effective tool for corporate strategy."
—Kosei Tashiro, Chairman, Japan Investigative Services Association

"Larry Kahaner turns a sea of information into a firehouse of opportunity."
—Vint Cerf, President, The Internet Society

"A highly entertaining and valuable account on the secret art of information espionage."
—*Consultants News*

"Tailor made for your CEO's bedtime reading."
—*Profiles Magazine*

"Marketing intelligence—long the jealously guarded province of marketing and promotion companies—enters the public domain with Larry Kahaner's *Competitive Intelligence.*"
—John Zweig, CEO, Specialist Communications,
WPP Group USA, Inc.

"For those business leaders challenged to excel, Kahaner explains in everyday language what competitive intelligence is, why you must have it, and how to develop it."
—E. Peter Earnest, President, Association of Former
Intelligence Officers

"This book brilliantly demonstrates the impact of competitive intelligence on revenues, and ultimately a company's success in the marketplace."
—Svetlana Shaknes, Manager, Competitive Intelligence,
American Express

"*Competitive Intelligence* elucidates why companies need to develop effective intelligence programs—and how to do it. Highly recommended reading."
—Mark Dingle, Senior Business Consultant, Bristol-Myers Squibb

"Finally, a clearly articulated approach to analyzing the competition and a fresh perspective on investment analysis."
—Steve McMenamin, Director of Equity Research, Cantor Fitzgerald

"A first class introduction to the art and practice of competitive intelligence. Kahaner explains how firms use competitive intelligence in all aspects of business—from mergers and acquisitions to marketing—to gain real competitive advantage, and he describes the organisational system that makes it possible. The chapter on analysis alone is easily worth the price of the book."
—Douglas C. Bernhardt, Managing Consultant, Business Research
Group, Geneva, Switzerland

COMPETITIVE INTELLIGENCE

**HOW TO GATHER,
ANALYZE, AND USE
INFORMATION TO MOVE
YOUR BUSINESS TO
THE TOP**

Larry Kahaner

A TOUCHSTONE BOOK

Published by Simon & Schuster

TOUCHSTONE
Rockefeller Center
1230 Avenue of the Americas
New York, NY 10020

Copyright © 1996 by KANE Associates International, Inc.
All rights reserved,
including the right of reproduction
in whole or in part in any form.

First Touchstone Edition 1997

TOUCHSTONE and colophon are registered trademarks
of Simon & Schuster Inc.

Designed by Levavi & Levavi

Manufactured in the United States of America

10   9

The Library of Congress has cataloged the Simon & Schuster edition as follows:
   Kahaner, Larry
      Competitive intelligence : how to gather, analyze, and use information to move
   your business to the top
   Larry Kahaner
         p.   cm.
      Includes index.
      1. Business intelligence.   I. Title.
   HD38.7.K339   1996
      658.4'7—dc20   95-26837   CIP
   ISBN-13: 978-0-684-81074-4
   ISBN-10:   0-684-81074-3
   ISBN-13: 978-0-684-84404-6 (Pbk.)
   ISBN-10:   0-684-84404-4 (Pbk.)

Contents

Part Three: Issues, Opportunities, and the Future

Being a Hero
and Not a Bum

"What enables the wise sovereign and the good general to strike and conquer, and achieve things beyond the reach of ordinary men, is foreknowledge."
—Sun Tzu, *The Art of War*

While reporting for *Business Week* magazine in Washington during the early 1980s, I covered the telecommunications industry during its greatest time of change. There was the divestiture of AT&T, the growth of the competitive long-distance industry, and the upheaval that followed from burgeoning technologies like cellular phones, nationwide paging, cable TV, and satellite communications. It's only now that I realize I was one of the first people in Washington to use a cellular phone. Motorola let me try one for a day—until the batteries ran out—during their Washington, D.C., trial. I remember the curious looks I got from people who saw me walking down the street with this weighty, brick-shaped telephone against my ear.

It was an exciting time and one of the best parts was getting to know many decision makers at innovative corporations during the course of my work.

I relished the chats I used to have with people like Bill McGowan, the late chairman and CEO of MCI, the person responsible for much of the upheaval that I was covering. McGowan was a clear and elegant thinker, and I enjoyed talking with him. His take on subjects was often outlandish but businesslike nonetheless. He possessed the ability to see through clutter and come up with simple solutions to complex problems. It was easy to be distracted and disarmed by his eccentric, flamboyant demeanor, which hid an orderly, analytical mind.

I had traveled with McGowan on the company's jet and looked in awe at his reading pile, or should I say mountain. On the seat next to him were stacks of magazines, newspapers, and catalogues. There were trade magazines and industry newsletters; I expected these. But there were also things I didn't expect like the *National Enquirer*, the *Racing Form*, the J.C. Whitney (automotive) catalogue, *Good House-keeping*, and newspapers from small towns whose names I can't recall. The newspapers were usually only four pages long.

It was a joke in the company that McGowan traveled with two suitcases—one for his clothes and one for his reading material.

McGowan didn't have any hobbies or interests that would account for this wide array of reading materials. In fact, he was a workaholic with little time for any outside activities beyond building his company. I was perplexed by his odd choices in reading.

I got to know McGowan better when I wrote a book about MCI called *On the Line,* which was published in 1986. One of my reasons for writing the book was to understand how a company as small as MCI could not only beat Ma Bell, but go on to create an entire new industry. My other reason was to understand how companies compete and how the people in those companies increase their company's competitive advantage.

After all, companies don't compete; *people* in companies compete.

Journalists are lucky. We have the most latitude of almost anyone to ask questions of people at all levels of society. The questions can be simple and naive or they can be in-depth and cutting. Sometimes, they can be both.

One day I asked McGowan: "What's the essence of your job?"

Without hesitation he said: "Making decisions. If I make the right decision, I'm a hero. If I make the wrong decision, I'm a bum."

"How do you make decisions?"

"I gather as much information as I can, from as many places as I can, I think about it, then I decide what to do."

That's why he read so much of everything. It was his way of turning information into usable intelligence.

Now, many published books and hundreds of interviews later, I still remember what McGowan said about the crux of being a manager, about making the right decisions.

The secret to business success is no secret at all.

If you make the right decisions you will succeed. If you make the wrong decisions, you will fail.

You'll either be a hero or a bum.

This book is about making the right decisions. It's about a business system for making decisions that has been hidden in some companies—highly successful companies—for years because nobody wanted to talk about it openly. Why? Because others may think it's unethical and shady.

It's about a discipline that is growing steadily every day, but few companies want to discuss it for a different reason. They understand its power, and they don't want their competitors to know about it.

Interestingly, though, a few companies *will* discuss it. They're certain that even if others know about it, they will still perform better. That's the nature of this tool. The same basic techniques and information are out there for anyone to use—if they have the brains, motivation, and the skills to do so.

This book is about managers having a better way to make decisions, and not having to spend enormous amounts of time—like McGowan did—reading everything in sight to do so.

I will show you the new world of competitive intelligence. You will learn how companies efficiently, systematically, and economically collect information, analyze it, and use it to make decisions. It's about how intelligence—not simply information as most people believe—can flow through your company for the benefit of everyone. It's about beating your competitors both here and abroad and never being surprised or blindsided by their actions or other outside events again.

Above all, this book is about being a hero . . . and not being a bum.

"Knowledge is power."
　　　　　—Francis Bacon

"If a little knowledge is dangerous, where is the man who has so much to be out of danger."
　　　　　—Thomas Henry Huxley

PART ONE

What Is Competitive Intelligence?

CHAPTER ONE

The Rise of Competitive Intelligence

"It is pardonable to be defeated, but never to be surprised."
—Frederick the Great

In today's business environment, having the right information is not enough anymore.

In a world where competitors are fiercer than ever, rapidly changing technologies alter the rules of the game daily and one wrong business move can destroy your company, managers are seeking new ways to make decisions.

Many managers believe that information is the key. They think that if they have enough information, they will make the right decision.

Nothing could be further from the truth.

As you will see, information is merely the starting point of the decision-making process and not the end. And while the quality of your information is important, what you do with it—how you analyze and then use it—is much more important.

Turning raw information and data into actionable intelligence is fast becoming the most critical management tool of cutting-edge business leaders.

For them and other forward-thinking, successful managers, the age of information is over and the age of intelligence has begun.

The process these people use to turn information into intelligence and enter the age of intelligence is called Competitive Intelligence. Adapted from techniques used by political and military intelligence agencies during the Cold War era, competitive intelligence is a simple four-step process that ultimately can make or break companies of any size, in any business.

What is competitive intelligence?

Competitive intelligence is a systematic program for gathering and analyzing information about your competitors' activities and general business trends to further your own company's goals.

When practiced responsibly it's legal and ethical, although some companies have been known to cross the line—stealing information, wiretapping phones, and burglarizing offices—entering the darker realm of the world of industrial espionage.

Most companies don't enter this illegal world. In fact, it's unnecessary. Virtually everything they need to know is available, albeit sometimes purposely hidden or hard to find. These experts gather information by employing the latest technology and ingenious methods, including satellite photoreconnaissance, combing government databases, filing Freedom of Information Act requests, back-engineering, and even hiring psychiatrists to analyze a competitor's decision makers. Companies often employ super-speed computers designed specifically for analyzing mountains of data.

These skilled corporate agents ferret out information from the most unlikely of places and transform it into intelligence that can turn their company around, build market share, launch new products, or destroy a competitor. It's a hardball world that turns raw data into millions of dollars if done well. If done poorly, their own company might perish as a result of their miscalculations.

Competitive intelligence is relatively new and as yet undeveloped among the majority of U.S. companies. Less than 7 percent of large American companies have their own full-blown competitive intelligence divisions and most of these are relatively new. Eighty percent are less than five years old.

Japanese companies, by contrast, have had well-established competitive intelligence systems in place since World War II, although their economic intelligence-gathering history goes back many centuries. Their current competitive intelligence infrastructure includes trading companies (*sogo shosha*) and government agencies that place operatives around the world to collect information and funnel it to huge depositories in Japan for use by company decision makers.

Mitsubishi, for example, has about thirteen thousand employees in more than two hundred offices worldwide. They collect more than thirty thousand pieces of business and competitive information *daily*. This data is filtered, analyzed, and disseminated to companies within the Mitsubishi family to be used as ammunition in the ongoing global war against competitors.

In Europe, the situation is somewhat similar in that government agencies also have taken an active interest in competitive intelligence. In Germany, the state-run banks play a large role in running businesses and therefore want to protect their investments. The banks have traditionally used their power and influence to collect confidential information about foreign companies and quietly disseminate it to German companies.

In France, the government works with companies more covertly—often illegally by American standards—to collect information about foreign competitors. Between 1987 and 1989, a twenty-person branch of the Direction Générale de la Sécurité Extérieure (DGSE), France's equivalent of the CIA, spied on companies like IBM and Texas Instruments and turned information over to their French competitors. The former head, Pierre Marion, said: "It would not be normal that we spy on the United States in political matters or in military matters. We are allied, but in the economic competition, in the technological competition, we are competitors. We are not allied."

Competitive intelligence has become the latest weapon in the world war of economics, which pits nation against nation. While the major powers are moving away from traditional weapons of destruction, they are moving toward economic weapons like competitive intelligence to ensure their national sovereignty and survival.

Many of the emerging economies such as China, Vietnam, Korea, and Thailand see competitive intelligence as a way to win economic wars against larger, more industrialized countries. By using their wits instead of weapons, these countries are able to turn raw information into usable intelligence to further their economic status in the world market.

Although the number of U.S. companies using competitive intelligence is relatively low, it is the fastest growing corporate discipline. Only ten years ago, a handful of people met in a hotel in Washington to discuss forming a group that would foster professionalism among those involved with competitive intelligence. They established the Society of Competitive Intelligence Professionals (SCIP), which has since grown to more than five thousand members with affiliates all over the world. The group is now signing up about a hundred new members each month.

This book will show you the best and brightest in the burgeoning world of competitive intelligence. You will learn how companies around the world employ competitive intelligence and how American companies in particular are beginning to understand its value in an age of fierce global competition.

You will see how, without competitive intelligence, some companies have failed. Conversely, you will see examples of competitive intelligence by large and small companies and how it was used to increase market share, profits, and competitiveness.

You will learn what competitive intelligence can do for your company, how it can help you enter new businesses, learn about hidden competitors, understand your marketplace, and increase the range and quality of potential acquisition candidates.

This book will change the way you make decisions and show you why information is not critical anymore. Forget about living in the age of information. We are living in the age of intelligence and the two are very different.

Competitive intelligence, long a part of Japan's industrial policy, is becoming an official part of the industrial policy of many European countries. This has not escaped notice by the CIA, which has already taken the first steps toward becoming an economic intelligence provider for American businesses. Applauded by some and jeered by others, the CIA has quietly helped some U.S. firms win large overseas contracts using pilot competitive intelligence programs.

What makes competitive intelligence even more critical in the new, post-industrial era is the growth of high-tech industries such as telecommunications, biotechnology, fiber optics, pharmaceuticals, chemicals, and computers. These cutting-edge industries require large research and development expenditures, have razor-thin margins, fast development cycles, and are global in scope.

Unlike manufactured products of the past, the cornerstone of these exploding industries is knowledge—not raw materials. Turning information into usable intelligence is what will ultimately separate successful companies from those that fall by the wayside not only in the high-technology sector but every other business sector as well.

CHAPTER TWO

What Competitive Intelligence Can Do for Your Company: Information Versus Intelligence

"I've got too much to read."
—Most company managers

The basis of competitive intelligence is knowing the difference between information and intelligence.

When executives say that they have too many reports to read, too much information to go through before making a decision, they're making the mistake of confusing information with intelligence. What they really mean is that they have too much information and not enough intelligence.

Understanding the difference will help them get on the road to more efficient decision making.

Here's the difference:

Information is factual. It's numbers, statistics, scattered bits of data about people and companies and what they've been doing that seems to be of interest. Information often appears to be telling you something but in reality it's not. You can't make good decisions based on information no matter how accurate or comprehensive the information is.

Intelligence, on the other hand, is a collection of information pieces that have been filtered, distilled, and analyzed. It has been turned into something that can be acted upon.

Intelligence, not information, is what managers need to make decisions. Another term for intelligence is knowledge.

The United States is the most information-rich nation in the world. We have more information produced, more information stored, and more information flowing through our computers and networks than anywhere else in the world. This massive amount of facts makes us think that data is important. Indeed, we think we live in the information age, but we couldn't be more wrong. While that was true several years ago, it is no longer the case.

When computers and telecommunications merged in the mid-1980s (Koji Kobayashi, former chairman of NEC, had the vision to realize that communications and computers were intertwined and so set his company on that course), information became so important that we traded it, moved it, and worshipped it. However, since that time, information has become a commodity.

With the advent of massive commercial and government databases, information has become cheap and accessible at the same time. So, while we continue to establish new sources of data, it has become less important.

Take the example of pocket pagers that allow us to receive commodity prices almost instantly anywhere we roam. If everyone who wants that capability can have it—and the prices have come to the

Modern Business Eras

Machinery	Capital and Labor	Information	Intelligence (Knowledge)
1940s	1950s-1960s	1980s	1990s-

Mechanical Technology	Investment	Computers	Information and Analysis	Competitive aka Intelligence Systems

BUSINESS DRIVERS

Figure 2-1

point where even the amateur trader can afford the service—does that make the information less valuable?

Yes, it does.

If everyone has the same information, who has the edge over his competitors? Because the commodities market usually is a zero sum game—somebody wins when somebody loses—pure information is no longer an edge. What gives a trader the competitive advantage over someone else is his analysis of the prices, their movements, and other factors. How he turns raw information into usable intelligence is what separates the successful trader from the one who fails.

This is true of all businesses.

The company that knows how to turn information into intelligence will succeed, and the company that doesn't will fail.

What Competitive Intelligence Can Do for Companies

Suppose you were going to hire a consulting firm. Both come highly recommended, both have the same capabilities, but one was much less expensive than the other. Be honest. Would your first thought be that the lower-cost consultant could not be as good as the more expensive one?

Of course. It's human nature to think so.

Even though there might be other factors involved, the fact that one consultant's services are priced lower would bring up questions of their competency.

Now, suppose I told you that instituting a competitive intelligence system would require only minimal resources and a minute change in organizational structure. In other words, the start-up costs are low and the rewards extremely high.

Would that change how you felt about it? Would the low cost make it seem unworthy?

I'm sure it would. It's only human nature.

But you'll find that instituting a full-blown competitive intelligence system is neither costly nor disruptive and pays off in ways you can't yet imagine.

Okay, so if it's so good, why doesn't every company do it? Why, according to the Society of Competitive Intelligence Professionals, do only 7 percent of large U.S. companies have a full-scale, formalized competitive intelligence system? For small companies the number is lower, about 5 percent.

Before I answer that question, let me stack the deck a bit and tell you what a competitive intelligence system can do for you and your company.

First, competitive intelligence is not a function; it's a process. Therefore it should appear in all aspects of your business as one seamless, continuous activity not relegated to one area, division, or unit.

Although the main job of competitive intelligence is to support management decision making, having a formalized competitive intelligence system in place can help your company address many different issues.

A formalized competitive intelligence program can:

• Anticipate changes in the marketplace.

Companies that direct their intelligence efforts at tracking changes in the marketplace are rarely surprised by events that affect their businesses. On the other hand, not paying attention can exact a high price.

The classic case here was the misreading of the changing marketplace in the 1970s by the Big Three U.S. automakers. The increased cost of gasoline and the changing demographics of smaller families were two of several factors that transformed the face of the U.S. marketplace. American consumers had a pent-up demand for smaller cars and for cars with better gas mileage. They also wanted higher quality cars. While Detroit carmakers didn't respond to these needs, Japanese automakers employing competitive intelligence methods did. That led to their successful bid for the American auto market.

• Anticipate actions of competitors.

Bell Atlantic Mobile Systems regularly monitors its cellular phone coverage area with mobile vans that can pick up radio signals (not phone conversations!) from the towers of its competitor Metrophone. Listeners try to determine if Metrophone has turned on spare channels that are held in reserve for expansion. These extra channels would not only give customers better service—fewer busy signals for instance—but better coverage in outlying areas. If they have indeed activated these channels, it could mean that Bell Atlantic had better respond with its own plans to activate its bank of spare channels. If Metrophone is "heard" field-testing its extra channels, Bell Atlantic would have to respond by activating its spare channels or lose customers to Metrophone. If Bell Atlantic didn't have this early-warning system, it might not learn that its rival was using its spare channels until it was too late to retain customers who would migrate to the company with better service and larger coverage.

• Discover new or potential competitors.

AT&T has one of the corporate world's most advanced competitive intelligence systems. One facet, known as "Access to AT&T Analysts," is a database of in-company experts, about one thousand people, who make themselves available to other employees in their area of expertise.

For example, an employee might be researching segments of the Chinese market. An inquiry might produce someone at the company who has lived in China.

One part of the service is a flagging system that tracks the ten companies in which employees have expressed the most interest or about which have asked the most questions. Usually, they are the competitors you would expect such as Sprint or MCI but not always.

According to Strategic Planning Manager Marty Stark a company he had never heard of suddenly appeared on the list. A study was commissioned to find out about the company and why AT&T employees were interested in it. After some research, it was discovered that the company was entering one of AT&T's lines of business. The competitive intelligence system warned AT&T about the company's potential activity months before there was a story about it in the *Wall Street Journal*.

• Learn from the successes and failures of others.

Sam Walton, founder of Wal-Mart stores, was brilliant at learning from competitors' mistakes and successes. He learned that customers were unhappy with retail giant Sears because they were often out of stock on items. Sears's poor distribution system was the root of the problem. So Walton decided to build a state-of-the-art distribution system, including his own fleet, which gave his customers the service they desired.

In another instance, Walton saw how poorly retail salespeople were treated by Wal-Mart management. He set out to build a program to motivate and train employees, to built esprit de corps among his salespeople, who would now be called "associates." He instituted stock options and bonuses. Walton copied many of these positive aspects from a very successful retailer, J.C. Penney. Penney pioneered in 1913 the practice of calling salespeople associates and giving them a financial stake in the company's performance.

• Increase the range and quality of acquisition targets.

Mike Meurisse of 3M United Kingdom PLC was looking at a company for possible acquisition because it was nibbling away at one of 3M's product lines. It was growing and gaining market share.

It was a private company, run by a tyrannical owner who played his cards close to the vest. He had several factories in Europe, but there was very little information available about the company or its operations.

Further sleuthing led Meurisse to believe that the owner had lied about his production capabilities. His products actually were coming from rock-bottom-priced factories in the Far East and not from his European facilities. In addition, although he was increasing market share, it turned out he was making very little profit—he was growing through low pricing. In that regard, he was a threat, but that threat would be short-lived, Meurisse concluded. "The bottom line is that he really wasn't making any low-priced European-made products despite the fact that originally we thought he was. Competitive intelligence saved us from buying the wrong company. It was not a threat after all."

• Learn about new technologies, products, and processes that affect your business.

The pharmaceutical industry has unique challenges, including very long lead times—sometimes ten to fifteen years for certain drugs—coupled with high research and development costs. The long time line allows continual tracking of competitors' similar projects and allows you to make strategic decisions along the way about your own projects.

According to Pat Bryant, Marion Merrell Dow's manager of global scientific competitive intelligence, the company continually monitors competitors' progress through public records at the Food and Drug Administration and through research journals and elsewhere. "Competitive intelligence helps us determine if we want to continue our own development, put in additional resources, or shut our program down because the problems are not worth the extra expense. In some cases, we have done just that and saved the company a lot of money which would have been wasted."

- **Learn about political, legislative, or regulatory changes that can affect your business.**

A Samsung employee in Los Angeles read in the newspaper that one of America's last guitar factories was going to close mainly due to less expensive Korean imports. He sent that information to company headquarters in Seoul, which engaged in the following analysis:

Guitars are symbols of America's independence and free spirit. It might be likened to the disappearance of the cowboy. Intelligence analysts thought that there would be a backlash against imported guitars and that Congress might set higher tariffs to protect a genuinely American industry and all that it stood for.

Samsung shipped all the guitars they could to U.S. warehouses and stockpiled them. As they expected, Congress raised tariffs on imported guitars but Samsung had a huge supply on hand and was able to profit handsomely even after the tariffs took effect.

- **Enter new businesses.**

Not only can competitive intelligence help you decide if you should enter a new business, it can give you a running start. For example, a Japanese naval architect who designed huge oil tankers was assigned to design Japan's first tourist ship, the *Crystal Harmony*. He and two other designers took cruises all over the world. Just before dinner, they would take photos of the dining arrangements in luxury liner restaurants. After dinner they would count how many people were in the bar, how many were dancing, and how many were strolling along the deck. They checked out people at the pool and in lounge chairs. They took notes about everything they could visually inspect.

They worked every day until the early morning hours, at which time they went back to their rooms and put the numbers into a database for later analysis.

After several years of competitive intelligence cruising, the *Crystal Harmony,* a 49,000 ton version of the *Queen Elizabeth 2* was on the high seas. Japan's entry into the cruise ship business was successful.

• Look at your own business practices with an open mind.

Many companies, especially large corporations, think internally. Methods become stale and outmoded. Competitive intelligence exposes you to new ideas and concepts. It causes you to become externally focused.

A good example of that is W. Edwards Deming, the father of quality control manufacturing. When Deming's ideas were rejected by American firms after World War II, he went to Japan where he found an eager audience.

Even though his concepts were responsible in part for Japan becoming a world leader in the manufacturing of high-quality products, nobody in the United States was interested.in implementing what he was advocating until decades later. It was business as usual for American firms even though old methods didn't work anymore. Now, Total Quality Management (TQM) concepts are being implemented at many manufacturing facilities in the United States with excellent results.

Had U.S. companies been looking at Japanese business practices with an open mind, or for that matter paid attention to Deming back in the 1940s, they would have seen the usefulness of his theories.

• Help implement the latest management tools.

Lately, some companies have reported trouble implementing and sustaining valuable tools like TQM, reengineering, and customer satisfaction. One of the reasons is the lack of information. According to a 1993 survey of managers who were trying to implement TQM, most stated that a lack of information caused them to fail in their attempts to bring TQM to their companies. Their complaints mainly concerned what survey authors Fuld & Company called "internal information bottlenecks." Respondents said they couldn't get internal company information that they needed because they didn't know where to find it. Or when they finally located what they needed, the information wasn't timely.

In short, their companies tried to implement TQM without an intelligence infrastructure—without a competitive intelligence system—and failed.

The same could be said of tools like customer satisfaction, which is crucial to a company's success. Efforts there have also failed due to lack of information and an intelligence infrastructure.

Why Companies Need Competitive Intelligence Now More Than Ever

Efforts at getting competitive intelligence up and running in the 1980s were often scattershot although the best programs have endured. For companies that made halfhearted or no attempts at establishing a formal competitive intelligence program, perhaps it still wasn't deemed important enough. However, most American companies now are starting to understand that the 1980s were a cakewalk compared to the 1990s and the coming decades.

Consider this: Today, less than 40 percent of the U.S. companies on the 1979 Fortune 500 list are still on the list.

Competitive intelligence is an absolute imperative because of events and changes that occurred in the 1980s and show no sign of abating.

For example:

- **The pace of business is increasing rapidly.**

The pace of our daily business (and personal) lives is increasing dramatically.

Think how much more quickly you're expected to respond to queries from suppliers and customers. Remember the days when you could mail someone papers for delivery in a few days and that was good enough? Then remember how overnight delivery services changed that and next-day delivery became standard for some projects? Now think about how fax machines and e-mail have changed the game again. Suddenly, projects that took weeks must be accomplished in days.

Think about how your own company expects you to handle more projects with more speed than ever before—and perhaps with fewer resources.

Chances are you're also making more decisions and making them faster than ever before. The key to keeping pace with the *new speed* of business is through the efficient management and use of competitive intelligence.

• Information overload.

The only thing worse than having too little information is having too much information. How many managers can say that they return all phone calls, handle their mail, or read an important industry journal in a timely fashion? It's not because these sources of information aren't important—who knows if that one phone call or one article will improve your performance—it's because there's too much of it.

We pride ourselves on how much information we have. Don't we believe that information in itself is power? On the other hand, we all complain about how much information we must wade through to learn what we need to know to conduct our business. If information is power, why should we complain about having too much power? Because information alone is not enough.

Competitive intelligence is not just about collecting information. It's about analyzing this information, filtering it, learning what's useful and what's not—and then using it to our benefit.

• Increased global competition from new competitors.

For the first time in history, we are experiencing a global economy. Companies no longer think in terms of political borders when it comes to running their businesses or selling their products. This trend is growing as world and regional trade agreements such as GATT (General Agreement on Tariffs and Trade) and the European Union, and NAFTA (North American Free Trade Agreement) become institutionalized.

Countries such as Korea, China, Indonesia, and Brazil that were never world economic players in the past are now part of the global economy.

Industrialized countries are building facilities all over the world, even in other industrialized countries—so it's not just a matter of finding cheap labor as in the past. Japanese and German automakers now have plants in North America.

Because of better telecommunications, financial firms can be located anywhere and global banking is commonplace. A few years ago you had to carry paper money or traveler's checks when you traveled overseas. Now, your hometown money card can get you local currency almost anywhere in the world. Your personal portfolio of mutual funds is not considered well rounded unless you have international funds containing shares of overseas companies.

For your business, it means that competition can come from any country. Competitive intelligence can help identify new and emerging competitors.

• Existing competition is becoming more aggressive.

Along with the growing global marketplace comes a maturing market in industrialized countries such as the United States. This means that companies will increase market share at the expense of their competitors.

No one has to tell you that competitors will find and capitalize on any weakness in your organization, whether it's in production, marketing, advertising, or distribution. In any business it's more expensive to acquire new customers than it is to keep current ones. The fight for customers is fierce, with many companies willing to sacrifice profits for market share.

Competitive intelligence can help you forecast competitors' actions and allow you to be proactive.

• Political changes affect us quickly and forcefully.

Never before in history has political change been so massive or so quick to affect our lives. The crumbling of the Berlin Wall, a coup in a Caribbean nation, or the signing of a peace accord in the Middle East can change the face of business overnight. Suddenly, there are new players and new markets. Think about the end of the Cold War and what it did to the defense industry. What about the highly trained labor force that it left in its wake and the products it left behind? What possibilities does it give us?

Within our own borders, look at the deregulation of businesses such as telecommunications, airlines, and electric utilities. Within a few years, businesses that never existed before are operating. Electric utilities used to be government-sanctioned monopolies. No longer. There are positive opportunities for some and losses for others.

Competitive intelligence can keep you informed of political changes that affect your business.

• Rapid technological change.

Just the way political change can alter markets, so can technological change. Do you remember when there was no business called "the computer business"? Although it took years to become established, change now comes in leaps and bounds, and fast-moving technology alters the rules of the game continually. Now, almost daily, something happens in the computer industry—some new technological break-through—that can mean new opportunities.

Look at biotechnology. If ever an industry changes fast, this is it. Who knows where the next breakthrough will occur? Who knows when a disease will be cured or a new organic compound manufactured using gene technology? What would happen to certain industry sectors if chemical pesticides could be replaced by nonpolluting, gene-produced compounds?

Keeping track of technological changes in your own industry and other industries is vital for survival.

Why Companies Don't Use Competitive Intelligence

Despite the fact that everything a company does—from managers making decisions to using management tools like TQM and customer satisfaction—involves the flow of information and intelligence, only a handful of companies have a fully developed, systematic way for dealing with these two drivers.

That's strange, isn't it?

If competitive intelligence is such a strong process and the basis for everything a company does, why do so few U.S. companies embrace it?

The most important reason is attitude, the way managers think about intelligence.

Have you heard the following statements? Have you thought or said them yourself?

"Nothing goes on in this industry that I don't already know about."

Humbleness isn't a characteristic that we see in many American managers. There's a tendency for executives and managers to read the *Wall Street Journal*, the local newspaper, skim a few trade journals, and think they know everything that's going on in their own particular industry.

Worse yet, managers think they know what's going on in the general marketplace by reading a few magazines.

For anyone who has visited Japanese companies, one of the biggest eye-openers is how much Japanese managers—even at the highest levels—read. They peruse their competitors' publications, their annual reports, technical publications, everything they can to understand the competition. How much does the average U.S. manager read outside his company's own reports? Very little in comparison to his Japanese counterparts.

Surveys of U.S. upper management show that they get much of their information from their peers, hobnobbing with other CEOs. While this is a good source of information, it's skewed. It's not the whole picture, simply one view from the rarefied world of upper management.

"Nothing goes on outside this company or outside this country that's worth watching."

You laugh, but many company managers believe this one. The U.S. character often is one of misplaced superiority compared to the rest of the world. The "everything is better in the United States" attitude does exist and this belief spills over into business. How many years did it take for American carmakers to believe that the Japanese were making better cars than Detroit? How long did it take before American steel companies realized that Japan and other countries could make better steel? Was it because American businesspeople were stupid? No, it's because they had blinders on to the world outside the United States.

Fortunately, this superiority complex is fading and American industry is beginning to learn from those in other countries.

Most multinational companies understand this, but companies that are not in the global arena—who are very local or regionally focused —can also learn from what's happening in other countries. However, they rarely look outside their immediate area for information that could be useful.

"Competitive intelligence is spying. It's unethical."

Many high-level managers don't understand that 85 to 90 percent of the information your company needs can be found legally and ethically. Unfortunately, they equate competitive intelligence with industrial espionage—two separate and different pursuits. The only answer is education.

"It's not taught in business school, therefore it's not vital."

Schools in other countries teach competitive intelligence. In Sweden, for instance, you can now obtain a Ph.D. in competitive intelligence. In Japan and France there are government-affiliated schools and courses of study dedicated to competitive intelligence. But a person can obtain a master of business administration degree in the United States without ever taking a class in competitive intelligence. In fact, several professors have said that they have tried to institute these courses and ran into resistance. This is to be expected with something new. Schools, like other institutions, don't embrace change. On the other hand, as you'll see in later chapters, some U.S. schools are making a start. Awareness among academics is spreading, albeit slowly.

"Competitive intelligence is a cost center, not a profit center. It's too expensive to implement a program."

What CEOs are really saying is: "I can't quantify the benefits of competitive intelligence."

The effects of competitive intelligence are indirect. "No simple correlation exists. Everything works through an intermediary," says Bernard Jaworski, a professor at the University of Arizona who tried to quantify the effects of competitive intelligence programs.

According to Jaworski and others, competitive intelligence leads to increased quality, better strategic planning, and a greater knowledge of markets. However, putting a dollar figure on those facets is difficult if not impossible in many cases.

Looking at it another way, though, how much money did your company lose by not doing something? For example, how much market share did you lose by not knowing your competitors' activities?

How much did you lose by not getting that contract? Was it because you didn't have enough information about your competitor?

Japanese companies don't ask these questions. They don't have to count beans to know that competitive intelligence pays off in the long run. In Japan, competitive intelligence is considered part of how companies are run every day. The cost of competitive intelligence is considered the cost of doing business. Its cost-effectiveness is not questioned.

In the late 1980s, Fuji introduced a single-use camera in Japan. Even though Kodak had patented the camera for use by tourists who forgot to bring their own, Kodak was slow in getting it to market. Fuji used public-domain sources, including patents, and came up with a competing product first.

Kodak learned through competitive intelligence methods that Fuji was planning to market the camera in the United States and introduced their model just one day before Fuji came out with theirs. As a result, Kodak got the bulk of news coverage while Fuji had to settle for being an also-ran in consumers' and retailers' eyes. Could Kodak quantify the price of competitive intelligence that allowed them to steal Fuji's thunder, not to mention the sales? Single-use cameras are no small market. It's the fastest growing photography segment. In 1988, six million units were sold, with sales reaching 29 million by 1993.

"American CEOs are financial in nature and not technical in nature."

As opposed to CEOs in other countries, American CEOs often come from financial backgrounds and not from technical or engineering backgrounds. This emphasis on financials is important, of course—companies must make a profit to survive—but it also leads to a bias against information sources that are technical in nature.

For example, while many U.S. CEOs want to know about a competitor's financial situation, its market share for instance, they may not appreciate their competitor's technical prowess. It's been said lately that U.S. firms look to numbers to keep profitable while foreign firms look to technology for their future profit. The importance of learning about the latest technology through competitive intelligence methods is often overlooked by American CEOs.

"We tried doing some competitive intelligence, and it was a failure. I didn't see results."

Many companies jump on the competitive intelligence bandwagon because of something they read or heard about the subject. The CEO decides to get a clipping service and maybe asks the librarian to subscribe to an on-line data-bank service or two. Someone is pulled out of marketing to work on competitive intelligence in their spare time. Surprise. It doesn't work. Everyone is disappointed, and the thought of doing competitive intelligence disappears.

Faye Brill, formerly of NutraSweet, now at Ryder Truck, says it best: "What I've seen in company after company is that they don't put the resources behind competitive intelligence. Of course it fails. Competitive intelligence is doomed without full-time resources—people and money."

If you look at the Fortune 500 companies, about 7 percent have a highly developed competitive intelligence system. However, about 80 percent of firms have some informal system or ad hoc methods that they use. It can be anything from subscribing to a clipping service that looks for key words in articles to using on-line databases. When you poll these companies and ask if they have a competitive intelligence system they'll say yes.

Unfortunately, while these informal systems are better than nothing, they don't give users the full benefits that they could get by employing a formalized system.

Because competitive intelligence is such a powerful process, companies see large returns with even a small, informal effort. This leads them to believe that they're doing all they can in that area. This can lull managers into a false sense of security about their competitors.

Then, one day, they get a nasty surprise.

CHAPTER THREE

Why Most Managers Are Still Stuck in the Information Age

"Knowledge is the true organ of sight, not the eyes."
—Panchatantra

While many managers and their companies have begun to understand that intelligence is the key to success, most still receive their information in the old ways and continue to think that information—not intelligence—is paramount.

In 1979, in a *Harvard Business Review* article, John R. Rockart of MIT's Sloan School of Management identified four ways that managers get their information. (He didn't use the word "intelligence" to identify what they really needed.)

First there's the *by-product technique*. In this method, reports and studies produced for various departments come across the executive's desk. The by-product method assumes that if the report was written, it will contain information pertinent to the manager's job.

For example, the sales department produces a report about their quarterly sales figures, breakouts of market segments, market share, and so forth. Although the report may be extensive, there is little if any thought as to what's in the report to help the manager make better decisions. In fact, most of these reports are simply pages and pages of computer-generated information.

The by-product method is by far the most common kind of information to reach the executive. It's what brings many executives to the point of screaming about all the reports they have to read, that they can't possibly handle it all.

On the other hand, there is a class of executive who revels in having mounds of reports on his desk. He can then a) brag about how he doesn't read any of them or b) brag that he reads every word of every report.

Sadly, this method, which does have some advantages—it's cheap to produce and is comprehensive—often submits information that is out of context. That is, a report about sales may not show how it impacts marketing or how payroll affects production. There are no links to the information.

The second approach, called the *null approach*, encompasses the belief that managers are fast-moving, always thinking of the future, so there is no way to adequately satisfy their information needs. Therefore, reports like those found in the by-product method are useless because they only discuss historical informatior. not future needs.

This approach hopes to replace the by-product method with oral, subjective information from close advisors who are always keeping a watch on business conditions and report their findings to the executive.

Unfortunately, this approach dismisses all computer-generated reports, some of which can be useful to the executive. The other drawback is that it places the executive in the position of spending a lot of time listening to opinions that may be unrelated. There may be no contextual link to the information he's receiving.

One of the good points of this approach is that it contains some intelligence, not just information. As people are telling their stories, they're also giving some analysis, making some guesses and estimations on scenarios and courses of action.

The third method, the *key indicator system*, is composed of two related concepts. The first involves selecting a set of key indicators that reflect the company's health and collecting information on these key points. In an obvious example, an executive may choose to look at the profit-and-loss statement. However, depending upon the business, other key indicators are crucial, such as product returns, customer complaints, and miles per gallon of the firm's fleet. These indicators may be critical to the company's survival from the executive's point of view.

The second concept is like the first except that instead of looking at all the figures involved with specific key indicators, only those numbers that are out of whack are given to the executive. For example, a level of acceptable inventories is established but only when figures go above that level does the executive receive a report.

The prime advantage of this method is that the executive receives some early-warning signals of trouble in areas that can sink the company. However, the drawback is clear. Although the executive knows something is wrong, there are no ideas on how to fix it.

The last approach is called the *total study process*. Managers are questioned about their total information needs and those requests are compared to what information systems the company already has in place. The gaps are noted and plans are implemented to fill the holes with additional information systems.

This approach has some merit in that it takes into account what managers want. The main disadvantage is that it doesn't take into account what managers actually require. It also can lead to massive information collection programs only to satisfy a few managers.

Unfortunately, not much has changed since these methods were identified. It's amazing that most managers still use these four methods in their decision-making process. Old paradigms die hard.

A Better Way

Clearly, none of these approaches is adequate. Managers and everyone else in companies need a new way to make decisions, gain insight into their businesses, and beat their competitors.

Moreover, companies need a formal system for moving information *and* intelligence around their firms. Only when both are available can a company become successful.

MANAGERS MUST VIEW INTELLIGENCE AS A PROCESS THAT MOVES THROUGHOUT THEIR ORGANIZATION, TOUCHING EVERY FACET OF EVERYTHING THEIR COMPANY DOES.

They must be willing to see this new idea and embrace it, to tear down old notions about information and understand that only through the orderly flow of information and intelligence can their companies succeed.

And this is where managers begin to feel uncomfortable.

They ask: What kind of animal is competitive intelligence?

Managers and those who practice competitive intelligence agonize and debate about what competitive intelligence is all the time, and it's one of the reasons it has taken so long to catch on.

Is it a process, function, skill, capability, or product? By being able to pigeonhole it into one of these familiar slots, managers are often more at ease with the concept of competitive intelligence and more likely to implement it.

Some successful companies consider competitive intelligence a function and treat it as such. Others think of it as a product produced for executives. Some forward-thinking companies are beginning to consider competitive intelligence as one of their capabilities, a core competency that every unit, indeed every person, must possess.

Many companies can't even decide what to call it—competitive intelligence, competitor intelligence, competitive analysis, competitor analysis; there are a few others around, too.

Does it matter?

Yes . . . and no.

Competitive intelligence must fit into your company's unique culture and structure. Look at it any way that works for you; call it whatever you want. However, you should know that some approaches can limit the power available with competitive intelligence.

The worst thing you can do, though, is not use competitive intelligence because you can't precisely define what it is. That shouldn't be an excuse.

IDEALLY, COMPETITIVE INTELLIGENCE IS BEST THOUGHT OF AS A PROCESS THAT IS USED TO MAKE DECISIONS FROM THE LARGEST STRATEGIC DECISION TO THE SMALLEST TACTICAL MOVE. IT'S A PROCESS THAT PERMEATES YOUR ENTIRE COMPANY.

But competitive intelligence is more than that.

In the future, intelligence-based companies that have become efficient, learning, prosperous entities will be one part of a larger, worldwide intelligence community. This network will embrace countries, governments, social structures, and individuals, all of which will be connected by the concept we call intelligence.

And your company, no matter what its size, will be an integral part of this community.

PART TWO

Real-World Competitive Intelligence

CHAPTER FOUR

The Intelligence Cycle

"Many shall run to and fro, and knowledge shall be increased."
—Daniel 12:4

The basic unit of a competitive intelligence system is the intelligence cycle. It is the process by which raw information is turned into intelligence.

The process that is used by companies is similar to that which is employed by the CIA and others in the intelligence community worldwide.

The beauty lies in its simplicity. There are only four steps.

I. PLANNING AND DIRECTION

This is the step when management gets involved and decides what intelligence it requires. This is also the part of the cycle in which the competitive intelligence practitioner decides which course he should take in fulfilling his task.

This stage can also be thought of as the other end of the intelligence

1. Planning and Direction
2. Collection
3. Analysis
4. Dissemination

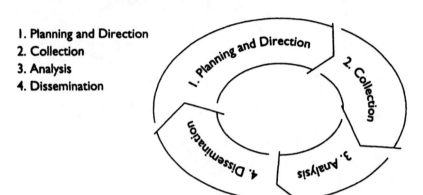

The Intelligence Cycle

Figure 4-1

cycle, because once specific intelligence is delivered to the decision maker his subsequent actions—based on that intelligence—will spur further intelligence needs. The company's situation undoubtedly will change based on those actions.

2. COLLECTION

This phase involves the actual gathering of raw information from which intelligence will be produced. The vast majority of collection materials are in the public domain, meaning they are available to anyone who knows where to look. Sources include periodicals, annual reports, books, broadcasts, speeches, databases, and so on.

Creative collectors can usually find most anything they need legally and ethically.

Collection also involves processing information so that it can be transmitted and stored electronically if desired. Once in electronic form it can be manipulated into a form that allows it to be analyzed.

3. ANALYSIS

This is generally considered the most difficult part of the intelligence cycle. Analysis requires great skills and guts because it requires the analyst to weigh information, look for patterns, and come up with different scenarios based on what he has learned.

Even though analysis is based on logic and hard information, analysts must sometimes "fill in the blanks" and make educated guesses about possible outcomes.

4. DISSEMINATION

This is the last step (and the first, too) in the cycle, and involves distributing the intelligence product to those who requested it.

It's the time when the analyst will suggest possible courses of action based on his work. He must be able to articulate his recommendations and defend them with logical arguments.

The resulting intelligence will also be distributed to others in the company who can use it.

Why Intelligence Is Better As a Process

You may remember I mentioned that competitive intelligence works best when considered a process instead of a function.

First, the structure of the intelligence cycle is clearly a process, and when you run a large-scale intelligence system in your company all you have to do is expand the steps outwardly to include more people to accommodate its growth.

In addition, even though some very successful companies consider competitive intelligence as a function and attach it to the offices of top management (an obvious plus for its stature), that configuration can sometimes be thought of by the rest of the company as some kind of "executive spy agency." By keeping competitive intelligence at the highest levels only, it can sometimes cut the group off from the rest of the company, including those who might want to know more about it and could benefit from it. Moreover, employees who might otherwise contribute information into the system might be discouraged from doing so.

Where to Put Your Competitive Intelligence Unit

In many large companies the competitive intelligence unit is placed in the strategic-planning office, which reports directly to top management. This makes the most sense if the competitive intelligence unit's

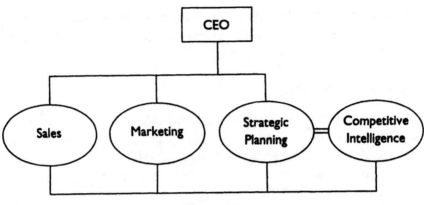

Figure 4-2

main job is to support strategic planning, and in most companies this is the case (figure 4-2).

In other companies you may find a competitive intelligence unit in each business division, attached to a senior vice president or president as seen in figure 4-3.

What you don't want to happen is for each function such as marketing, sales, and R&D to have their own competitive intelligence units *unless* they talk to each other. This communication can be difficult to accomplish in some companies.

Where the unit is placed is not as important as how its lines of communications are configured. In many companies information flows from the top down or from the bottom up. It rarely moves around the company freely and that's a mistake. Some of the recent work with organization concepts such as the Learning Corporation has taught us that.

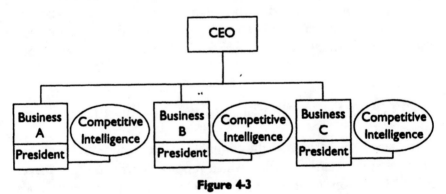

Figure 4-3

ximum efficiency and power, the competitive intelligence ould be placed high enough in the organization so people ct it and see that it has a senior champion. However, it should o be accessible by everyone in the company and not be part of any one division.

The competitive intelligence unit should be close to the prime users but accessible to everyone in the corporation.

CHAPTER FIVE

Planning and Direction

"Would you tell me, please, which way I ought to go from here?"

"That depends a good deal on where you want to get to," said the Cat.

"I don't much care where ———," said Alice.

"Then it doesn't matter which way you go," said the Cat.

"——— so long as I get *somewhere*," Alice added as an explanation.

"Oh, then you're sure to do that," said the Cat, "if you only walk long enough."

—Lewis Carroll, *Alice in Wonderland*

The first part of the intelligence cycle is planning and direction. In many respects, it's the most important part of the cycle, because all other tasks rely on the plan that has been established.

Having a plan and direction will keep you from walking too long. If you go off looking for every piece of information related to a topic, you will run out of time and resources and may not have found your answer. If, however, your plan is focused and sharply aimed at your target, you increase your chances of a successful intelligence project.

Planning and direction requires a three-pronged approach:

I. A clear understanding of the user's needs, including his time constraints.

You must understand what the intelligence will be used for, why it is needed, and exactly which people or department will use it. Intelligence has many uses: strategic planning, research and development, entry strategies, acquisitions, market timing, and technology assessment. Find out what top management needs to know and why.

This bears repeating: Unless competitive intelligence serves the needs of top management (its prime customer), it will fail.

The competitive intelligence team can learn this in many ways. Interviewing or surveying top management about their interests is the most effective method.

For example, in 1984 the chairman and CEO of McDonnell Douglas in St. Louis requested that each of the company's major components establish a competitive intelligence unit. According to Robert Margulies, then manager of competitive assessment, the assignment was to cover three elements:

* the overall business environment
* the customer's needs
* the competitor's activities

While this may seem broad and open-ended, it was, in fact, tempered and focused by a survey of management. Margulies noted that management set priorities within these elements that ensured that they got the intelligence they needed as opposed to what the producers wanted to present. Call it internal customer service.

The time frame involved is critical. It will determine how to allocate your resources and what types of collection processes to use. For example, if a piece of information you think you'll need might be found by a Freedom of Information Act request, the data won't be forthcoming anytime soon. These requests can take months for a response. If you don't have months, you'd better look in another area.

This is the part of the intelligence cycle when management must be involved. Simply supporting the ideas and concepts of competitive intelligence isn't enough. Management must be part of the process from the beginning.

Critical Success Factors

One of the main items that a manager and his competitive intelligence unit should focus on is the company's Critical Success Factors.

Critical Success Factors were discussed as far back as 1961 by D. Ronald Daniel, who went on to become managing director of McKinsey & Company. Critical Success Factors were defined as those tasks that had to be completed for the company to succeed.

According to Daniel, supermarkets might deem critical success factors as having the right product mix in each store, having it on the shelves, having it priced competitively, and effectively advertising their availability. If they focused their efforts in these areas, the company would flourish.

Of course, the CSFs might vary from executive to executive and from manager to manager although they would most likely remain the same or mostly the same within an industry.

CSFs vary because of a company's geographical area, its competitive environment, and other differences. For example, a large company might consider managing government regulation a CSF because they are so large that their actions may spark questions of market overhang. A smaller company, in that same industry, may not consider regulation something critical to their survival. For the smaller company, regulation is an issue, but it may not be necessary to focus too many resources on it.

Another example is a manufacturing company that is located in a rural area as opposed to a competitor in the city. Because of higher electricity rates in the rural area, managing utility costs may be a CSF. For the urban company, managing the cost of electricity may not be a factor to its success. On the other hand, managing delivery vehicles in heavy traffic areas might be a CSF for the urban firm.

The question arose: How do we determine our company's Critical Success Factors? At the time, in the early 1960s, a groundbreaking method was offered that gave managers a way to pinpoint their company's CSFs. The manager was interviewed about what he believed was absolutely necessary for the company to survive, items that if not secured would lead to the company's failure no matter what else it did or accomplished.

Interviews could take hours and sometimes they would be handled over sessions of several days. Much the way a psychologist might keep asking the patient to think harder and clearer about a single issue, the questioner encouraged the manager to think about his CSF. It sounds so simple now, but this was not the case then, almost thirty years ago.

Although CSFs remain an important focal point for managers, its worth to modern competitive intelligence is monumental because it gives us a method—interrogation about vital issues—to determine a manager's intelligence needs.

In the same way that a manager learn his company's CSFs, he can discover his own competitive intelligence needs.

This question-and-answer approach is used daily by companies in their customer surveys. However, customer surveys are usually in a written question-and-answer format with little opportunity for the customer to focus on his exact needs. So-called focus groups are closer to the kind of interview that yields useful answers.

So it is with executives. While many competitive intelligence professionals use written question-and-answer surveys, the best way to learn about managers' needs is by direct, interactive interviews. Some people suggest two interviewers, one to ask questions and the other to take notes.

The more focused the responses about the manager's needs, the more efficient the information-collection process and subsequent analysis can be.

2. Establish a collection and analysis plan.

Depending upon the time available and the intelligence items requested, set up a plan outlining what information should be collected. The plan should include contingencies in case a piece of the puzzle isn't available. If not, try to get the next best information.

3. Keep the user informed.

Once you have a plan of attack, go back to your "customer." Make certain that the intelligence you're planning to provide will fit his needs. Let him know what you think is possible and what may not be possible. Let him know the time frame and resources necessary to do the job.

This process will focus your efforts even further. As the user studies your plan, he may have further needs or may decide that what he wanted at first isn't worth the effort.

Most important, this process ensures that you will deliver to the "customer" exactly what he needs.

Planning and direction are also at the end of the intelligence cycle because intelligence leads to action, which then results in new situations and yields new opportunities.

For example, if intelligence is being used to support a tactical plan, the company will need a new plan once it is accomplished. The new tactics will bring with it new intelligence demands.

CHAPTER SIX

Collection

"You can see a lot by watching."
—Yogi Berra

Collection involves obtaining the raw information that will be turned into usable intelligence—something that can be used by management. It's like raw material being shipped to a factory to be transformed into a finished product.

There are many types of information, but for now let us divide it into two categories: primary and secondary.

Types of Information

Primary sources are unadulterated facts directly from the source. It could be a company CEO, president, government agency, or someone else who has access to absolute and correct information. It's information that has not been changed, altered, or otherwise tainted by opinion or selection. (By selection we mean what happens in the media. Even though a quote may be accurate, it was still chosen by the reporter from a slew of other quotes that could have been published.)

Examples of primary sources are speeches in which a company president gives information or clues about his company's plans, their financials, technology, or anything else. Annual reports and other company publications are also considered primary sources. Securities and Exchange Commission reports are primary sources as well. You get the idea.

Unless the source is deliberately lying, primary sources should be considered absolutely accurate. You should always be on the lookout for slips of the tongue and other mistakes. Although it doesn't often happen, more than one CEO has quoted the wrong figures in his presentation to Wall Street analysts and has had to backtrack the following day in the *Wall Street Journal*.

Items that you observe yourself are also primary sources. If you count the number of cars in a parking lot in an effort to determine the number of employees on the night shift, that's primary source data. The same goes for things you see at trade shows and from reading product literature. Photos and unedited videotapes are also primary sources.

Government data is also considered primary source material. Government information collectors usually obtain the information from the industry itself, often through surveys and questionnaires, and that information is about as good as is available anywhere. Government filings in regulatory agencies are excellent sources of primary source information, as are court documents and records.

Primary sources are the holy grail of source information. Obtaining primary material should be your ultimate goal, but it is not always possible to obtain it.

The other category of information is secondary sources. *Secondary sources offer altered information.* Secondary information is more commonly found than primary information, and sometimes it's the only kind of information you can get on a subject.

Secondary information includes sources such as newspapers, magazines, television, and radio. Information written about companies in directories or in trade association publications should be considered secondary. Academic papers and theses, as well as analysts' reports about companies should be considered secondary information.

What separates primary from secondary material is that primary material is raw, unchanged, and usually in its entirety, while second-

Primary Sources

❑ Annual Reports

❑ Government Documents

❑ Speeches

❑ Live TV and Radio Interviews

❑ Company Financial Reports

❑ Personal Observations

Secondary Sources

❑ Newspapers

❑ Magazines

❑ Books

❑ Taped and Edited TV and Radio Programs

❑ Analysts' Reports

Figure 6-1

ary sources have been selectively pared from larger information sources (such as a speech excerpted on a TV show) or altered by opinion (such as an analyst's industry report).

This does not mean that secondary sources are less important or even less accurate than primary sources. What it means for you, as you collect information, is that you must give each bit of information a different weight based on where it comes from and what it has been through.

Secondary sources can sometimes be better sources of information than primary sources. You can often get insightful opinions from analysts and journalists. These people often see an entire industry and can offer sides you don't see. They observe trends you didn't notice and have confidential sources within the industry.

For example, a company president may give a speech in which he says that he expects his company to grow at 15 percent in the next fiscal year. Things sound peachy, but a newspaper account of the speech goes further as the reporter fills out her story with comments from industry analysts that suggest that the 15 percent figure may not be as easy to reach as the company official suggested.

What does this mean to you?

You've learned several things. First, you know what the president believes and you know what "the Street" thinks—both useful bits of information.

Had you just read the newspaper account you would have missed the president's reasons why the company is expected to grow. Had you only heard or read the speech you would have missed the rebuttal.

A good rule for using a secondary source is to check it against a primary source whenever possible. It goes the other way, too, although there isn't always media coverage of something that's primary information.

As you collect secondary sources you'll become more familiar with the idiosyncrasies of the source. Some are more accurate than others; some are more complete; some oversimplify; some have biases; and so on. Eventually, you'll learn what weight to give secondary sources based on where they are published and what person, in particular, did the work.

When collecting information from overseas media, it's important to be aware of the differences between American journalism and foreign journalism. For the most part, U.S. newspaper journalists (we're not talking about columnists) try to be unbiased—almost to a fault it seems. They strive to get both sides of a story and try not to inject their own personal opinion. However, British journalists, as an example, don't always follow that rule. Stories have a point of view; they may be injected with opinion or bias.

This is not necessarily a bad thing as long as you know what the bias of the writer or publication bias is. You can then factor that in. The information becomes more valuable than if you didn't know about the person or the publication's particular prejudice.

Now and Later

Companies with competitive intelligence programs engage in two kinds of collection procedures. First, they collect information (either the answer to a problem or the first step in solving a problem) for a specific reason or in response to a request from management.

Second, they collect information that is saved and built into an ongoing data bank about one company, one industry, and so on. This information is updated regularly so it can be consulted when needed. Ideally, both of these activities are going on at the same time.

Easy Versus Difficult

In a perfect, nice world you will be presented with a question from management, and you go about looking for the answer. Lo and behold you find what you need in some newspaper article or in a company's annual report.

For example, suppose you wanted to know what a competitor's growth plans were for the coming year. You look in the annual report and there it is: The chairman outlines his program for 10 percent growth.

Then, there is real life.

Most often, you're asked for information that isn't readily available, and trying to answer management's query becomes a matter of being creative—very creative.

People who are prone to using brute-force techniques in solving problems don't last very long in the information-collection business. Certainly, there are basic methods that may find the answer quickly—like the preceding example—but finding other information requires that you have a broad knowledge of business, industry, government, and sometimes a narrow knowledge of a specific industry or sector.

It may require you to think in terms of several steps before even finding a number to analyze.

For example, in 1989, Coors's managers were worried by reports that Anheuser-Busch was going to make a big push into its Rocky Mountain market with Budweiser and Bud Light. Anheuser-Busch had been blitzing cities on the East and West Coasts with advertising and promotion and making some inroads at the expense of Coors. Coors is the weakest of the big-three breweries (Miller is the third). The Rocky Mountain area had always been a stronghold for Coors and to lose market share in its home territory would not only be costly but humiliating.

The question was this: Did Anheuser-Busch have the brewing capacity in its Denver-area plants to follow up a promotional and advertising offensive with enough products to make it a cost-effective campaign?

The answer was elegant. Using only public records, an outside competitive intelligence consultant studied the Environmental Protection Agency filings of Anheuser-Busch's wastewater discharge. From that he was able to determine their maximum capacity. As it turned out, they did not have enough brewing capacity to make a successful launch in the area. Coors, which at first had planned to spend millions on counterpromotion and advertising, was able to hold off and put its resources elsewhere.

All companies of this kind must file wastewater statements with the EPA. How did the collector know that? It's one of those things that a well-rounded businessperson knows. At the very least, upon review of that specific industry, it's one of those facts that should pop out as a feature that can be exploited.

This story also nicely shows the three facets of competitive intelligence.

- Information: the amount of wastewater that was discharged.
- Analysis: given that figure, the factory's capacity was extrapolated.
- Using the information: Coors decided to postpone a possible countercampaign.

Here's another example: A Japanese firm wanted to build a paper-processing plant in Georgia and needed to know the capacity of a nearby plant and how much paper they were producing. If the plant was underutilized, it wouldn't make much sense to build another one. On the other hand, if it was at full capacity there might be room for another plant in the area because there were plenty of tree farms in the region.

An outside consultant hired someone to count the number of railroad cars leaving the plant; however, there was no guarantee that the cars were full. Working with a chemist and metallurgist, the consultant was able to determine how much weight had passed over the tracks by measuring the amount of rust still remaining on the tracks after each train trip. Subtracting the weight of the railroad cars, she then determined how much load the cars were carrying. From that number, she extrapolated the amount of paper produced. But that was only part of the answer. Were the plant's machines operating at 100 percent capacity?

Next, she learned how many and what kind of machines the plant used simply by asking some workers. She found out from the manufacturer how much material these machines were capable of producing.

It turns out that the plant was at 90 percent capacity most of the time, and the Japanese firm decided to pursue the possibility of building a new plant.

Again, this story shows how a creative person finds the answer to a specific question.

- The information: weight and number of the railroad cars and how many trips they took; the capacity of the paper-making machines.
- Analysis: given those numbers, what capacity the plant was operating was estimated.
- Using the information: room in the region for another plant.

Although both of these examples are creative, the first case is one that used public-domain information as its foundation. The second case involved a more complicated and imaginative use of nonpublic information collection. Both approaches got the job done.

First, let's look at public-domain information and where you can get it.

Public-Domain Information

Public-domain information is a vast sea of data that is open and available to anyone who seeks it. Some of it is generated by the government and some is produced by the media, trade associations, and companies.

Because we live in a society of laws and regulations, there is a certain amount of paperwork that is involved in day-to-day business. This is especially true for industries that are heavily regulated, such as food processing, agriculture, pharmaceuticals, airlines, and so on. The common thread is one of public and environmental safety. When safety is an issue, there is a lot of paperwork that must be filed. Almost all of it is in the public domain.

A paper trail also follows companies that are traded publicly. When this is the case, Securities and Exchange Commission reports and documents from state corporation councils are available.

Even on a local level many forms must be filed. Clever restaurateurs often check on potential competitors by looking at their building and fire code applications. It will outline how many people are expected to be in the restaurant ("Maximum allowed by fire regulations"), how many grills the kitchen will have (blueprints of the sprinkler system), and if they expect to have valet parking.

One restaurateur in Omaha learned that a potential competitor had filed a request for "no parking" signage in front of his doors. The reason for the request was stated plainly on the form: "To allow for valet parking pickup area." The restaurateur promptly worked on getting valet parking for his customers as well.

A Simple Guide on Where to Start Looking for Public-Domain Information

When looking at companies and the information you can get about them in the public domain, you should first look in three government jurisdictions: federal, state, and local.

FEDERAL

Publicly traded companies have to file a slew of paperwork with the Securities and Exchange Commission. These filings are crucial for building a financial profile of your competitors.

The most useful are the 10-K annual filings, which contain such items as:

Income statement, balance sheet, breakout of sales by product line, debt structure, depreciation, dilution, opinion of auditors, analysis by management, ownership overseas, properties, subsidiaries, description of the industry and discussion of the industry's future (especially important for burgeoning industries like biotechnology), and court actions such as bankruptcy, patent infringement cases, and lawsuits by shareholders.

The 10-K can help you paint a picture of a company's financial status, its strategic plans based on management comments, and marketing plans. The true worth of 10-K reports comes with comparing the current 10-K to past years' reports. You can get a good idea of where the company is heading and how it may have changed its focus over the years.

Along with the 10-K, companies must file 10-Qs, which are statements of quarterly income, earnings per share, and so on. 10-Qs can point out, for example, a company's consistent weak quarters, which you might be able to exploit.

Public companies must file other reports, which your own auditor can help you identify. Don't forget to study companies that are undergoing an initial public offering. You will learn about your new competitors by looking at their prospectus and other required forms.

While SEC forms are common to all publicly traded companies, most federal filings are specific to an industry. For example, radio and TV stations must file papers with the Federal Communications Commission, trucking companies must file forms with the Interstate Commerce Commission, and pharmaceutical companies must file forms with the Food and Drug Administration. In addition, any company that produces water or air wastes must file forms with the Environmental Protection Agency.

How do you know what agencies handle each industry? How do you know what information they must submit? If you're in the industry, you already know. If not, you might be able to figure it out based on the obvious situations just mentioned. Have someone in your company or group research the question. Or ask a consultant who works in that particular industry. At the same time, find out how you can obtain the records. Learn which documents are publicly available and which are not.

For example, some FDA information about drug testing is confidential, because it may expose a company's trade secrets. On the other hand, some information is in the public domain free for the asking. In the middle is information that the government will release only if you file a Freedom of Information Act request.

The FOIA was first enacted by Congress in 1966 to provide people the right to obtain information from the government. Originally established to help private citizens and the news media, it is now being heavily used by companies seeking information about other companies.

The law applies to federal government agencies except the president, vice president, Congress, and the federal courts. (All states have their own version of the FOIA, and you should check with each state.)

Each federal agency is required by the act to publish in the Federal Register its procedures and regulations concerning the FOIA. It's easier, however, to contact the agency directly and ask for the FOIA officer. He or she will send you the regulations.

In general, the FOIA states that the requestor must specify what records he wants. You must be as precise as you can, and the more information you supply the better. You don't have to explain your reason for requesting the information.

Each agency must determine within ten days after receipt of your request whether to grant access or deny these records. The agency may determine to give you part of the records and deny others based on rules of exemption. If they deny any records they must give you a reason as well as the name and title of the person responsible for the decision. The letter will also explain your right to appeal.

Your appeal letter must be responded to within twenty working days.

While on the face of it, the FOIA sounds pretty good, it doesn't always work as you'd like it to or as the Congress had hoped it would work.

Although an agency must respond within ten working days and tell you about access, you'll often get a letter saying that because of the caseload all they can promise is that they will get to your request as soon as possible.

The reason for the backlog isn't necessarily because agencies don't want to process your requests. It's because they allocate few resources to their FOIA responsibilities.

Some requests have been known to take years to answer, and there's no way of knowing beforehand whether the information you'll get will even be of any use until you get it.

Clearly, FOIA requests should be part of an ongoing collection process and not for information that you need quickly.

FEDERAL GOVERNMENT REPORTS

The U.S. government is the largest publisher in the world—books, reports, studies—millions of documents annually.

Among all these is information that you can use in competitive intelligence programs.

The Department of Commerce, for instance, publishes *Current In-*

dustrial Reports, which details inventory, production, and demand for more than five thousand products produced in the United States.

Although these booklets don't mention companies by name, they give the number of companies competing in a market, total production, and the total market. If you're willing to make some estimates, you might be able to guess at some numbers for your competitor such as his share of the market based on his production.

This is just a teeny example of what's out there. I could write a separate book on what the government has to offer in general industrial and economic information, but I'll leave that to someone else. The important thing to know is that a lot of what you need is available and easy to obtain.

STATE

At the minimum, states require that companies—even those that are not publicly traded—register each year with the state government, usually the secretary of state, if they are incorporated.

States vary as to how much information is contained in these public filings, but they may hold some clues about your competitor.

For example, the president of a computer modem company in California heard a rumor from one of his salespeople that a competitor was planning a joint venture with a software company to produce new communications software and sell it along with their modems. Depending upon which company it was, it could hurt the first modem company, which had prided itself on buying the latest software to pack with its modems.

The company tried to learn who the software company was but failed and the arrangement occurred about three months later. The first modem company was caught off guard. It cost them sales as business users believed the new software to be better than what the first company could offer.

The information was so obvious, and it shouldn't have come as any surprise to anyone. The president of the software company in question sat on the board of directors of the second modem company but nobody paid any attention. Although they were a private company, the list of directors is public-domain information. This is the kind of information that should have been gotten by all competitors as a matter of course and updated annually. Although there was no guarantee that just because the president of the software company sat on the board that the two companies would do a deal, it certainly was a logical choice. In this case it turned out to be true.

States also regulate such diverse things as vehicle licenses and liquor licenses for bars and restaurants.

One small highway construction company in Annandale, Virginia, does a semiannual check of motor vehicle ownership of its competitors with the Department of Motor Vehicles. Why? It wants to know what kinds of equipment its competition is buying and how many pieces it owns. The owner told me: "I also want to know which equipment they've gotten rid off, which equipment wasn't re-registered. It gives me an idea of how long I should keep my equipment compared to other companies."

Another source of information about equipment comes from Uniform Commercial Code filings. Each state has a department that handles these filings. UCC filings are made by banks, finance companies, and other lenders describing liens against properties such as buildings and office equipment. Lenders employ UCC filings to protect themselves against companies who want to use the same property again as collateral for different loans.

Through UCC filings you will learn what new equipment your competitor has purchased; you already know he didn't pay cash for it. The filings don't just tell the kind of equipment but the model number and a rather detailed description of its characteristics. This information could tell you a great deal about what your competitor may be planning.

Be sure to check for UCC filings on the county level, too.

LOCAL

Most counties and municipalities require companies within their jurisdiction to obtain business or operating licenses. These licenses, which are public-domain, tell who owns the company, where they're located, and whether it's a subsidiary of another entity.

One of the most useful of local records is requests for building and construction permits. These filings can tell you what your competitors are planning. Almost all developers keep close track of their competitors by following the construction permit process. This is especially true when a project needs a zoning variance. Variances require that the petitioner give detailed information about site plans, plumbing and electrical requirements, and so on.

The October 1992 issue of *Progressive Architecture* discussed how architecture firms now are using intelligence-gathering services for leads to bid on jobs. These services comb through building and zoning permits and list potential projects and their needs.

In this instance, intelligence is crucial because competition for jobs among architects is keen. In fact, the share of architectural revenues received from developers, traditionally the strongest source of work, has fallen from a high of 22 percent in the boom year of 1986 to around 10 percent in 1993. To make up for the lack of developer work, architects must search for other builders. That's where competitive intelligence enters the picture. Jeffrey Blydenburgh, associate director of HOK Hospitality in St. Louis, said: "[These services] help to identify the names of people who *are* building."

THE MEDIA

Because the news media is a secondary source, it not only contains raw information but usually some analysis.

As I've already mentioned, you should factor in a news organization's bias (intentional and unintentional) in covering some industries, companies, and government agencies.

Surveys have shown that Japanese companies use their nation's newspapers more than any other single source of information because the business newspapers in Japan contain much more in-depth information than anywhere else in the world. However, newspaper articles from U.S. newspapers are excellent sources for competitive intelligence practitioners in this country.

You should also know that not every newspaper carries the full text of a story. For example, when a wire service, such as Associated Press or Reuters, sends out a story, its member newspapers pick up the story in its entirety but may cut it for space. News stories, as opposed to features, are usually cut from the bottom but you don't know how much was cut, if anything, unless you see the original story. So, if you read an article in the newspaper that interests you, and it originated with a wire service or even another newspaper, you should find the original. Otherwise you may be missing some crucial information.

One of the best things about newspapers is that most stories can be obtained using on-line databases. Newspapers allow databases to re-produce and distribute their stories to users. Most agreements divide user's fees among the newspapers and the database provider. Because the stories are on an electronic database you can search them by company names, product names, people's names, or any key word or term you desire.

This procedure is also fast. You can obtain information immediately, although be aware that there may be a lag time of a few days to a few weeks for a newspaper story to show up. Magazine stories may take a little longer.

Another way to obtain newspaper and magazine articles is through a clipping service. You provide the key words and a service will fax you the articles on a daily, weekly, or monthly basis. This is not only con-venient but often these clipping services read very small-circulation newspapers, magazines, and newsletters that are not on any database.

Don't overlook TV talk and news shows or televised government hearings as information sources.

Don't expect to find out everything you want to know about a competitor through one or two sources. Your job is to collect nuggets that can be built on, added to, and enhanced.

Some of the best information sources are trade journals. Articles pub-lished in them are always more focused than stories in the general press, and are often written by company officials—your competitors. Certainly, an engineer writing in an engineering trade publication is not going to reveal any trade secrets; however, he may tell you some things about his firm's ongoing projects or products that you didn't know. You may find a gem or two. And, because it comes from someone intimately involved in the company, the information is accurate and reliable.

One other aspect of perusing the media is worth mentioning. Com-petitive intelligence information is not only found in the news and feature sections but in other parts of a newspaper or magazine, namely display and classified advertising.

Retailers have studied their competitors' advertising for years to see what products they're highlighting as well as the prices. Grocery stores follow their competitors' ads very closely.

But other companies should pay attention to ads because of what it can reveal about competitors.

Figure 6-2 is an advertisement from Bell Atlantic seeking assistant managers in human resources and a manager in labor relations. The

Figure 6-2

Washington, D.C., region had been abuzz about Bell Atlantic getting into the cable TV business with their own service competing against local cable franchises. This ad marks a definitive move in that area. It shows that Bell Atlantic Communications and Construction Services, Inc. (BACCSI) is *a new separate subsidiary* that will install, repair, and

Figure 6-3

maintain cable systems for any *Video Information Provider*. The ad says they are up and running with enough expertise and staff to look for outside contracts. They promise *competitive rates and short service intervals*, two traits that have been lacking in local cable companies, which were, until now, monopolies. Interestingly, this ad was placed before they had delivered their first cable TV picture beyond the testing phase.

In figure 6-3 we see that American Personal Communications is seeking several people for positions because they are *bringing Personal Communication Services to the Washington-Baltimore area*—a new expansion for the wireless communications company. If they are your potential competitor, there is no doubt they have arrived to battle for your customers.

TRADE ASSOCIATIONS

Industry trade associations are good sources of information about a particular industrial sector, but you won't find specific information about its member companies. What you will find is data about the industry, projections, markets, and so forth. Obviously, this can be useful in learning about an industry in general, especially about issues facing them.

However, there's one trick that may help you learn about individual companies. If the trade association is dominated by several large companies, any information about the industry that they have probably reflects those large companies disproportionately.

Say, for example, the trade association claims that its members comprise 70 percent of the overall market. If you estimate that two companies equally dominate the trade association, then you can get a pretty good estimate of how much of the overall market share one company maintains. In this case, it's probably around half of 70 percent, or about 35 percent of the total market. (This example is really one of analysis, which will be discussed in the next chapter.)

DATABASES

Databases are excellent tools for casting a wide net to begin your information search. You can either hook up directly to the database itself or have a company do the search for you based on your key words (figure 6-4).

I like to divide databases into two categories: those with *stories* and those with *data*.

Those databases with stories contain articles from newspapers, magazines, transcriptions of TV and radio shows, newsletters, press releases, government reports. These are usually secondary sources but a few primary ones, too.

Those databases with data carry patents, financial information, advertising, stock exchange information, statistics, sales—unfiltered, raw data. These are mainly primary sources but a few secondary sources as well.

This list is just a tiny fraction of what is available on-line. Many service companies like Compuserve and America OnLine offer many of the most popular databases to their customers so you don't have to subscribe to each one individually. However, for the more obscure or esoteric databases you may have to deal directly with the database compiler.

Also, many of these databases are now offered on CD-ROM. While

Databases with Stories

INVESTEXT	Reports from Wall Street analysts
ABI/INFORM	Abstracts and full text of business journals
DOW JONES NEWS RETRIEVAL	Full text of *Wall Street Journal* and other periodicals
DATATIMES	Full text of hundreds of newspapers
NEWSNET	Full text of more than 300 newsletters

Databases with Data

DUN'S MARKET IDENTIFIERS	More than 6 million records about companies
DRI INTERNATIONAL AUTO	Automobile production figures in many countries
FINANCIAL TIMES CURRENCY AND SHARE INDEX	Data on international exchange rates
TELERATE	Securities prices

Figure 6-4

they may not contain the most up-to-date information, they are easy to search and can help you get a historical perspective on your competitors and the competitive environment.

There are several directories and electronic databases of databases, including the multivolume *Gale Directory of Databases*.

THE INTERNET

No legitimate business book is permitted to be published today without mentioning the Internet. Fortunately, I can fulfill my obligation without stretching the truth, because the Internet can be one of the most important elements of any company's competitive intelligence program.

For those of you who may not be familiar with the Internet, it's a bit difficult to explain because its operation is not organized or very businesslike. In fact, it is very unbusinesslike and somewhat chaotic by nature.

Quite simply, the Internet is a network that connects computers all over the world. The system started as a Department of Defense program in the late 1960s to see if computers at colleges and universities involved in defense contracts could be connected to government computers and to one another. The program was a success and soon every college and university wanted to hook in. By the early 1980s, the desktop computer came along and instead of large, mainframe computers hooking into the network, individuals began connecting directly.

Next, the National Science Foundation wanted to establish a network of five extremely high speed supercomputer centers that could be accessed by anyone needing intensive computing power. It was so effective that the original Department of Defense network virtually disappeared and the people who were on it began to use the NSF network. However, the need for these supercomputers didn't work out for various political and technical reasons but the network they established continues today. Although the NSF only allows noncommercial, research-, or educational-oriented information to be connected directly to its network, independent commercial operators—sometimes called Information Providers or IPs—may now tap into the larger network through a connection called a gateway.

So what do we have? We have millions of people "entering" Internet, or the Net as it's known to aficionados, through colleges, universities, hospitals, government agencies. In the past few years, private citizens and companies have been accessing the Internet through commercial IPs. The Internet reaches outside the United States into virtually every nation in the world.

How many people are on the Internet? Nobody knows because nobody has bothered to count how many people have access to a mainframe computer at, say, a large university. Clearly there are tens of millions of people with access to the Internet, considering the growth of about 100,000 computers a month. Most are individuals but each time a computer comes onto the network, it may have many more users.

Once you're on the Internet you can use it for e-mail and exchange messages with anyone else on the network, or you can use it for other information services.

For companies with worldwide offices, the Internet makes having your own private network unnecessary. Employees can easily send and receive information and intelligence worldwide without the costs involved in maintaining a dedicated network.

Because of its government involvement, almost all U.S. government agencies are on the Net. Indeed, almost every college, university, and research facility in the world is also on the Net. So are foreign government agencies operating both in and outside the United States. The French embassy in Washington has its own bulletin board on the Internet as do French agencies in France. All are accessible by anyone on the Net. These government databases are excellent sources of information for competitive intelligence use.

If keeping abreast of government regulations is one of your competitive intelligence imperatives, you can get full texts of agency regulations and proceedings from the Internet.

Before we go further, let's talk about the Web and Web Pages because they're the most important thing to happen to the Internet since its inception.

Until recently, commercial users did not have access to the Internet. Now that situation has changed and many companies are on the Net. However, the Internet is still very much a noncommercial entity. One of the reasons for this change is the World Wide Web, sometimes called WWW, and its *pages*. The Web is a unique configuration of everything that's on the Internet but made user-friendly with hypertext functions. Hypertext is a system where you read text and when you get to a word or phrase in bold or in a different color, you click your mouse (or press enter) on your computer and that links to information about the subject in another part of the Net.

These hypertext links use these pages as their foundation.

Figure 6-5 shows a Web page for the U.S. government's executive branch. Click *Independent Federal Agencies & Commissions,* and you link to Figure 6-6. From there you can dig deeper into those agencies. There are many federal government Web pages from many sponsors.

The CIA has a page on the Web that discusses the CIA's mission, organization, and functions. There are graphics, including an aerial · shot of the Langley, Virginia, headquarters. It's an especially interesting page to access, because it has information about their intelligence cycle, which is the model for industry.

Some Web pages also contain *search engines*. These are software programs embedded within the Web that allow you to search for information by key words and phrases, as shown in Figure 6-7.

Although no one search engine is all-encompassing, they can search vast areas of the Internet. Considering how much information is on the

There are four ways to use this service to look for government information.
- By selecting a government agency from one of the categories in the image above.
- By agency using a map of Washington, D.C.
- By a subject index to government information online, which is provided by FedWorld.
- By a government information locator service (GILS), which is an index being built to all government information

 Find Information from Other Branches of the Government

Choose this for a textual representation of this page.

feedback@www.whitehouse.gov

Figure 6-5

Internet, these searches can be amazingly comprehensive. In essence, by using several of these search engines, you can find all the information available on the Internet about any subject.

For example, searching with the key words *Asia business* yielded the *Asia Business Directories*. Like much of the commercial activity on the Internet, it's still being built, but you can see how much raw information is there today (Fig. 6-8).

Many companies are putting pages on the Internet and these contain advertising and information about their services. Several competitive intelligence consultancies have Web pages. Kodak's Web page is enormous, with a hypertext menu that branches out into many areas (Fig. 6-9). The Japanese company NEC's Web page site reveals in depth the company's history, divisions, products, and even an organizational chart.

The strength of the Net is not just in how much information is on it

Choose this for a textual representation of this page

Figure 6-6

Lycos

The Catalog of the Internet

A 1995 GNN Best of the Net Nominee
Rated number 1 in content by Point Survey

Enter search keywords Search Options Formless

Lycos users: We want your feedback! You could win a CD-ROM!

- Employment Opportunities at Lycos, Inc
- Advertising Information
- Licensing Information
- Lycos Inc Business Partners
- Frontier Technologies licenses Lycos Internet Catalog software
- Lycos Frequently Asked Questions
- Lycos Register your own pages, or Delete your own pages
- Lycos Results
- Lycos Documentation
- Lycos Legal Notices

The Lycos(tm) "Catalog of the Internet" copyright © 1994, 1995 Carnegie-Mellon University
All Rights Reserved

Last updated 20-Aug-95 by webmaster@lycos com

Figure 6-7

but also how many people are on it. The brain trust on the Net is immense.

If you ask a question in the right place, you may find exactly the answer you're looking for.

People meet in *newsgroups* or *listservs,* which are composed of those interested in the same topic. Most of these news groups are academic in nature or research-oriented; however, we're beginning to see a growing number of business- and commerce-oriented groups (figures 6-10 and 6-11). These groups don't meet in real time. You leave a question or comment and other people respond. You read their response later. If you *subscribe* to one of these groups, every day or every few days you will have e-mail sent to you automatically. Other groups allow people to browse or *lurk* without necessarily having e-mail sent to them.

Because so many people are on the Net, no matter how obscure your query you may find someone who knows something.

There are also very specific groups that will automatically put you on their mailing list. To subscribe, send an e-mail message to the listserv address with the requested words in the body of the text. The list server is handled automatically by a computer.

It is safe to say that there is more raw electronic information contained on the Internet than in other entity on earth.

There is also some intelligence there as well.

Welcome to Asia Business Directories

Bringing the world to Asia and bringing Asia to the world.

Asia Business Directories is a service brought to you by **Bruno Internet Information** are a Singapore-based company which specialises in developing the Internet as a medium to facilitate global business to business communications.

We are here to assist companies who would like to do business with companies in Asia. We understand that it can be quite difficult to establish contacts in Asia, especially if you are halfwa round the world. We intend to facilitate **effective communications** between companies outsi Asia who are interested to do business in Asia and companies in Asia.

Asia Business News Headlines Today

Today's News

Our Services

Directories

- **Singapore Online Business Directory**
  We are kicking off the service with a directory of 4000 different Singapore-based companies. Many of these conduct business throughout the region and may potentially serve as your contact to reach out to other parts of the region

  We have implemented a friendly search interface to help you find the **right companies** to b your business partners. If you so desire, we will fax your enquiries to the companies **at no cost.**

  For the users of our directory of Singapore companies, the two Singapore government agencies listed below are the primary points of contact for trade and investment related information about Singapore. They are excellent sources of additional information and assistance for entering the Singapore market and/or investing in Singapore.

Figure 6-8

- Singapore Economic Development Board

The Singapore Economic Development Board is the main government agency responsible for economic development in Singapore. They promote foreign investment into Singapore and offer a variety of assistance to potential investors, including tax incentive and grants, well as guidance and support on the process of starting a new investment in Singapore

- Singapore Trade Development Board

The Singapore trade Development Board is thee main government agency responsible for developing and administering the trading sector of Singapore's economy. They can assist companies outside Singapore in contacting potential trading partners in Singapore throug their far-flung network of offices

In the future we intend to carry on-line business directories of all major Asian countries.

Company Advertising and Internet Presence Services

We will also design, maintain and display on-line advertising and information for our corporate clients. Do you wish to be listed on our directories? Are you a Singaporean company interested in developing a Net Presence? Please contact us for more details on this service Click here to find out about our **Global Reach** services

For an example of the type of information and services which you can put online please browse the information provided by the World Publications Group. The Group provides a wide range of **marketing support and distribution services across Asia**   , with offices in **Singapore, Ho Kong, Taiwan, Beijing, Korea and Malaysia.**

- **The World Publications Group**

Information Sources on Asia

We intend to be the **DEFINITIVE**   information resource on Asia. This home page should be everyone's first stop on the Internet when they are looking for information on Asia.

We have made an effort to arrange the information in a useful structured manner. Please start your information search by browsing the various sections below
- **Information by region and country**

Your Feedback

We value your feedback. If you have any questions, suggestions or comments at all, please send mail to bruno@wwa.com, or use our feedback form We'll be happy to modify our site to better serve your needs.

Thank you for visiting Asia Business Directories We hope this service has been valuable to you

Figure 6-8 (continued)

| About Kodak | Digital Images | Customer Forum |
| Product Information | Contact Kodak | Guest Book | Search |

Events & Announcements

● Business Imaging Systems (AIIM)
● Picturing The Digital Age

Text representation of this image.

Last Update: Friday, 07-Apr-95 18:58:19 EDT
Contact *webmaster@www.kodak.com* if this server presents any problems.

Copyright, Eastman Kodak Company, 1994

Figure 6-9

Non-Public-Domain Information

Just because some information isn't publicly available doesn't mean that it's private or confidential. All it means is that you must be a little more persistent and clever to find the information that you want.

MOMENT OF CHANGE

Leonard Fuld of Fuld & Company has come upon a unique concept he calls the *moment of change.* It is during times of massive change or upheaval that there is increased attention to certain companies. During these times the media produces loads of stories, a large quantity of paperwork must be filed, and many public-domain documents are produced.

General Business News Groups

clari.nb.business:	contains company press releases worldwide
clari.biz.market.report:	stock market information
clari.biz.mergers:	press releases about mergers
clari.biz.finance:	financial-related information

(*clari* is short for clarinet. In Internet circles that means information that is time-sensitive.)

Figure 6-10

A good example of this phenomenon was when the Manville Corporation, facing more than seventeen thousand unsettled asbestos-related lawsuits, declared bankruptcy in 1981. The court records that the company had to file filled an entire federal courtroom. In addition, Manville had to file papers with the Environmental Protection Agency explaining how it would put its machinery back into service and under what conditions it would operate it.

Specific Business News Groups

E. Europe Business:	listserv@pucc.princeton.edu

(Type "subscribe e-europe" in body of message)

Caribbean Economics:	listserv@vml.yorku.ca

(Type "subscribe carecon" in body of message)

ISO9000 INFO:	listserv@vml.nodak.edu

(About Worldwide Technical Standards; Type "subscribe ISO9000" in body of message)

Japan Business:	listserv@pucc.princeton.edu

(Type "subscribe Japan" in body of text; it's the same address as E. Europe Business, but you'll be put on a different mailing list)

Insurance Info:	listserve@bongo.cc.utexas.edu

(Type "subscribe risknet" in body of text)

Figure 6-11

Regulatory changes also bring out a lot of information. When AT&T underwent divestiture in 1984, massive amounts of paperwork were produced revealing every single detail of the Bell Operating Companies (the local phone companies), Western Electric (the manufacturing arm), and AT&T's long-distance division. This is in addition to the enormous amount of information the company revealed during the court trial that led to divestiture.

Other moments of change and their resulting spurt in public domain information occur during acquisitions and mergers, industry privatizations, regulatory changes, turnovers in management, and geographic relocation of company offices and facilities.

HUMAN INTELLIGENCE

Government intelligence agencies like to call it *humint,* and it means human intelligence or, put another way, what somebody tells you.

When someone on your sales force tells you about a customer whose company may be up for sale, that's humint. When you hear a rumor at the country club about a new manager coming on board one of your competitors, that's humint. When you send one of your employees to an open house at a competitor's new factory and he takes notes on what he saw, that's humint.

JUST ASK

One of the most direct ways of finding information about competitors is to ask. Current customers will often share their thoughts about your competitors' services, products, and pricing if you ask them. The customer is willing to tell you because it serves his purposes of getting the best products at the best prices. However, keep in mind that your competitor may be asking him as well.

Customer surveys are one of the most used management tools. These surveys, which are filled out by your customers, will help you compare yourself to your competitors from your customer's perspective.

Customer surveys can be written, in which case they should be kept short. Or you can use a phone survey. Again, keep it short. It goes without saying that you must identify yourself and tell people the reason for your inquiries.

Asking questions such as, How does our product compare to XYZ Company's product? or, How would you change their product? can go a long way toward increasing your knowledge of your competitor and the industry in general.

There is nothing illegal or unethical about calling your competitor and asking for their sales brochures, rates, and products catalogue. There is even nothing wrong about calling and asking your competitor's salespeople about the size of their departments, how long it takes to ship products, and what kind of inventory they keep on hand. These are questions that a regular customer might ask, so the company is not trying to keep this information confidential.

In fact, advertising agencies have for years collected rate cards and brochures from TV, radio, and cable stations to have on hand when they need the information for a customer. There's no reason why you can't have that kind of information as well.

Many companies put themselves on mailing lists to receive sales brochures or direct-mail offerings as a way to monitor their competitors. This has a twofold benefit. Not only do you keep up on their products but you can extrapolate how much they're spending on direct-mail advertising, another piece of the overall intelligence jigsaw puzzle.

In Japan company officials talk to one another with the understanding that when information is passed around everyone benefits. We don't have that sort of attitude in the United States.

However, we do see people in the same industry gathering at trade shows, luncheons, and so on and this allows us the chance to talk with our counterparts. While no one expects deep trade secrets to be exchanged, people who trust each other—especially those have worked together previously—often talk about their companies. The key is to trade information with the emphasis on *trade*. We both give and we both get.

Through these meetings you might be able to set up a network of companies like yourself that don't compete because of geographic considerations. This is very common with freelancers and those with a small independent service or retail companies. You can freely share information with those in your industry but not have to worry about giving away your secrets to a nearby competitor.

Retailers do, on occasion, send people to other stores to test their customer service, products, and inventories. There's nothing wrong with asking a salesperson how some processes are handled and which products are selling well.' A friendly store clerk might even tell a customer how their sales commission structure works or how well the store is managed. These are all tidbits that can help your business.

Lest you think the direct approach of "just ask" doesn't work, look at what software giant Lotus Development Corp. did in the early 1990s. The company put together teams of people from sales, marketing, and engineering and each team was assigned to gather information about a competitor.

Teams did the usual document searches but in addition they asked for interviews with their competitors' workers and managers. The response was mixed. Software maker Borland had their lawyer meet the Lotus people and ask them to leave. Microsoft's Bill Gates, on the other hand, happily went on about his business philosophy and vision of the future. What Lotus learned most importantly from this exercise was what their competitors think about them and their products. This has helped them stay competitive.

SALESPEOPLE

By far, the best source of human competitive intelligence comes from your sales force. They are out there, on the front lines, learning about their competitors, trying to understand how to outsell them.

In fact, salespeople instinctively collect information that gives them an edge but most of them keep it to themselves or share it only with their colleagues or direct manager.

The information doesn't seem to make it to the top decision makers.

One of the reasons is that salespeople have so much paperwork to do that adding another paper to fill out is a low priority. One way to counteract that is to make it easy to share things that have been learned. Some companies have an 800 number or allow quick notes to be jotted down and faxed. An e-mail message works well, too. There's nothing wrong with an informal, low-tech system to collect information from salespeople or anyone else.

Another sure way to entice participation is to make certain that any information that works its way up also works its ways down. In other words, salespeople must get useful feedback based on information that they or some other salesperson shared with the competitive intelligence unit or manager.

One paper company's competitive intelligence unit learned from its account executives that a competitor's product was being heavily advertised in newspapers in Midwest markets. This prompted the competitive intelligence unit to let sales reps on the East and West Coasts know that the competitor may be gearing up to hit their area as well. We'll talk more about dissemination of intelligence in another chapter.

It's important that all data be treated as if it were important—because it is. Even unsubstantiated rumors can be helpful, especially if they're being heard in different parts of the country.

Because some rumors turn out to be untrue, a lot of people don't want to pass them along. So, it behooves the competitive intelligence unit to let people know that while accurate information is always prized, hunches or guesses about something may be worthy, too. It's important for salespeople to know that they won't be penalized for turning in something that turns out not to be true.

Digital Equipment Corp. is a good example of a company that collects information about competitors gleaned from their sales force and funnels it into the competitive intelligence unit. The information can be any tidbit such as the price change on a product or a new sales brochure. Even rumors are given more than passing attention.

In a related area, companies like Motorola and Johnson & Johnson ask that customer-service representatives fill out forms about tidbits they've picked up about their competitors. This information is directed upward to the competitive intelligence unit.

OBSERVATION

There is a tendency to think of competitive intelligence as a totally intellectual pursuit. That is, some people would like to sit in their offices, punch up a database, read the newspaper or talk on the phone and thereby try to get everything they need.

While this ivory tower tactic works for many situations, it's not the whole story. Sometimes you just have to get out of the office and see what's going on. Again, that's why salespeople are such valuable information resources.

One loading dock supervisor says that about once a month he watches, from a public sidewalk, stopwatch in hand, his competitor's workers load trucks. "I see how many people they have loading, how many breaks they take, how many boxes are on a pallet and like that. It gives me a good idea how my people compare." '

The supervisor says that he's particularly interested in how they load trucks in inclement weather. Part of the loading dock is exposed to the elements and he notices that in wet weather the flow slows as workers become careful not to slip. "I've figured out that they drop about 15 percent in loading speed during the rain. Sometimes I'm tempted to tell them that it would be cost-effective to build an overhanging awning that would keep the rain off the platform, but it's an edge that we have over them. I'm not about to give that up."

While low-tech observations such as this are often effective, we're beginning to see high-tech observations integrated more and more into competitive intelligence programs.

AERIAL OBSERVATION

In the late 1970s, the Dow Chemical Company plant in Midland, Michigan, had a $3 million security system, an eight-foot-high fence, a twenty-five-person security force, and a sophisticated alarm system all designed to keep out intruders.

The Environmental Protection Agency visited the plant in 1977 to investigate allegations of emissions violations. A second visit was requested but this time the company balked. The EPA thought about obtaining a court-ordered warrant but decided on a different approach.

The government agency flew over the plant and took photographs. Their contention was that Dow didn't own the skies above the plant and therefore the company could not accuse the government of invasion of privacy. In addition, they argued the plant was observable from commercial planes taking off from a nearby runway.

Dow disagreed and both sides went to court.

In November 1984, a Circuit Court of Appeals reversed a lower court decision that had sided with Dow Chemical. This decision was upheld by the Supreme Court (there was a similar case involving a marijuana grower who claimed that law enforcement planes were invading his privacy; he lost) and these cases set the stage for legal flyovers of business facilities.

If these surveillances are done by government agencies, they may be available from the agency itself, perhaps through a Freedom of Information Act filing.

However, you may, if you want, rent a plane and fly over a site and take pictures of the area.

In fact, a form of aerial reconnaissance was employed by Ray Kroc in the early days of McDonald's. Kroc would fly over a burgeoning suburban area, see where new homes and roads were being built, and look at sites for his restaurants to serve the growing population.

Many county and state governments take aerial photographs on a regular basis to help their planning process. Governments use aerial photos to help design roads, wastewater facilities, parks, industrial areas, as well as for recording the effects of natural disasters such as tornadoes and hurricanes. These photos are often available for a fee to anyone who requests them.

What can you learn from these photos?

In the case of chemical or other processing plants where products are moved along the facility through piping, for instance, you can see the flow of work. This will tell you the kind of processing that is going on based on the configuration. You can estimate the width of pipes and size of storage tanks. That can help determine the plant's input and output.

With the ending of the Cold War, a new wrinkle in aerial surveillance has been added: satellite photos. The only problem for nongovernment users is that the photos are *too* good.

Military satellites are capable of resolutions to one meter. Such excellent resolution is considered classified information out of concern that unfriendly governments could buy the satellite images if they were on the open market and use the information they contain against us.

During the Iran-Iraq war, U.S. intelligence agencies shared satellite images of Iran with Iraqi forces. As a result, during the Gulf War, when Iraq became an enemy, Saddam Hussein's forces knew the ability of these satellite images and used that knowledge to help them hide their mobile Scud missile launchers.

It is with this concern that the U.S. government is considering plans to sell desensitized or fuzzied-up military satellite images for commercial use. Several private U.S. companies have decided not to wait for the federal government and are planning to launch their own satellites. Images could cost as little as a few hundred dollars each. The most likely first customers are businesses and local governments who will use the images for planning purposes.

TRADE SHOWS

The face of trade shows has changed in the past decade. They are no longer simply places to schmooze, meet with colleagues, and try to make sales. Trade shows have become prime opportunities for competitive intelligence activities.

Trade shows are unique in that they are one of the few forums where it's okay to openly talk with competitors. In addition, while most companies try to hide the details and intricacies of their products from competitors, they bring forth this information boastfully during shows.

Japanese companies have perfected the art of trade show intelligence. Teams of people swoop down on the show, pick up whatever printed materials they can find, ask lots of questions, take loads of pictures, and learn as much as they can from the exhibiting companies.

We're starting to see that same sort of activity among U.S. companies as well.

This is especially true for *category killer* retailers such as Circuit City and Best Buy. They send teams of people to the consumer electronic shows, which are some of the largest and most extensive trade shows in the world. These twice-a-year events attract companies that show off the latest electronic gadgets, including audio and video gear. Traditionally, vendors will wait for the show to publicly introduce their newest equipment. The category killers are there to see what's hot and what they may want to carry in the future. They also expect to cut deals that preempt their competitors.

For manufacturers, the consumer electronic shows are a place to learn about their competitors' sales and marketing tactics, pricing, and publicity programs. An official of a Japanese manufacturer said that he learned from a salesperson in a competitor's booth that the company was planning a major advertising campaign during the next quarter. The booth person was eager to give him the details.

In order to take the fullest advantage of trade show intelligence, you must plan ahead. You must decide how many people to send and what areas you want to cover. Like any competitive intelligence foray, you should start with some specific questions about your competitors or the industry in general. (Although just cruising around the hall can be laborious, it can give you a good idea of general trends based on what people are exhibiting.)

Many companies send several kinds of people to trade shows, such as a marketing person, a salesperson, and an engineer. Each will focus on his area of expertise and collect pertinent information.

Preplanning helps as you identify the booths or exhibits to visit and also which speeches or seminars to attend.

During the show the team should meet regularly and discuss what they've learned and either change their focus based on new information or continue as planned to finish their coverage. Meeting regularly also gives people an opportunity to read over the brochures and press releases they've received to see if there are any follow-up questions they need to ask of booth personnel (figure 6-12).

It goes without saying that everyone should collect every brochure, every business card, and every specification sheet they can for later reference and use.

While at a competitor's booth, everyone should know who you are and what company you represent. It's only ethical that you wear an accurate name tag like everyone else. This doesn't preclude you from talking with your competitor about his product or service. Nor does it preclude him from asking you about your company's offerings.

There is also no ethical reason why you cannot observe the kinds of people who are visiting the booth, the companies they represent, and the kinds of questions they're asking. You can learn a great deal by listening to what potential buyers are asking your competitors. It's also useful to see which company representatives are taken to the private lounge area for serious discussions.

Presumably (but not always) your competitors are visiting your booth as well and asking the same kinds of probing questions. Everything is fair game. Your edge is to try to conduct your competitive intelligence activities better than they do.

Gathering International Intelligence

Gathering information on companies and conditions outside the United States presents special challenges for American competitive intelligence professionals.

The United States is far and away the most advanced nation when it comes to the world of information. We produce more databases and publish more written material than any other country. In addition,

What to Bring Back from Trade Shows

In addition to notes of your own observations, demonstrations, conversations, and any photos you took, bring back to your office the following items that are usually available.

☐ List of Attendees

☐ List of Exhibitors

☐ List of Seminars, Speeches, or Lectures

☐ Taped or Written Transcript of Seminars, Speeches, and Lectures (if not available, how to obtain by mail)

☐ Brochures, Pamphlets, and One-Sheeters

☐ Press Releases

☐ Price Lists

☐ Technical Data Sheets

☐ Magazine Articles Given as Reprints

☐ Product Photos

☐ Product Samples (often, small samples of new materials are offered)

Figure 6-12

because of our open society more information is available at low cost than anywhere else in the world. This availability is coupled with one of the most reliable and low-cost telecommunication systems in the world.

Although it may not always seem so to those of us living in the United States, our government agencies, legislatures, and courts are extremely open compared to those in many other countries.

Now for the rest of the world.

Getting information about companies and conditions overseas is a lot trickier than in the United States. Moreover, the information we want may not be available or difficult to obtain.

In the countries of the European Union, for instance, there are sixteen countries speaking twelve languages. This in itself presents problems even though English is becoming more common as the language of commerce. However, information from various countries is, of course, not in English.

When looking for information from the Far East, U.S. information collectors are often stymied by the language. While you may be able to find someone in your company who can translate documents in French, Spanish, or German, what are the chances that you will find someone fluent in a certain Chinese dialect?

On-line databases are not as advanced in Europe as in the United States. Moreover, the conversion of written information to computers is slow. Sometimes data can be one to two years behind.

When looking at countries in Eastern Europe, the problem is not only one of outmoded technology but of accuracy. Competitive intelligence professionals report that some government statistics are not reliable. This is a holdover from the days of Communism when accurate reporting wasn't a priority.

HERE OR THERE?

Can a competitive intelligence professional based in the United States collect information about overseas companies without being there? The answer is yes and no but mostly no.

There are some steps that can be taken in the States but many pieces—the nitty-gritty—must be collected overseas by someone familiar with the language, culture, and business practices..

First, what you can do without leaving home.

The foreign media is vital to overseas information collection. Certainly, you will want to monitor English language newspapers and magazines that you can obtain here such as the *Financial Times,* the *International Herald Tribune,* and the overseas editions of the *Wall Street Journal.* You also will want to subscribe to the major foreign language business publications such as France's *La Tribune de l'Economie,* which has specific articles about industries or companies translated into English.

The U.S. government can help collect overseas information. The Department of Commerce has taken the lead role in this area. For example, the Foreign Broadcast Information Service listens to and translates into English radio and TV broadcasts from around the world and disseminates a daily summary.

The Department of Commerce will often pass along reports from overseas offices to companies and trade associations. The department also runs the International Trade Administration, which investigates instances of *dumping* and other unfair trade practices. A target company may have been part of an investigation from which you can obtain information.

Another good source is trade groups either stationed in the United States or with offices located here. The same goes for international organizations with U.S. offices. The United Nations's World Bank in Washington is a good example of that and so are some of its other economic entities such as the International Monetary Fund and the International Finance Corporation.

BEING THERE

As much as you'd like to believe that you never have to leave home to collect foreign information, it's not true. At some point you will have to hire a competitive intelligence professional to collect information for you overseas or assign one of your overseas employees to the job. The main reasons are culture and access.

In the United States for example, it's acceptable to *cold-call* someone we don't know, introduce ourselves, and ask questions. Americans are very direct people.

This behavior rarely occurs in Europe, and in Japan it is considered downright rude.

If you do get the information you want, you're still looking at it from an American perspective. For example, how many Americans know that West European managers usually have technical backgrounds as opposed to financial backgrounds? This will color what they say in interviews and how they will react.

Managers in other countries, especially Japan, don't rely on Wall Street investors and the public for their capital needs. Money comes from banks. So, while foreign managers want to look the best they can in public, there is little need to give a good news spin to the media as is done in the United States. There is little fear of scaring away investors—the banks—as long as they know exactly what's going on in the company in spite of a negative news story.

Here's another difference. In Europe, companies are generally stable in that there is a long-term management mandate and companies are not considered on the block or managers' jobs in jeopardy just because of a few bad quarters. In the United States, because of public stock ownership, every company is considered fair game and managers are judged almost quarter to quarter. Long-term planning often takes a back seat to keeping the share price high.

Another example: Suppose you're interested in a foreign competitor's R&D expenditures. You study their financial reports and find the figure, but are you aware that some foreign governments subsidize corporate R&D?

Do you, as an American information collector, know how to interpret and factor in these cultural differences to the information you gathered?

Unless you've spent a great deal of time in the foreign country, know the business culture, and speak the language, the answer is no.

FINDING SOMEONE

Clearly, the best choice for obtaining competitive intelligence from overseas countries is from someone familiar with the language, culture, and practices, and the best person, of course, is someone in your company. However, what if you don't have overseas offices but still need to monitor foreign businesses?

Hire a competitive intelligence consultant.

In the past few years, businesspeople in Europe and Asia have been establishing consultancies for competitive intelligence. All of these people are native-born and many have worked as competitive intelligence professionals in their countries or regions.

Also, many U.S. competitive intelligence consultancies have established offices in Europe and Asia that they use for their American clients. Some U.S. companies have simply established relationships with overseas individuals who are skilled in competitive intelligence. You can reach these people through their U.S. affiliates.

Organizing Information

Some competitive intelligence professionals think that a company needs a sophisticated system for organizing, storing, and disseminating data. This is not true. In most cases, the simpler the better.

Some small companies rely on file folders with information people can easily access. These folders contain annual reports, competitor pricing charts, advertisements, newspaper clippings, and so on.

Which people should have access to this information?

Anyone with a need.

Information must be shared in order for the system to work. If salespeople are encouraged to gather and share information with the competitive intelligence unit, then they must have access to that raw information and any other information that comes into the unit.

The only question is how.

For small companies with one location, file folders in a centrally located room can work. Anyone can come into the room, read through a folder, and take notes or make copies. Whatever analysis they wish to do on their own should be encouraged by the competitive intelligence unit.

For companies that have local area networks, or wide area networks for that matter, information should be made accessible from a central data bank for anyone who needs it.

The Golden Rule: Information collected by the competitive intelligence unit—either by competitive intelligence personnel or anyone else in the company—must be available to everyone who needs it.

The information, of course, is analyzed by the competitive intelligence unit for management but anyone who needs it for tactical planning, making simple decisions, or just wanting to learn more about a subject should have access as well.

Corning has an enlightening way of sharing information. Management learned that although people were willing to share their information, they still wanted control over it. For example, they wanted to update it when necessary but also expunge it if they discovered something was in error without having to jump through hoops to do so or be embarrassed by their mistakes.

The company designed a computerized central database with local control. Each record has an owner and that owner can do whatever he wants with the information even though everyone has access to it. If you don't want the information anymore—or don't need it—you can transfer it to someone else. This feature comes in handy when people change jobs within the company.

Another interesting feature is that information is flagged each time it is accessed. This serves two purposes. One, it tells the research people what kinds of information people need and are using, and second, it gives some feedback to the person who has contributed the information. It's a good feeling to know that people find useful the information you have gathered and shared.

This kind of computerization is becoming more common. According to a survey conducted by Fuld & Company, computer use in intelligence operations rose from 31 percent in 1983 to 44 percent in 1991. This should not be surprising. As companies become more computerized and we see PCs on people's desks, it's only natural that they be used for competitive intelligence.

All that is required is that written material be scanned along with pictures, graphs, and charts and placed into a file that can then be called up by the user.

Users should have the option of searching for material using key words and phrases much as they do with magazine or newspaper databases.

Some companies buy software packages that are geared toward competitive intelligence use. One example is a software program called WINCITE from WINCITE Systems. One particular feature (Fig. 6-13) allows you, among other things, to produce profile reports about individual competitors, their products, and services. The program also lets you distribute reports throughout your local area network.

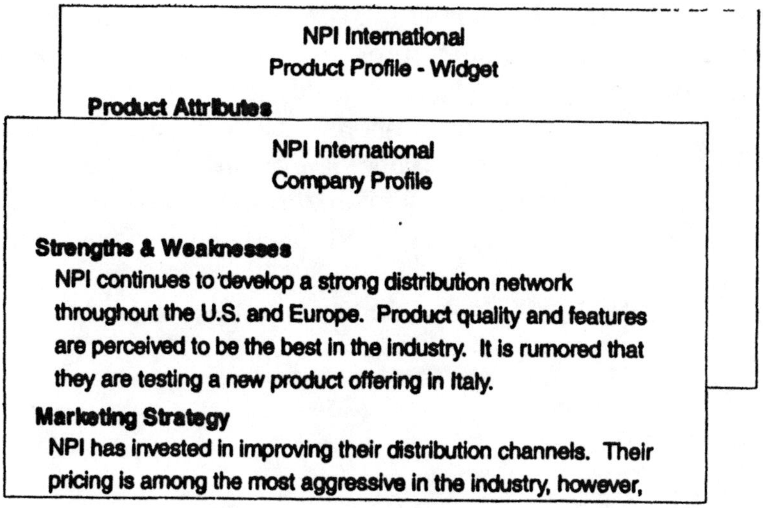

NPI International
Product Profile - Widget

Product Attributes

NPI International
Company Profile

Strengths & Weaknesses
NPI continues to develop a strong distribution network throughout the U.S. and Europe. Product quality and features are perceived to be the best in the industry. It is rumored that they are testing a new product offering in Italy.

Marketing Strategy
NPI has invested in improving their distribution channels. Their pricing is among the most aggressive in the industry, however,

Figure 6-13

MassMutual's Corporate Strategy Department started monitoring the competition from a strategic point of view in 1990. It built a text database using the WordPerfect word-processing program. This allowed key word searches and text retrieval using a program familiar to most everyone in the company because they were already using it daily.

CRITERIA FOR ORGANIZING AND DISSEMINATING DATA

1. It must be easy for anyone to input data into the system.
2. It must be easy for anyone to retrieve data from the system.
3. The system must be able to hold all media collected such as pictures, graphs, and brochures.
4. The system must be able to grow as a company's competitive intelligence services grow.
5. Data must be accurate. Information based on guesses, estimates, and rumors must be noted as such. These pieces of information are useful. Some companies attach a 1 to 10 rating on data so users know how much weight to give each item.
6. The system should be centrally located although anyone can take information and use it to produce their own local database. They should be encouraged to share back with the central system whatever enhancements or filtering of information they have made.
7. Large chunks of data should be broken down into smaller pieces so people can access only what they need without having to wade through large databases. Information files should be organized by competing company name, technology, pricing, or other categories, based on how people want to use the information. It will take time to learn what people really need. Questionnaires and surveys can help.
8. The system should be secure from unauthorized users.

CHAPTER SEVEN

Analysis

"All the people out there give the impression that business intelligence is nothing more than collecting data. It's unfortunate, because the real value added comes with the intervention of humans."

—Professor Liam Fahey, formerly of Boston University and Babson College

Before World War II, countries relied on spies. If a country needed to know something about its enemy, such as the number of troops, their movements, or how well their munitions were holding out, they had spies infiltrate the enemy's ranks. The spy observed what he needed to know or he recruited a traitor to get the information for him.

This is an efficient way of learning about your enemy. Not only is it accurate, but it doesn't require any extrapolation of the facts. What you see is what you get.

However, starting with World War II, spying became tougher. The Allies had few spies in Nazi Germany and Japan and therefore had to rely on bits and pieces of information gathered from radio transmissions, unclassified documents, captured military personnel, and aircraft reconnaissance. Although the Allies never had a complete set of the pieces to the puzzle, they had begun to learn how to turn what pieces they had into usable intelligence. This process became known as military analysis.

After World War II, the United States became a leader in analysis techniques as it sought to gain insight into the Soviet Union during the Cold War years. Much of the information the CIA and other intelligence-gathering organizations obtained was from publicly available sources such as reports, newspaper articles, broadcasts, satellite pictures. James Bond and his American counterparts notwithstanding, most national intelligence needs were met by activities other than spying.

Analysis is the process of taking information—often seemingly unconnected information—and turning it into intelligence.

The first objective of any intelligence project is to find the answer. The preferred method is for the answer to be there when you look. Why risk the inherent inaccuracies of analysis when you don't have to?

Jan Herring, a vice president of the Futures Group and former CIA analyst, illustrates this concept with a story about Aerospatiale, the French aerospace company. "Years ago we were trying to learn the strategic plans of Aerospatiale. If I can't find it, I thought, I'm going to read the papers and get other pieces, then infer their plans. We found the European Space Agency database—a rather obscure database at the time—and Aerospatiale's plans were right there. We got lucky, and we didn't have to do the analysis."

Unfortunately, these kinds of instances are not always going to happen. The analyst isn't always going to be this lucky.

Good Analysts Are Born, Not Made—Usually

Good analysts are hard to find. It takes a unique person with many skills and a certain temperament to be a successful analyst.

Intelligence agencies like the CIA look for potential analysts who can think linearly and in patterns. They don't always think sequentially; they can leap ahead when necessary. They make remote relationships from things they have learned and know about from outside the realm of their immediate investigation. They relate this outside information to what's going on inside their own situation.

Good analysts do not necessarily have an MBA in the particular area in which they're involved but have a wide base of experiences and knowledge.

The CIA tries to recruit college graduates who are at the top of their class. They are put under the tutelage of a branch chief, who, after six months of training, teases an assessment out of him or her based on a mock-intelligence gathering situation. Making assessments, estimations, and guesses is not something that comes easy to most of us. These apprentices are asked about implications for U.S. policy and reaction from allies.

The second time around the recruit must defend his assessment before a board. The third time around the recruit must be willing to draw conclusions without prompting or pushing. The CIA analyst-training program takes about eighteen months.

According to Herring, the most important trait of an analyst is to be able to say: "This is what I think will happen based on what I know. This is what it means to the company."

It takes personal courage, intellectual fortitude, and conviction to take guesses based on analyzed information.

Assessments always involve unknowns and uncertainties. The traditional way many businesses treat those who make errors—demotion, dismissal, or ostracism—isn't conducive to breeding analysts. Although no one advocates making illogical, unfounded assessments, at some point companies and the people in those companies must make an educated guess.

Most of the time, assessments are presented as options. Often an analyst examines several different scenarios and assesses the potential effect on the company. Although he may not be able to know with certainty what a competitor will do, he should be able to articulate several probable courses of action and their effects.

Sometimes, advanced analysts can take this a step further. In some cases, they can actually test a scenario by watching a target company's reaction to their own company's programs. This provides a real-life test to an analyst's theories. Of course, part of an analyst's assessment should also include how a target company responded in the past to your or another company's actions.

A good analyst, in the end, must guess what will be the most likely scenarios. He must take a stand. The good news is most of the time a practiced analyst will make the correct assessment. .

When Will It Happen?

While a good analyst is right most of the time, most analysts trip up when it comes to timing. The CIA knew for some time that the Soviet Union was going to dissolve into chaos. The one thing they didn't know was when.

Analysts at competing companies were sure that IBM would enter the personal computer business. It was the only way they could go if they were to remain competitive. Everywhere, PCs were in, and mainframes were out. However, the PC program at IBM wasn't funded (which confused and confounded many analysts in itself) and it seemed to outsiders that IBM would remain with their mainframe business. It was only a matter of time, most analysts concluded, that the company revenues would dip, the stock would drop, and layoffs would occur. This took place in 1989 and 1990 when the balance sheet still showed a profit, but it wasn't until 1991 that most IBM watchers agreed that the company was in deep trouble with no end in sight to the free fall. Most analysts were correctly predicting IBM's troubles in the late 1980s; they just didn't know exactly when.

Another example of good analysis but errant timing concerns Bill Gates, chairman of Microsoft. Gates gave a speech before attendees of a computer show in 1990. He and his staff predicted that the days of using personal data assistants that turn your script into text readable by computer were coming soon. In 1994, Gates made another speech during which he noted that his timing was off about the PDAs. In fact, even in 1994, the technology still wasn't quite right.

SWOT

One of the basic, but not necessarily simple, forms of analysis is something called SWOT: Strength, Weaknesses, Opportunities, and Threats.

SWOT gives a basic way of analyzing a competitor by filling in a matrix of the company's characteristics. This method is particularly useful in cases where an analysis must be done quickly or when you want to take a big-picture look at a competitor. It's also useful as a preliminary analysis that can be taken further when you have the time and resources to do so.

Once accomplished, SWOT analysis gives you a good look at your competitor in comparison to your own company. It gives you the highlights of his past with an eye toward his future moves—or moves that you should take to preempt the target's most likely activities.

Although your assessment includes rankings, from most important to least important within each matrix, SWOT is more of a qualitative analysis as opposed to a financial analysis that relies on numbers and statistics.

Strength includes the competitor's most powerful attributes, including the patents it holds, its technology, market share, depth of management, financial position, customer loyalty, quality of product, and so forth.

Weaknesses are the opposite of strengths and include the competitor's liabilities such as weighty debt, unskilled workers, labor strife, poor-quality products, poor image, and outmoded equipment or processes.

Opportunities are chances to prosper from a changing marketplace, industry situation, or other environmental condition. Opportunities include things like pending government regulation that would benefit the company, changing demographics that boost the potential customer base, a competitor's patent that is expiring, or a drastic drop in the cost of raw materials.

Threats are the opposite of opportunities in that they are external conditions that can harm a company. These include raw materials shortages, costly government regulations, new competitors, or, for companies that rely on borrowing money, interest rates that are heading higher.

Strengths and weaknesses are internal characteristics and opportunities and threats are external characteristics.

How Do Companies Compete?

Before looking at a typical SWOT matrix, step back a moment and understand how companies compete. This may seem obvious, but many companies never think about how their competitors compete against them. They don't understand the areas in which their competitors exhibit their characteristics.

What makes a company competitive and in what areas do you and your competitor go head-to-head?

First, companies compete with products. They strive for quality, market share, performance of their product, low returns, and customer satisfaction with the product.

Second, companies compete in the financial area. Companies want high returns on investment, high share price, low costs, and access to capital when necessary.

Third, companies compete in technology. They want to bring products to market quickly. They want to exploit their patents and prevent others from using them. They want to get high returns on research and development dollars.

Fourth, companies compete with their organizations and their people. They want depth in management, a corporate culture that breeds success, and a highly trained, intelligent workforce.

Fifth, companies compete by strategic alliances with other companies. To build strength they acquire the skills of other companies by merger or joint ventures. Sucessful companies have strong alliances with suppliers, distributors, and manufacturers.

Sixth, companies compete in manufacturing. Some of this can overlap with product competition, but mainly we're talking about plant capacity, special processes and machinery, motivated and skilled labor force, and, of course, quality.

Seventh, companies compete with marketing and advertising. Areas such as service and strong promotion are key factors here.

Eighth, companies compete with their reputation. How they are perceived by the media, customers, suppliers, financial institutions, and government agencies are important factors in a firm's competitive edge (figure 7-1).

Not all companies compete in all of these areas.

Figure 7-2 is a typical matrix with an example of company A's SWOT. As you assess your competitors look in the above eight areas to decide which factors are crucial to their success. Also notice in the matrix that it not only has implications but possible scenarios as well. There won't be a one-to-one correlation on every cross factor nor will only one

How Companies Compete

Products	Alliances
❏ quality	❏ strong joint ventures
❏ market share	❏ strong relationships with
❏ performance	other companies,
❏ low returns	suppliers, distributors,
	and customers
Financials	**Manufacturing**
❏ low debt	❏ special processes
❏ high share price	❏ necessary capacity
❏ access to capital	❏ up-to-date machinery
Technology	**Marketing/Advertising**
❏ cutting-edge	❏ strong promotions
❏ fast cycle times	❏ healthy budget
❏ high patent exploitation	
Organization	**Reputation/Image**
❏ skilled/trained workers	❏ positive perception
❏ motivated workforce	❏ name recognition
❏ depth in management	❏ trademark recognition

Figure 7-1

implication spring from each cross factoring of SWO and T. In this example, there are many more possible scenarios.

Our Mental Models

According to Professor Liam Fahey formerly of Boston University and Babson College, even good analysts show weakness in one behavioral area. "Most analysis is done to confirm our assertions or theorems. It's not done in an open forum of inquiry."

In two words, it's the problem of preconceived notions.

All of us are reluctant to disparage our own mental models of how we'd like the world to be or how we think other people act. For example, an analyst who believes that companies should increase revenue through cost cutting might be looking for that trait in a competitor while all the time their plan may really be to gain market share (and increased revenues) through increased advertising.

SWOT MATRIX of Company A

Internal Factors ⟶ External Factors ⟶	Strengths (S) 1. Best technology 2. Skilled workforce	Weaknesses (W) 1. No management depth 2. Spotty distribution
Opportunities (O) 1. Demographics favor product consumption 2. Failing of other competitor, B	SO Implications 1-1 Keep technology current 2-2 Might hire skilled workers from B	WO Implications 2-1 Must satisfy growing market segment to remain competitive
Threats (T) 1. Possible regulation 2. Growing of competitor C	ST Implications 1-1 Might have to share technology to avoid regulation 2-2 Keep current workforce satisfied	WT Implications 1-1 Management may not be able to thwart regulation 2-2 C may take market share away

Figure 7-2

Doing an accurate assessment requires that we put aside our personal biases and our preconceived notions and look at each case with an open mind. This doesn't mean that you can't build theories along the way based on what you see or what you know. It does mean that you must wait until you have solid evidence and a strong logical argument before you come to any conclusions.

Crystal Ball: Seeing the Future by Understanding the Present

Some of the criticism of business intelligence is that it's historical. It looks at past events or at current numbers. True enough. It's the only thing we have, but if the search is done correctly, analysis can offer several possible scenarios for future actions by your competitors. These scenarios will then allow you to counter them, preempt them, or do nothing based on your goals and plans.

When trying to figure out a competitor's future actions, you should look at several areas.

Leila Kight, president of Washington Researchers and one of the earliest competitive intelligence practitioners, suggests that there are four key perspectives when forecasting a company's actions.

1. The company's public forecast.
2. Industry experts' forecasts.
3. What the company's current or past actions indicate for the future.
4. How the competitive environment will affect the company's future.

All of these factors should be judged against the company's strength and weakness or, put another way, their capabilities.

For example, suppose a company says it is going to embark on an acquisition campaign. Perhaps the president mentioned it in his letter to shareholders as part of the annual report. However, after you analyze their financial position—maybe the market changed to their detriment—you believe that they don't have the wherewithal to buy another company. Their public forecast about acquisitions, no matter how well intended and honest at the time, is unlikely.

While the annual report is one type of public forecast there are others, including speeches, trade show exhibits, newspaper articles, and regulatory filings. All of these may contain signals of future actions.

One public forecast that I particularly like are mission statements.

MISSION STATEMENTS

One of the main goals of analysis is to forecast what a company is likely to do.

Aside from looking at the numbers and knowing what the company has done in the past, it would help to know the goals and philosophies by which they set their compass and make their decisions.

Believe it or not, many companies do that and an analyst doesn't have to look far for it. The source is mission statements.

Like the previous example about getting lucky and finding the published strategic plans of Aerospatiale—saving the trouble and uncertainty of analysis—mission statements often tell you exactly what you want to know about a company's strategy and plans.

In addition, by studying how a company's mission statement has changed over the years, you can get an excellent insight into how the company may be moving in a new direction or field of activity.

First a definition: Corporate mission statements are the operational, ethical, and financial guides of companies. They expound the goals, dreams, behavior, culture, and strategies of companies more than any other document.

Mission statements go by many different names, including philosophies, goals, game plan, beliefs, vision, and values. They are as short as one sentence or as long as a booklet.

These documents are not just slogans or mottoes. Most companies actually pay attention to their mission statements and try to live up to their words. This is because mission statements often express the beliefs of top management on how they want the company run. Also, these documents usually take a long time to compose and when the process is done management is loath to see their efforts wasted.

Interestingly enough, mission statements are one of the most used management tools, according to a 1994 study by the Planning Forum and Bain & Company.

Mission statements are often written during times of crisis, such as when a company is changing strategy, management, or the industry is in upheaval. Because of this, it's something that analysts should pay attention to as part of a firm's remade overall picture.

Let's look at a few mission statement excerpts and see what you can learn from them.

Suppose you had been watching the real estate developer Trammell Crow in the 1980s. At the time, it was the largest private-sector developer, but like many real estate developers it was being bashed by the drop in the real estate market. So in 1989, the company made plans to change the way it did business. That change, to those who knew where to look, was articulated in the company's mission statement, which was altered to reflect their change in strategy.

The company's "Vision" went from: *To be the premier customer-driven real estate company in the U.S.* to: *To be the premier customer-driven real estate services company in the U.S.*

One word, *services*, changed the company's focus. No longer would they play the role of being a traditional real estate developer—make decisions, then consult people to see if they like the decision—Trammell Crow would become a services business, where you consult people to see what they want and then build it, manage it —whatever services the client requests.

Under "Guiding Principles" the company states: *We build long-term customer relationships by listening to, understanding, and exceeding our customers' needs—timely and hassle-free.*

What's interesting here is the phrase *hassle-free*. It's not a term you often see in company documents. To a skilled analyst it imparts a feeling of familiarity, simplicity, and a down-to-earth attitude that clearly shows the kind of relationship the company would like to have with its clients.

Let's look at Intel. The 1994 mission statement and the statement of "Values" show clearly the kind of company they are through the words they use. An analyst from a competitor knows very well how they want to operate and how they will accomplish their goals. The mission statement shows they take risks and reward people for doing so. It also outlines the kind of people they want to work there and what is expected of them

Want to know where, geographically, they will spend their re-sources? Under "Our Objectives" it says: *Capitalize on growing PC consumption in Asia.* Want to know what new products they're inter-ested in? *Extend the Intel architecture to mobile products.* And what about people? What is their philosophy about layoffs or downsizing? *Continuously redeploy people and assets with greater value added.* One day you're working in a chip factory, the next day you're driving a truck.

Suppose you're an ice cream maker and you're analyzing Ben & Jerry's. You know that the company gets all its milk products from Vermont dairies, which charge a little higher than dairies out of state. Will the company stay with them or go elsewhere to get a better price? Their mission statement states: *To make, distribute, and sell the finest all-natural ice cream and related products in a wide variety of inno-vative flavors made from Vermont dairy products.*

Further exploration will show you that Ben & Jerry's has honored its mission statement in the past and will probably do so in the future.

Thinking about buying Hallmark or Smuckers? Probably not. Their mission statements state emphatically that they will remain private and family-owned.

Want to understand companies that are undergoing vast transformations like AT&T or IBM? Take a look at their mission statements. All the information about their revised corporate strategy is there in black-and-white.

INDUSTRY ANALYSTS

The second crystal ball tool is industry experts' forecasts. In other words, what close observers of the industry have to say. These include Wall Street analysts, newsletter reporters, trade associations, and unions.

WHAT THE COMPETITION IS DOING

A third tool is the company's actions that indicate a future course. For example, if a company buys land, it's pretty clear they will build a facility on that property. If they place ads in newspapers looking for lots of people, they may be embarking on new projects or anticipate increases in production. (Of course, you have to know more of the specifics. They could just be replacing retired workers or even striking workers. Don't take anything for granted.)

Other actions to look for include mergers and acquisitions, and buying licensing rights to patents and technology.

MACRO INDICATORS

The fourth indication of future actions, the environment in which the company operates, includes market demands, environmental regulations, and demographics. Assuming you are in the same industry as your target company, you should already know what factors affect the company and are likely to impact its decisions and activities.

I would like to add a fifth factor to this well-used and well-accepted list of crucial factors that can help predict future actions.

The behavior of the decision makers. The human factor.

Many competitive intelligence strategists often overlook this important factor because it can't be quantified. You can't put it into numbers. It also resides in the area of psychology, which makes many people in business uncomfortable.

The Human Factor

"Decision makers know where a company is going."
—Cheryl Poirier, The Futures Group

One area of competitive intelligence that is not often addressed is the personality of decision makers. Intelligence practitioners tend to look at the hard numbers of a company, but many fail to take into account the behavioral traits of management that are responsible for decisions.

This important piece of the puzzle is often neglected because it can't be quantified. However, if done correctly a personality profile can give some of the best clues to a company's future plans.

Cheryl Poirier of The Futures Group tells the following story:

"There was a large conglomerate of about six or seven companies who had brought in a new CEO and chairman. We wanted to look and see what he would focus on. Which business would receive his attention and what would he change about them?

"We performed a financial analysis, looking at return on investment, and learned that all the companies came in at about 9 or 10 percent.

"Then we found an article in which the CEO said he measured a company's performance based on their return on assets. He said that everything came out of that figure. It was important to him. So we looked again at the companies but this time we focused on the return on assets. They all came out at about 9 or 10 percent except one, which was 2.5 percent.

"We decided he would focus on that company, and sure enough, later on he did."

This story not only illustrates the power of personality profiling to predict a company's movements but also highlights one of the three key elements to personal profiling: a person's history and background.

People tend to repeat successful behaviors. The CEO in this example preferred to focus on return on assets because it had helped him succeed in the past.

People also tend to learn from past mistakes. If they couldn't increase market share by cutting prices in the past, for example, they probably won't use that strategy again.

Interestingly, some competitive intelligence practitioners who per-

formed a personality profile of John Sculley (the former head of PepsiCo who went to Apple as CEO), predicted that he would fail in his
new job. They saw him implementing tried-and-true tactics that
worked at PepsiCo but probably would not work at Apple because the
two companies are so different.

Sculley used brand loyalty at Pepsi to charge high prices for his
product. That revenue was plowed back into advertising to increase
market share. This tactic worked at Pepsi but was a disaster at Apple
where Macintosh sales dropped precipitously.

Sculley eventually left Apple under less than amiable circumstances.

The second key element to profiling is a person's overall behavior.
Are they aggressive, boastful, do they take risks or are they conserva-
tive by nature?

People rarely change their basic personalities and these can give
you clues to their future behavior. Interviews and profiles written
about businesspeople give good indications of their personality
traits.

Ross Perot gives very clear signals about how he will react to certain
situations. He appears to be friendly, genial—until someone threatens
his status or questions his integrity. Then he becomes nasty and acts in
an autocratic manner.

The third element concerns a person's environment. What kind of
external environment are they dealing with at their company? What
barriers or constraints are they operating under and how will they
react? For example, how will a CEO react to a hostile board or a nasty
takeover attempt? Sometimes, a decision maker is thrust into a situation he never had to deal with before. You will have to guess about his
possible reaction.

Body language and speech also play an important role in guessing
the moves of a decision maker.

U.K. consultant Andrew Pollard in the Summer 1990 *Competitive*

Three Keys to Personality Profiling

1. Past behavior: successes and failures

2. Overall behavioral traits

3. Current environment

Figure 7-3

Intelligence Review related a story about a TV interview in which Sir John Egan, the head of Jaguar, was asked about his company's poor performance. The interviewer asked if Jaguar was considering a merger. His reply was: "No, I think we intend to remain fully independent."

Pollard notes that his slightly hesitant words were amplified by a tone and manner that gave the impression that he was not certain, that his determination in the matter was far from absolute.

It was not a surprise, according to Pollard, that Ford took over Jaguar nine months later.

Sometimes, profiling a competitor can help you decide your own best course of action.

In the early 1970s, fledgling telecommunications giant MCI was struggling to survive. AT&T had refused to give them interconnections to the local phone system and without these connections they would not be able to sell long-distance services. While mid-level officials of AT&T and MCI engaged in deep and lengthy negotiations, a personal profile of AT&T's chairman forecast the true outcome.

MCI chairman Bill McGowan had on two separate occasions, over a two-year period, met with AT&T chairman John deButts to discuss the matter. In both instances, McGowan came away with the impression that because of deButts's confrontational nature the company would never give MCI the connections it was entitled to receive under law. McGowan believed that deButts was willing and in fact relished a court battle with the upstart MCI. McGowan concluded that deButts's arrogance also would cause him to make mistakes along the way and lose the fight.

McGowan's assessment of deButts's nature was on the money. Instead of spending more effort in trying to negotiate an agreement, McGowan used his time and limited resources to marshal his forces in a massive lawsuit against AT&T. After many years, MCI won, which ultimately led to Ma Bell's divestiture.

Profiling would be easy if we could sit our subject down and administer a psychological test such as the Myers-Briggs. That's impossible, but there are methods that can get us as close as possible to a person's nature.

Here is some basic data that you will want to collect for your assessment:

- Childhood history. Where was he born, under what conditions did he grow up? Was he poor, well-to-do? What traits did his parents instill in him?
- Education. What did he study? Where? Has he spent time traveling; has he visited and studied other cultures?
- Who are his friends? What are his hobbies and interests?
- Where has he worked? How did he manage and make decisions in similar situations?
- What are his basic personality traits? Calm and thoughtful or excitable and vitriolic? How does he treat people in his company?
- What are his goals? What drives him? Is he a risk taker or does he reach his goals by slow and steady steps?
- What is his lifestyle? Lavish or simple?

There are other elements of course. Much of what you want to know will be in the person's writings, such as speeches where he mentions his business and personal beliefs. You should pay attention to TV and radio interviews and profiles written about the person by reporters or industry analysts. Question-and-answer interviews can be revealing. Sometimes managers will explain exactly how they make decisions and manage their companies.

A good source of information is people in your company or acquaintances who know the person. Don't forget obvious sources like *Who's Who* and the company's own biography of this person. Read the annual reports where he has written his letter to shareholders. This can give strong clues as to where he would like to go and how he may accomplish the journey.

It's important to remember that we're not dealing with numbers and graphs. We're dealing with people, and their actions cannot be quantified. Personality profiles require intuition and some estimating.

In Europe, emphasis is placed on handwriting analysis, a practice that is not often considered in the United States. In fact, if you've ever applied for a job in Europe you already know that cover letters are expected to be handwritten. This is so prospective employers can glean some indication of your character from your handwriting.

Some competitive intelligence practitioners build samples of a competing manager's handwriting to help build a picture of their personality. If you can get some handwriting samples, this may be a useful source of information. Although the signature on the annual letter to

John F. Welch, Jr.
Chairman of the Board and
Chief Executive Officer

February 11, 1994

Figure 7-4

shareholders is not enough, short memos to staff or notes to colleagues may be of some value in your overall assessment.

However, don't overlook signatures. While they don't tell you much
about the inner, true personality of a subject, signatures can tell you
about the public person. Signatures are our faces to the outside world.
It's the personality we want to project and it may or may not be the
same as the private person. (Usually it is not.)

Doodles and Personality
(geometric shapes)

Meticulous, may be a bit fussy

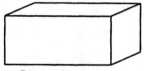

Practical, consistent

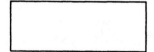

Practical, feasible, effective

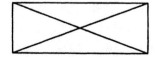

Strong self-control

Figure 7-5

Take Jack Welch's signature from General Electric's 1993 annual report (figure 7-4). Although we don't know anything about how much pressure he used to sign the letter to shareholders (an important factor in graphology analysis), the signature shows some interesting characteristics. The first letter of a person's name is usually indicative of how a person projects himself. The large, looping J shows courage, conviction, and a strong sense of self. The straight, nonlooping line that goes straight down shows a person's look at himself. In this case, the unfinished loop may show an inability to learn from past mistakes or that the writer may not want to deal with past mistakes or traumatic events.

As with signatures, doodles are also windows to a person's personality (figure 7-5).

For example, strong, logical planners often sketch geometric shapes. These people are precise and keep to the essentials. Shading these shapes or adding other shapes to them indicates an eye for detail and minutiae.

On the other hand, those who doodle people and characters are less analytical but may be more visionary. There are tens of more types of doodles which can be useful tidbits to add to your profile.

Patents

> "It took twenty years for optical fibers to show a profit. We keep track of patents to give us an indication if we're still maintaining leadership in that area."
> —Gary Rousch, Manager, Corporate Information
> Management, Corning Incorporated

Every day, around the world, more than a thousand patents and related documents are issued.

These documents provide information about your competitors and their products that are not available anywhere else. In fact, patents are the one place that your competitor is forced to reveal in public critical information that it never would let out otherwise. More than 75 percent of the information contained in U.S. patents is never released anywhere else.

While the patents themselves offer a great amount of technical and scientific information, the astute competitive intelligence analyst doesn't stop there. A patent's true worth is amplified after you've done some rather intensive, number-crunching analysis.

Patent analysis can tell you:

- Which companies are doing cutting-edge work; who the leaders are.
- Which individuals are doing cutting-edge work.
- Which countries are on the forefront of a technology.
- How long it takes companies to exploit a patent; how long it takes for research and development to turn into profits.
- Which technologies are trending up or down; where R&D dollars are being spent among industry leaders.
- Relationships (i.e., joint ventures) among companies engaged in similar research or producing the same products; research relationships among company subsidiaries.

These analyses are based on basic information contained in patent documents. All patents contain the following basic data:

1. Claims. Description about the product or process. Claims also include drawings and charts.
2. Inventor(s)/Author(s). This is the person or persons who actually invented the product or process.
3. Assignee. This is the person or company to whom the inventor assigned the patent. Usually, an inventor working for a company will assign the patent to that company.
4. Licensee. The person or company who has the right to produce the invention under agreement with the patent holder. In many cases, the assignee is also the licensee.
5. Citations. Although patents are issued only for new or novel inventions, no one has to reinvent the wheel. All patents must cite other patents from which the current work has used facets of or improved upon.

Seventy to 80 percent of all patents are never cited by another inventor in his patent. Therefore, when one particular patent is cited continually, it shows that the assignee owns some leading-edge technology. The following is a chart of citations of a Hitachi patent for

Direct Citation Neighbors for a Highly Cited Hitachi Patent
U.S. Patent Number: 4481573
Shared Virtual Address Translation Unit for a Multiprocessor System
Assignee: Hitachi

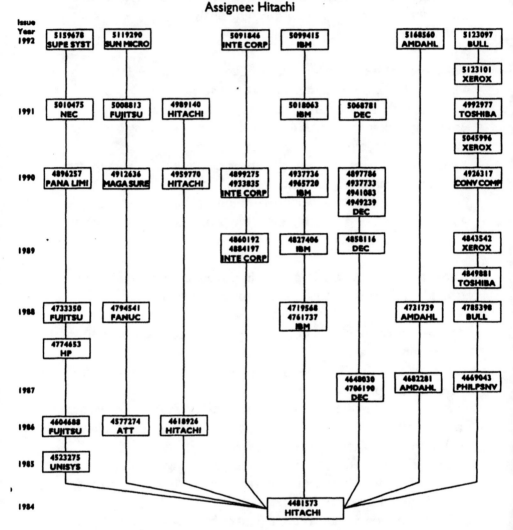

Figure 7-6

"shared virtual address translation unit for a multiprocessor system" (figure 7-6). In everyday English, it's a patent for a device that allows different computer devices, the main memory board in a PC for example, to use the same physical memory. In essence, this chip acts as a traffic cop equitably allocating memory among several users, making sure that they don't try to access the same piece of memory at the same time. This is an important device because sharing the same memory units saves money and makes computer systems more efficient.

You can see how many other patents used this technology and over what time period. You can also see which companies cited the patent and this gives you a good overview of Hitachi's most aggressive competitors in this field.

Now, if another company's patent in this field were beginning to be cited more, say in later years, that might suggest Hitachi was losing its dominant position.

The popular drug Tagamet was patented by SmithKline Beecham. The following chart shows citations based on the Tagamet patent from Merck & Co. as well as SmithKline from 1975 through 1988. This chart indicates that during that time period, and for this product area, Smith-Kline was losing scientific-technological ground while Merck was clearly gaining ground.

If you were looking to learn from an industry leader, it's pretty clear which company you would study.

Patent analysis can also show technology trends. By putting together

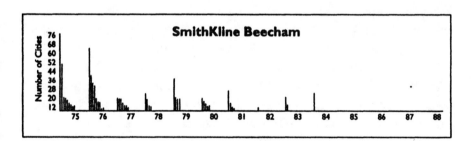

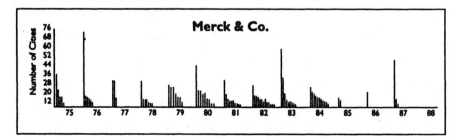

Figure 7-7

several patent trend indicators you can get a good picture of where a certain technology lies. This trend can help your company decide if it wants to enter a market and if so, how.

Richard Campbell, a patent researcher formerly with Batelle's Pacific Northwest Laboratories, developed a chart showing the life cycle of technology. He gives it four classifications: emerging, growing, maturing, and obsolescent. These four areas can be identified by doing patent analysis.

Figure 7-8 shows that when a certain technology is emerging, there is low patent activity with high concentration of the patent among a few companies. During the growth period, patent activity is high and concentration decreases as more companies enter the market. During the mature phase, activity is stable, the number of patents levels off, and the number of companies involved also stabilizes. When a technology become obsolete, patent activities decrease. Activity is at the lowest point but concentration is high as only a few major players remain.

The following chart. Figure 7-9, shows patent activities for optoelectric couplers. It was based on work by Mary Ellen Mogee of Mogee Research & Analysis Associates in Reston, Virginia. It shows the relationship between international patent activity and concentration among companies. At first, the number of companies involved in the technology is concentrated in the top four firms (100 percent). By 1974–77 concentration is down to 66.7 percent and still dropping. *Concentration is decreasing.* The activity level in all areas is increasing. *Activity level is high.* According to the technology cycle chart, the optoelectronics industry is still in the growing phase.

This kind of information is invaluable to a manager contemplating entering the business or for a company that is already in the business. By knowing which phase the optoelectronics industry is inhabiting, a

Life Cycle Stage	Patent Activity	Company Concentration
Emerging	Low, Increasing	High
Growing	High	Decreasing
Maturing	Stable	Stable
Obsolescent	Low, Decreasing	Increasing, High

Figure 7-8

Activity	1969–73	1974–77	1978–81	1982–85	1986–89
The same invention (family) patented in many countries	0.4	2.5	44.5	153.0	225.0
Number of companies receiving these patents	0.4	2.75	33.5	73.0	107.25
Concentration of companies (top four companies)	100%	66.7%	31.28%	29.35%	30.15%

(The numbers are an average indicator per year.)

Figure 7-9

manager can anticipate a certain set of problems, situations, and conditions. Different acquisition, marketing, and sales strategies are employed by firms, depending upon which phase their core technology is in: emerging, growing, maturing, or obsolescent.

Company strategies and characteristics also can be discovered with other kinds of patent analysis.

If a company is heavily citing its own patents this indicates that it is building a large body of knowledge in that area and will exploit that technology to its fullest. Mogee suggests these companies are employing a *pioneer* strategy.

On the other hand, companies that cite other companies' patents are engaging in an *imitator* strategy, relying on the work of others to boost their own efforts. Looked at another way, a company whose patents are cited more often than it cites itself may be losing its technological lead to its competitors.

In the chart of optoelectronic couplers, figure 7-10, the 45-degree line is a citation balance. Below the line, the company is being cited more than it is citing. Those above the line are being cited less than they are citing. Those near the line are in pretty good balance between the two conditions.

There is also a line separating *teaching* and *protecting*. Those companies that teach allow other companies to use their technology. Those that protect, keep their technology to themselves and try to keep others from learning what they know.

Note that two firms, Hitachi and Mitsubishi, have engaged in a strategy of not only exploiting other companies' technologies (imita-

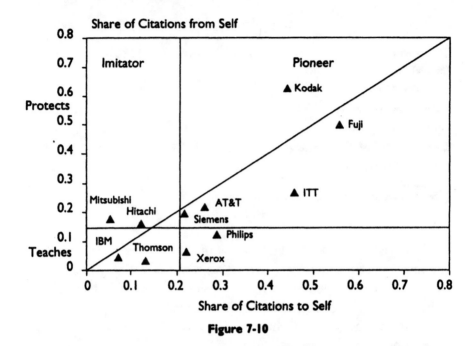

Figure 7-10

tor) but protecting their own technological advances from being used by other firms.

This is an enviable position.

Kodak and ITT are pioneers in the field and build on their own work, but ITT is having a harder time protecting its technology.

AT&T and Siemens, both near the 45 degree balance line, are more balanced. They're building on their own technologies yet protecting them at the same time.

Thomson and Philips produce inventions that are used by others but neither is very successful at capitalizing on its own research.

This type of analysis is cutting-edge work and should be considered preliminary. Researchers are continuing work on understanding these patent-strategy relationships in order to understand fully how to characterize a company's behavior based on patent activity.

Patent analysis also can be done for individuals, the inventors themselves.

This is especially important for acquisitions and mergers where your strategic intent is to "buy" the expertise to produce new products and processes because of the inventors in the company. Or, in another instance, you might try to hire key researchers from a competitor.

Not only do you want to identify the key inventors in cutting-edge technology but their associates or co-inventors who are also cited in patents. If you were trying to buy their expertise, which person would you choose? Could you break them up and still have the synergy that produced so many results? Analysis of their patents would tell you (figure 7-11).

Francis Narin of CHI Research likes to call this concept *brain mapping*, and that's an appropriate description. Not only does brain mapping show which persons are engaged in what research, it also indicates the exact work done by their specific project groups. In every company, key people work on key projects, and brain mapping can shed light on your competitor's priorities. You can also learn how long it takes your competitor's key people to work on projects.

Patent-related analysis is such a powerful tool that companies will try to hide their patent information from competitors. Despite the fact that patent information is in the public domain, companies in competitive fields will deliberately try to obfuscate their patents by using several ploys. You should be aware of these clever maneuvers.

The most common subterfuge is to assign patents to subsidiaries, holding companies, divisions, and other parts of the company. When doing a search, names of all closely associated companies should be covered.

Very often, a patent search of a small company on the leading edge of technology won't show any patents listed. Why? Because the founder kept them in his name or they're in the name of a co-founder or former partner. Looking at company names isn't enough when searching for patents.

When a patent is issued as a result of research conducted by a joint venture, it can be issued in either company's name. Make sure you check them both.

THE IMPORTANCE OF SEARCHING FOR PATENTS IN OTHER COUNTRIES

U.S. patent applications are kept secret while the patent process is underway. Not so in other countries.

While it takes about two years for most U.S. patents to be issued (longer in some backlogged fields like biotechnology and software) and material made public, it takes an average of eighteen months from application date for some other countries to make materials public.

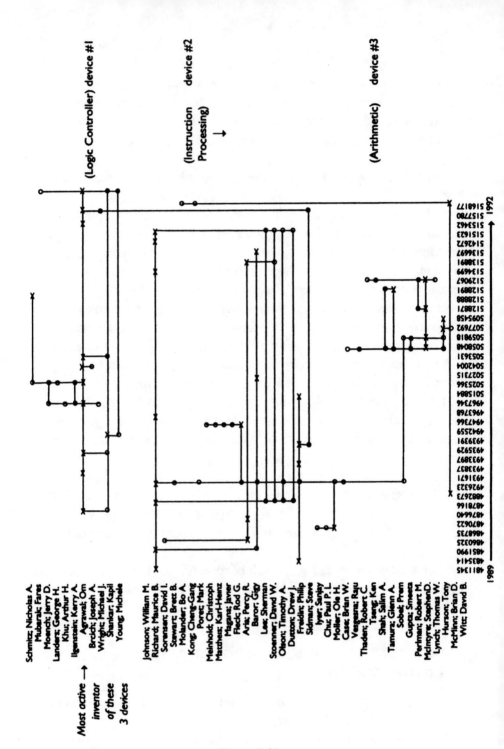

Figure 7-11

So, while you may not be able to get information about a competitor's patent in the United States—until the patent is actually issued—you may be able to get the same information from other countries about six months sooner even though a patent hasn't yet been issued.

Another reason to access foreign records is in instances when U.S. patent applications have been abandoned. Because the application process is secret in the United States, including the reason for abandonment, a researcher may never learn about a competitor's proposed patent application or discover the information it contains. Patents are abandoned for many reasons. One may be because of the inventor's death, lack of funds, loss of interest, or some legal squabble. In cases of very fast moving technology, a company may believe that it is too far behind its competitors to continue the patent process. It might learn this only after filing an application.

However, that application may be available in countries that publish such information even if the patent is never issued. The chances are good that the foreign application contains the same information as the withdrawn U.S. application.

Pending applications are available for public consumption in Belgium, France, Germany, Italy, Netherlands, and the United Kingdom. It's unclear what effect, if any, the increased role of the European Patent Office will have on the procedures of individual nations of the European Union. Other countries that allow public inspection of pending applications include Japan, South Korea, and China.

There's another aspect of foreign patenting that is of interest to analysts. An analysis of how many and which patents are patented abroad can be a measure of a company's commitment to that technology and how much it is willing to spend on its exploitation. Obtaining a patent in a foreign country can be more time-consuming and expensive than for a similar patent at home. An applicant needs to engage language translation assistance and foreign legal help. (This is less of a factor for some companies like Canon that have a team of patent lawyers and researchers on staff in the United States and other countries.) So, companies that engage in heavy foreign patenting are making a big commitment to using that technology on a broad scale. It shows they believe the technology to be valuable.

Likewise, companies that renew patents are showing their continued interest and commitment to that particular technology.

PATENT DATABASES

Searching for patent information should only be done by using databases. This is the only way you can go through the mass of available information and correlate it quickly enough to be useful.

There are hundreds of international patent databases with patent information from hundreds of countries, such as LEXPAT, from Mead Data Central, which contains U.S. patents; JAPIO, from the Japan Patent Information Organization, which contains Japanese patent abstracts; and INPADOC, from the European Patent Office representing more than fifty-five countries.

In addition, there are industry- and technology-specific databases, such as APTIC, from the U.S. Environmental Protection Agency, which contains patents for antipollution devices and processes; Metdex, from ASM International, which has metallurgical patents; and FLUIDEX, from Elsevier Science Publishers, which offers information about British patents relating to fluid engineering.

There are also databases that have information about patent court cases, mainly infringements. These can be enlightening, as the trial proceedings themselves often offer a close look at companies' research practices and procedures. One such database is WESTLAW's Intellectual Property Library, from West Publishing, which contains texts of federal court decisions about intellectual property cases.

Soft Information

"If we're not looking at soft information, we're not looking at *all* the information."
— Seena Sharp, Sharp Information Research

Several years ago, Nissan wanted to consolidate offices in one department that were scattered throughout the United States. The short list came down to four cities that seemed like good candidates. The company asked Seena Sharp of Sharp Information Research to build a matrix of about a dozen factors that would give management the advantages and disadvantages of each city. While researching the material, Sharp came up with about a dozen more factors that needed to be considered.

When the matrix was filled in with comparable statistics and figures, it became obvious that each city had pros and cons, so Sharp suggested that the client look at some different information—some *soft information*.

She recommended that Nissan look at a year's worth of editorials in each area's local newspaper. Although the statistics told a story about traffic, wages, taxes, skilled worker pools, and so on, they didn't tell anything about the future. "Facts and statistics tell you about what happened yesterday but not about tomorrow," says Sharp. The editorials were able to tell Nissan about upcoming issues and what they and their employees would face in the future.

Industry relies on hard numbers to make decisions, and that's been the focus of competitive intelligence collection. When companies engage in strategic planning, managers feel more comfortable with decisions based on numbers, charts, and graphs. However, Sharp and others believe that *soft* information should also be factored into the decision-making process and be part of the competitive intelligence landscape.

One of the most difficult parts of competitive intelligence analysis is forecasting what will happen in the future. Soft information can help.

To be sure, some soft information is being collected and used—rumors, op-ed pieces and anecdotes—but it is automatically given a lower rating for its utility.

Clearly, rumors should not be placed on the same level as hard facts when doing analysis. On the other hand, there should be a special place for soft information so management can see the whole picture before making decisions. And, as I've said, it helps with forecasting because numbers can show you the past but only guess at the future.

Because soft information can't be quantified, companies often disregard it. Avon is one example.

Skin So Soft is a lotion made by Avon for treating women's skin. Then President Jimmy Carter and other fishing enthusiasts discovered that this product aimed at women made an excellent insect repellent. Despite feedback from sportsmen who were buying the lotion by the carload, the company refused to acknowledge this new use. Because the company could not quantify the sales to this new market, mainly men and mainly fishermen, the company discouraged its use in this way. It took ten years and additional sales of $100,000 to convince them that this was a viable market. By then, the market was cold and Avon lost the opportunity to capitalize on it.

Why? Because it chose to look only at the hard information and not the soft.

A more successful story is that of Plano, a company that produces fishing tackle boxes. They learned from sales reps and consumers that the boxes were being used to hold jewelry and also by meeting planners who liked putting pencils, pens, rulers, and other small office supplies in the little compartments. The company responded by manufacturing the same boxes in bright colors to appeal to these new markets. Plano made this lucrative move without being able to quantify the market. Their decision was based on soft information.

Intuitively, we know what hard and soft information means but let's list some examples.

Hard

Facts

Statistics

Raw Data

Financial Information

News

Soft

Rumors

Opinions

Anecdotes

Op-Ed Pieces

Customer Feedback

Figure 7-12

IN SHORT, HARD INFORMATION IS QUANTITATIVE AND SOFT INFORMATION IS QUALITATIVE.

LOOKING FOR SOFT INFORMATION

Soft information doesn't come from the same sources as hard information. To find soft information you must look in places you wouldn't normally look when doing competitive intelligence collection.

A good example of this is the observation and analysis of Donald Hall, chairman of Hallmark Cards. Hall noticed in the late 1980s that the comic strip character Garfield the cat was becoming softer, less hard edged about life. This was a change from his usual irascible self. Hall asked his marketing people if this was a trend in the United States. If so, how should their cards reflect it? It turns out that the 1990s are indeed a little softer than the 1980s and the comic strip was foreshadowing a trend. Hall was smart enough not to base an entire line of cards on one single comic strip, but what he saw suggested further investigation, and the content of cards did change as a result.

Soft information is found in other places like TV commercials, jokes, editorials, and movies. Clothing manufacturers are always looking at MTV to see what young adults are wearing.

As you can see, soft information is very useful in spotting trends, showing the need for products and services that aren't apparent while studying numbers and statistics.

Stepping out of the world of solid numbers, graphs, and charts is not something most managers are trained to do, nor do they feel comfortable presenting nonquantifiable information to top management.

However, soft information should be a part of every competitive intelligence analysis report.

Sharp notes that soft information can sometimes seem surprising or silly. It appears off the wall and makes us feel unsettled. "Sometimes, it seems all wrong, but it forces us to think in new ways, and that's always positive."

War-Gaming

War-gaming is a special form of analysis.

Sometimes called Red Team/Blue Team, it's a concept that has been used for many centuries by military generals and, in recent history, during the Cold War Years; CIA operatives used war-gaming to anticipate military and political moves by the Soviet Union. The Soviets did the same for the Western nations.

The concept applied to business is simple. Teams of people take on the roles of their competitors and themselves. In the course of the "game," strategies and plans are proposed, acted out, and tested in as real a simulation of business conditions as possible.

Not only are competitors and your company part of the game, but sometimes so are wild card players who represent government regulators, outside companies not generally considered part of the competitive landscape, and market conditions that spring surprises from time to time on players.

The game itself is usually played over a number of hours—two- to four-hour sessions are common—over a number of days or weeks with frequent time-outs to understand the lessons learned.

War-gaming has many goals:

- Gives management practice in making better decisions in real-life situations.
- Identifies any additional information necessary for future decisions before those decisions are actually needed.
- Identifies probable moves by your competitors and the best response you can make when that move occurs.
- Identifies probable responses by your competitors to your activities.
- Increases teamwork.
- Limits surprises.
- Identifies your company's strengths and weaknesses.
- Identifies your competitors' strengths and weaknesses.

Southwestern Bell Telephone has a version of war-gaming they call Red Team/Blue Team. One team, the Red, is chaired by someone from the competitive intelligence staff. The rest of the team is composed of people from other departments, especially those with needed expertise in a particular area such as finance or transportation.

The Red Team becomes the competitor in personality and in actions. This is accomplished by collecting and analyzing data about a particular competitor, including personal profiles of management. According to Karen Wolters, product developer in Network Services, this process takes at least six to eight weeks. Some of the business plans that the Red Team will look at ahead of time are expansion areas, new services and products, current and projected market share, industry trends, and projected revenues.

Clearly, the Red Team knows Southwestern Bell's vulnerabilities, making this exercise even more powerful.

The Blue Team represents Southwestern Bell, and their goal is to study Red Team's business plan and develop their own response. This may take about five to six weeks and will include strategic and tactical actions.

At the end of the project, both teams present their findings to management and to the business groups who will be most affected by the Red Team's moves.

One of the main areas that they will address is what information still needs to be gathered or analyzed to answer any remaining questions or clear up any ambiguities.

C.J. Kurtz, president of The Kappa Group, consults companies who perform war-gaming. He suggests that war-gaming scenarios offer the following steps:

1. *Preparation.* This is where participants decide what actions they want to test and what activities and competitive moves they want to study..

Competitive intelligence techniques play a crucial role in the preparation phase, which could take several weeks to accomplish. Intelligence is compiled and disseminated to the players.

2. *Introduction.* The war game sponsor establishes the purpose of the activity and what will be done with the results. If the participants aren't familiar with war-gaming, a briefing session may be necessary. This step takes about an hour.

3. *War Game Session.* This is the role-playing session—team against team. Teams act and counteract, and more than two teams may participate. There may be several sessions spread out over several days. Kurtz recommends that interim analyses take place so that players can absorb the lessons learned during the simulation. At the end of each session, teams will want to summarize what they've learned. It's also a time to see if anyone could have benefited from additional data or analysis of that data to make better decisions. One of the prime reasons for performing war-gaming is that it gives you an idea of what information your company may be missing to respond to any competitor action.

During the engagement, umpires or referees are used to decide winners of skirmishes based on each side's action and reaction.

4. *Analysis.* When all sessions have been completed, participants review what they have learned, decide what information they should have collected or analyzed, and begin to develop action plans. The action plans might include programs to collect additional information, develop contingency plans to respond to possible events, reduce the probability that a competitor will take a certain action, and activities to block competitor actions.

5. *Wrap-up.* Tasks based on the analysis are assigned to specific individuals and groups.

6. *Follow-up.* Relatively soon after a war game is completed, a follow-up should be undertaken to ensure that all action steps are being performed. In addition, the wealth of knowledge learned from the war game should be disseminated to others in the company who could benefit from it.

COMPUTER WAR-GAMING

When Pacific Bell wanted to learn more about their new competitors in the regional telephone business they decided to use a computer version of war-gaming. The computer simulation, TeleSim, developed by Thinking Tools, Inc. under contract with consultants Coopers & Lybrand, allowed Pacific Bell to look at possible moves by cable TV operators and even the local utility companies—any company that had a telecommunications network in place capable of competing with them.

Pacific Bell would load large amounts of information into the program and plot a marketing or pricing strategy and the computer would give a likely outcome.

TeleSim is actually a business version of the popular SimCity, which allows urban planners (and gamesters) to design a city. Players watch the city grow and change as more variables such as population and vehicle traffic are added.

The outcomes are only as good as the competitive intelligence that goes in. In Pacific Bell's case, it might input information about a competitor's working capital, technology, and basic strategies such as whether it is going after market share or increased revenues. The game will calculate the cost to Pacific Bell of pursuing its strategies and accompanying costs such as stringing fiber in sparse neighborhoods as opposed to densely populated office areas.

By playing out each company's strategy over a long time period, say ten years, the computer will show each company's position at any point along the way. For example, will a company run out of cash before it completes its fiber optic network?

The game can also be programmed to inject wild cards like earthquakes and floods that can set strategic programs behind schedule and cost lots of money to fix.

The games act somewhat like spreadsheets, pondering what-ifs for many years to come, but are more sophisticated both graphically and in the amount of information they can handle.

As with human-powered war games, the key to success with computer war games is collecting the right information to feed the game as well as inputing information that has been analyzed to set the wheels in motion.

Word-Pattern Analysis

The Soviet Union built their new embassy compound in Washington atop a hill. It was purposely located in the microwave transmission path between the Pentagon and Fort Meade. The position also gave them a direct shot at intercepting other microwave telephone transmissions in and out of the capital area.

Like their spy counterparts in the U.S. government, the Soviets collected massive amounts of telephone and fax transmissions, which were fed into computers to be analyzed for their content. What they were looking for were individual key words such as *nuclear, Moscow,* and *troops.* When these words were found, the entire transmission would be further analyzed to see if these words were part of important groupings such as *troop movement* and *nuclear bomb.*

The CIA also is adept at listening on commercial and personal telephone transmissions searching for words and phrases that compromise national security. (The Secret Service also is interested in certain key words juxtaposed with others such as *president* and *assassinate* when combing wiretaps.)

As the Cold War recedes behind us, some of these military technologies are filtering into the private sector, and they can be used for competitive intelligence purposes in a legal manner.

Much of this technology is an outgrowth of national intelligence services but also, more openly, from defense-related operations such as the Foreign Applied Sciences Assessment Center. Its job was to study public-domain information from the Soviet Union and identify foreign technologies that could be important to military, economic, and political sectors in the United States.

The purpose was to recognize high-frequency words in texts such as *computer, data, materials,* and so on, with the emphasis on science and technology themes.

The program also looked at double-word groups such as *image processing, radio waves,* and *magnetic field.* Then it identified triple- word groups such as *spatial light modulators* and *space research institute.*

The idea is that when words or word groups are cited often, it's evidence of a thrust in that area.

For example, if documents reveal that *space research institute* is mentioned more than *spatial light modulators,* then there is much more interest in the Soviet Union about the *space research institute.*

Another analysis might reveal that there is a high incidence of word clusters appearing together such as *spatial light modulators* and *space research institute.* This tells us that the cutting-edge research taking place at the *space research institute* involves *spatial light modulators.*

This type of co-word or co-phrase analysis is very useful in showing where research thrusts are headed.

Another example of this might be searching a year's worth of biotechnology documents and papers and seeing a high incidence of the words *aquaculture* and *France.* Plotted over several years, incidences might show you that French companies or the government itself is ramping up its efforts in aquaculture or perhaps that interest has already peaked.

Still another analysis might show that other phrases are starting to show up that had not been seen before. This could indicate a direction that research is taking. For example, suppose the word *biotechnology* were starting to creep into documents, slowly at first, then increasingly so. That would indicate that French aquaculture researchers were just beginning to look at the role of biotechnology in the aquaculture field. If the number of incidences suddenly peaked, it might indicate that research on that tangent had reached its zenith.

While these examples are simplified, choosing the key words and phrases can be complicated. The discipline of linguistics research becomes a crucial element as prefixes, suffixes, and modifying words are chosen.

The effort to convert documents to computer-readable form is massive. The accepted method is to use an optical character reader program, which turns text into bits and bytes for the computer. OCR technology is developing rapidly and getting better and more accurate all the time. In fact, OCR technology is used in your fax modem to convert an incoming fax to text that will then appear on your computer screen. While the actual conversion takes a long time—as much as several minutes a page—the process is getting faster.

It is now within the realm of private companies to scan large amounts of documents and look for patterns using PCs.

For instance, Kodak could scan all the technical documents published by rival Fuji. By asking the computer program to identify recurring words and phrases, Kodak would have a good indication of Fuji's research and technical thrust. If this exercise were done over a long period of time, Kodak could discern Fuji's strategic directions and guess where they may be heading.

As seen in the example of the Foreign Applied Sciences Assessment Center, which was studying the Soviet Union's research interests, private industry could apply these methods to other countries as well. Companies like Motorola could learn which direction the Ministry of International Trade and Industry (MITI) is pushing chip research in Japan based on the technical words and phrases that keep popping up in its technical publications.

While some progressive companies are already doing this kind of analysis, it is largely limited to documents that are in computer-readable form such as on-line databases and CD-ROMs. There are also many companies that specialize in taking paper documents and having low-wage keyboard operators input the data into computers. These companies, often working offshore in the Caribbean islands, transmit the information by satellite back to the customer. While these methods may be cost-effective because of the cheap labor and inexpensive telecommunications channels, they are too reminiscent of the sweat-shop era to be palatable.

Technically and socially, the full benefits of this kind of analysis will only be enjoyed after large numbers of paper documents are quickly and inexpensively scanned into personal computers. That day is arriving.

Dissemination

"The great end of life is not knowledge, but action."
—Thomas Henry Huxley

The moment of truth has arrived.

After collection and analysis comes the most important part of any competitive intelligence project. This is when the findings are presented to key management.

This is when you give management the answers to their questions. What is competitor X likely to do? How will competitor Y respond to our price increases? When will competitor Z introduce its new product?

It's a time when you present your logical arguments based on your analysis of raw data. It's a time to defend your logic, to put up or shut up.

It's a time when most competitive intelligence projects fail.

Presenting Your Analysis

Those that succeed fulfill the following criteria:

The analysis must be responsive to management's needs.

Your assessment must answer the tough questions in a succinct manner. Your written report must be short and to the point. Your backup data can be long, but your recommendations must be simple and address the prime questions from management. Managers support competitive intelligence programs because they help them do their job better, i.e., make better decisions. If they don't do that the program has failed.

The analysis must be focused, not general.

Too often analysts don't have the courage of their convictions and present management with scenarios that are too general to be of any use in making decisions. Instead of coming down on one side or the other, analysts sometimes present scenarios with equal possibilities to happen. You must make a decision on the most likely choice and defend it.

The analysis must be timely.

This seems obvious but if you've been working on a project for a long time, a few months perhaps, is your information the latest that is available? If not, it should be updated.

One way to ensure timeliness is to use matrices as part of your analysis that allow new numbers to be plugged in when available. This will allow parts of your analysis to be useful for a long time to come.

High trust level.

Some senior managers support the idea of competitive intelligence, even fund it, but then don't trust the findings in their heart of hearts. Why? It may be new and untried. It's not how management is used to making decisions.

Competitive intelligence professionals say they are most successful when management knows them and trusts their work from other projects, perhaps in other positions at the company. Trust takes time to build, and it can only occur if your assessments help management make better decisions. One of your jobs is to make management feel comfortable with competitive intelligence methods and techniques.

Some competitive intelligence professionals are also starting to realize that they are actually taking on the role of a salesperson. They are selling their findings and ideas to management. If management doesn't buy it, they haven't done their job well enough.

Results must be in the best form for management.

Not only should intelligence reports have all the right components, they should also be in a form that will have the biggest impact on management.

Alan Bergstrom, a partner in Edgar, Dunn & Company, learned this lesson when he worked in the Reagan administration. His job was to present the president with intelligence reports. "I found that he wasn't paying attention to written reports," says Bergstrom. "He kept saying, 'Is that all?' "

Because of his background in the movies, Reagan responded better to visual stimuli so Bergstrom presented intelligence reports on videocassette.

Knowing how management accepts intelligence reports is crucial.

All of us take in information in three ways, visually, aurally, and kinesthetically (by sense or feeling). It's important for competitive intelligence presenters to understand their management's preferences.

Some people like to have a written report with charts and graphs that they can peruse on their own. Some people like big presentations with slides, video, and lots of fanfare. Some like a combination. Take the time to observe how management in your company prefers to learn.

For most managers, an oral presentation works best. It allows you to present your assessment and suggestions for action. The manager can then ask some additional questions or ask for clarification.

After making your presentation to senior management, copies of your assessment should also be distributed to key people outside the corporate office. If requested, they should be given full presentations in the form they find the most effective.

Later, you should conduct a session with senior management to see what you can do better next time, find out what areas need improvement.

What Else Do You Do with Your Analysis?

While competitive intelligence units should always be working on a major project or two for management—it's their reason for being— what about the rest of the company and their needs? And what about the downtime or free time between management's large projects?

A major chemical manufacturer uses an e-mail system to stay in touch with hundreds of its employees around the world. These people regularly transmit pieces of information to the competitive intelligence unit, which receives about twenty to thirty messages weekly. Some of the information is passed on to management and the rest is compiled into a report that is sent electronically to all the people who have sent in material during the month.

This is an excellent instance of collecting information, doing a quickie assessment to keep management informed of ad hoc conditions, and then turning loose the raw information back to people who can use it to make their own assessments.

Back to the Beginning

Delivering your findings to the user brings you back to the beginning phase of the intelligence cycle—planning and direction. Whatever action is taken as the result of your assessment will present the user (and the company) with new requirements and needs. After all, the company's status will change based on new actions that will be taken.

Competitive intelligence is never meant to be a one-shot activity; as the company changes so will its intelligence needs.

It's also at this point that some companies use the two-sided report card method of assessing how competitive intelligence worked or didn't work.

The user assesses how well his needs were met by the competitive intelligence unit and the competitive intelligence unit assesses how the users used the intelligence.

The only true measure of the success of competitive intelligence is whether or not the user used the intelligence he was presented.

Did it help management make better decisions?

CHAPTER NINE

Mergers and . Acquisitions

"Deals differ from the go-go '80s. Takeovers are more strategic. Firms are buying companies or suppliers to gain a competitive edge."
—The *Kiplinger Washington Letter*,
November 18, 1994

On the surface, the battery company looked like a great acquisition. Its financials were strong, and they were stealing market share from competitors.

The potential buyer hired a competitive intelligence consultant to check the company out, to look below the surface and see if it really was as good a potential buy as it seemed.

The consultant initially said yes; everything seemed fine. The take-over target was indeed increasing market share and making lots of money. However, when the consultant dug a little deeper, he learned something from customers that shocked him. They told him that the target company was using rubber separators between battery plates and the industry buzz was that plastic was the future. In fact, they said the reason the target's competitors weren't doing very well, and in fact were losing market share, was that they were retooling and reinvesting in the newer plastic technology.

A check with these companies proved that this was indeed the case.

The consultant then told the potential buyer about what he had learned.

When the buyer approached the seller with this information the seller got defensive, saying that it wasn't true about plastic being the future in separators.

The buyer then went back to the consultant, who in turn went out again to recheck his findings.

It checked out once more, and despite protestations from the buyer—who had his heart set on the acquisition—the consultant stuck to his story.

The company was purchased anyway, and I'd like to say the story has a happy ending, but I can't.

A year later the buyer told the consultant: "You were right." Saving face he added: "We bought the company for different reasons, and we did get it at a lower price."

The bought company never recovered.

This story is about a double failure of competitive intelligence. One, the purchaser not believing the information that the consultant discovered, and second, the battery company not knowing or not believing that plastic was the future in separators.

The Old and New Way of Buying Companies

After the flurry of mergers and acquisitions during the 1980s—many of which did not work out—the early 1990s brought a sobering, go-slow attitude. However, many acquisitions, or "strategic alliances" as many people like to think of them, are still being done the old-fashioned way. This is especially true when a public company buys a small, private company.

Until several years ago, the most common method for finding a takeover candidate was the old-boys' network. Companies found other companies based on relationships and acquaintances. (This is still the case with many acquisitions.) Nevertheless, the job of the so-called finder was to locate a company that was for sale and arrange a meeting between the buyer and the seller. The buyer took a tour of the facilities, the seller opened his books, and a deal was struck.

As you can readily see, this way of doing business has several flaws. The most obvious is that companies are limited only to buying companies that are for sale. This is a very small universe; maybe 1 percent of all companies are officially for sale at any given moment. However, it's been shown time and again that almost every company is for sale if conditions are right.

Now, enter competitive intelligence, which can help you find acquisitions in the entire universe of companies, not just those that are officially for sale. In addition, competitive intelligence practices can aid you in deciding if there is truly a fit between the two companies. This is particularly important as more and more companies are being bought for strategic reasons.

Competitive intelligence works very well in cases of companies buying another company for its technology or research acumen. One example is of a company that turned recycled newspapers into insulation for houses. The company embarked on a competitive intelligence project to learn about their competitors' programs. They wanted to know who had the most efficient operation.

They approached the problem by looking at an indicator unique to that particular business: how much newspaper went in and how much insulation came out. Who could turn out the most insulation per ton of newspaper?

They counted trucks, they counted chemicals used in the process, they studied EPA filings showing wastewater figures, they looked at the size of machines and facilities, personnel—they looked at all the clues they could to establish a picture of how much went in and how much came out.

It turned out, to the exploring company's pleasure, that they themselves were the most efficient converter of newspaper to insulation. However, their study pointed out the second-best company, which was doing a good job but lacked state-of-the-art technology. They approached that company and asked: Would you like to have our technology injected into your company? This ultimately led to a merger that led to the lion's share of the overall business.

Without competitive intelligence the acquiring company, which was looking to build market share, might have bought a different company on the basis of current financial figures and not how well they did their job of turning raw materials into finished products. They might not have learned that all that was needed to turn the second-best company into a first-rate company was a transfer of technology.

One electronics firm was interested in cutting-edge technologies that a competitor's subsidiary had developed and patented. The first firm was so keen on acquiring the technology that it made an offer for the subsidiary, which was accepted. The fit would be perfect and allow the first company to insert this technology into their overall strategic plan.

Sorry, this story has another sad ending.

Had the first company done more competitive intelligence homework, had they checked below the surface, they would have discovered that all the patents for this technology were in the name of one scientist and that particular scientist had moved to another firm months before the acquisition offer. So, while the buyer got use of the current technology because he now owned the subsidiary and this scientist's patents, it paid more than if it just bought a license to use it.

To add insult to injury, it didn't buy the promise of future technology advances as it had expected.

Competitive Intelligence in Offshore Acquisitions

Competitive intelligence can also play a special role in acquiring offshore companies. It allows the buyer to use competitive intelligence as compensation for not being a member of the culture. Nowhere is this more important than in Japan, where acquisitions are done differently than in the United States.

Foreign ownership of Japanese companies is not common, but it is increasing. One reason is that acquisitions were not, until recently, considered a legitimate transaction even among Japanese companies. Like layoffs, it's not been thought of as a correct way to conduct business.

However, acquisitions do occur in Japan and they are accomplished according to certain rules of behavior.

First and foremost, it's not considered a polite business practice to acquire another firm in a hostile takeover. Acquisitions occur between companies that are somehow connected or otherwise introduced through a third party like a bank or another company. The bottom line is that there must be an established relationship.

One strategy is to become a lender to the takeover company's largest customer, then use that entry to buy the company. Because of the complex, interlocking nature of Japanese companies it takes strong competitive intelligence skills to discover who the largest customer is.

Another technique is to learn who owns the target company's off-shore convertible bonds and buy that company. This is considered an acceptable method of entry.

Another point of entrance is to use competitive intelligence methods to discover the prime distributor for your target company. Once uncovered, you may be able to get an equity position and use that as leverage to purchase the target company.

For acquisitions, competitive intelligence can:

1. Increase the universe of possible takeover candidates. You're not limited to those companies on the block. Your investigation will uncover many possibilities.
2. Help you look below the surface and see if there is a true fit between the companies.
3. Help you look your best to lenders providing financing. A well-researched report employing competitive intelligence can show the true worth (not money value) of your potential acquisition and its contribution to your overall strategy.
4. Help you buy a company for its future, not its past.
5. Help you negotiate a better price.
6. Allow you to compensate for being an outsider when you want to purchase foreign companies.

CHAPTER TEN

Benchmarking and Competitive Intelligence

"Benchmarking is the process of continuously comparing and measuring an organization against business leaders anywhere in the world to gain information that will help the organization take action to improve its performance."
—International Benchmarking Clearinghouse

In the late 1970s Xerox was in dire condition. Not only couldn't they compete with the growing wave of Japanese firms making higher quality copiers, but these companies were also making less expensive copiers. In fact, Xerox discovered that companies like Ricoh and Canon could *sell* copiers for *less* than Xerox could manufacture them.

Fortunately for Xerox, they had a Japanese counterpart, Fuji Xerox, from which the parent company's salvation eventually sprang.

Fuji Xerox, itself a victim of the Japanese copier wars, had embarked on a program in 1976 called the New Xerox Movement, which was a total quality program designed to develop new products, bring costs under control, introduce new basic technologies, and strengthen the marketing organization. One of their tools was a technique called benchmarking in which you measure your company against other companies in many different areas. The concept was this: If you could learn from the best-in-class—and these competitors were indeed the best at the time—you could become the best as well.

Japanese companies routinely benchmark although they don't have a name for it. It's a practice that is ingrained and virtually automatic.

The quality program paid off for Fuji Xerox, and they were back in the race. By 1980, revenues and profits increased and they had won the coveted Deming Award.

Although there were some American competitors in the copier business (not that they were faring any better than Xerox) such as Kodak and 3M, these competitors didn't talk to each other. Unlike Japanese competitors, who often exchange information among themselves, American companies are reluctant to open themselves up to outsiders, let alone competitors.

So, while Fuji Xerox was able to glean information from other Japanese companies—even competitors—and funnel that information to the United States, Xerox still needed to set out on its own. The company decided to embark on a program that would make them the first American company to employ benchmarking.

It determined which processes it wanted to benchmark and found American companies—noncompetitors—to help them. Indeed, their goal was to find companies that did some processes even better than Japanese companies and learn from them.

One specific trouble area for Xerox was their logistics and distribution unit, which was responsible for inventory, warehousing, and distribution of parts and supplies. The question for Xerox became: Whom do we benchmark against?

Xerox's management found the perfect company, the one that everyone agreed had the best warehouse and distribution process: L.L. Bean.

By studying this outdoor equipment and clothing mail order company, Xerox management learned a few simple things that helped them right off the bat. For example, they learned that Bean employees kept the most frequently ordered items closest to the picking route. So, while Bean order handlers used this technique to save steps in packing orders, Xerox adapted this method to its repair people, who now more easily grabbed spare parts for their tool kits.

According to Xerox management, the L.L. Bean experiment gave them lots of little items that led to greater efficiency. (In fact, Xerox management claims that what they learned at L.L. Bean increased the division's productivity 3 to 5 percent and eventually it increased about 10 percent.)

Bean learned something from the experience, too—the value of benchmarking and going outside their industry to accomplish it.

Whom else did Xerox benchmark with? American Express for billing and collection processes, Westinghouse for bar-coding, and American Hospital Supply for automated inventory control. There were others, too.

Today, Xerox estimates it has identified almost seventy key work processes that it benchmarks. It also has the added benefit of benchmarking against the unique Japanese practices of Fuji Xerox.

How Competitive Intelligence Can Help Benchmarking

Competitive intelligence is a crucial element of almost every phase of benchmarking.

Unless you have a well-developed knowledge of competitive intelligence methods and techniques, you won't be able to get the most value out of your benchmarking program. Indeed, some facets of quality benchmarking are impossible without employing competitive intelligence.

Companies that have well-developed competitive intelligence programs, like Xerox, AT&T, and Corning, use the skills and knowledge from one to serve the other.

FIVE BENCHMARKING STEPS

1. Identify important functions or processes that need to be improved.

You might think that most companies know how they do what they do. Well, you would be wrong about that.

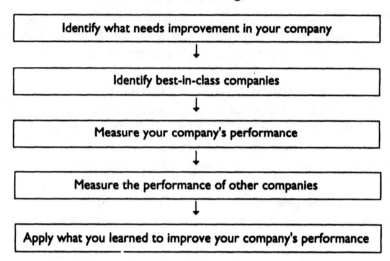

Benchmarking

Identify what needs improvement in your company

↓

Identify best-in-class companies

↓

Measure your company's performance

↓

Measure the performance of other companies

↓

Apply what you learned to improve your company's performance

Figure 10-1

Failing to examine internal processes is first among the top ten benchmarking mistakes developed by a team at Digital Equipment Corp. Just like managers embarking on a competitive intelligence project often overlook what information is already available within their walls, companies planning a benchmarking project may not have gathered everything they know about their internal processes. Without that solid information base, they won't be able to compare themselves to others.

* **APPLYING COMPETITIVE INTELLIGENCE METHODS TO YOUR OWN COMPANY CAN HELP IDENTIFY PROCESSES THAT YOU WANT TO MEASURE.**

2. Identify the best-in-class companies in specific areas of interest.

Motorola, one of the leaders in competitive intelligence, wanted to improve the cycle time between order receipt and delivery of its cellular telephones. Where did it look for help? To Domino's Pizza, clearly a leader in fast deliveries.

First Chicago Bank was interested in improving customer service in the area of lines. It doesn't take a genius to know that people hate waiting on lines. Where did the bank go for help? To several airlines who had improved their line services.

Although you may already know the leaders in your industry, you should not limit yourself to benchmarking with them. For one thing, competitors are often uneasy about benchmarking with direct competitors. (They also may be queasy about possible antitrust problems, although that usually isn't an issue unless pricing is discussed.)

Also, companies in the same industry tend to do the same tasks in the same way. Industries can become inbred. So, by looking outside your industry you increase the chances of finding something new and different.

The key is not to limit yourself either by industry or geography. Michael J. Spendolini in *The Benchmarking Book* calls this the "best in Cleveland syndrome" after a company he was consulting wanted to choose benchmarking partners on the basis of proximity to their home base in Cleveland. "Limited information resources produce information of limited value," says Spendolini.

Identifying your current competitors—those in your industry—may be fairly easy, but how do you go about finding best-in-class companies in industries of which you are not familiar?

The International Benchmarking Clearinghouse established by the America Productivity Quality Center in Houston runs a Common Interest Group that is composed of members interested in the same processes. IBC also helps match members who want to benchmark. While these services are helpful, they may not work for all companies. Or you may not find a benchmarking partner that you feel is suitable for your needs.

How's this for finding an unlikely partner? An ammunition company benchmarked with a company that made lipstick cases. Why? The bullet maker was looking for a way to brighten its shell casings and the lipstick maker was using nut shells to tumble with their lipstick cases. The method gave the cases a bright shine, just what the munitions maker was seeking. They adopted the practice and produced shinier bullets.

While competitive intelligence skills can help you find and work with a willing partner, its true strength comes into play when working with unwilling partners.

For example, some companies are considered so above every other company that everyone wants to benchmark against them. Officials at L.L. Bean report that, reluctantly, they must routinely turn down requests for companies to benchmark against their warehousing process because they don't have the personnel to accommodate everyone.

If a company is the best yet they can't help you, what do you do? For one thing, you can use competitive intelligence techniques to learn everything about their process without ever visiting them. Is that ideal? No, but it may be the only practical tactic. In fact, if you've really done your homework well, even companies that have refused your benchmark requests because of lack of time may be willing to answer a few finely focused questions that will complete your benchmarking project.

Additionally, while L.L. Bean may be the best warehouser around that people know about, what about some small company that nobody has heard about? They could have a warehousing process just as good (or better) than L.L. Bean's but nobody knows about it except the company itself—and they might not know how good they are either. Competitive intelligence methods can help you locate these gems.

* **COMPETITIVE INTELLIGENCE METHODS CAN HELP YOU FIND THE BEST-IN-CLASS COMPANY TO BENCHMARK AGAINST WHETHER IT'S IN YOUR INDUSTRY OR NOT AND WHETHER THEY'RE A WILLING PARTICIPANT OR NOT. COMPETITIVE INTELLIGENCE WILL ALLOW YOU TO BENCHMARK AGAINST ANY COMPANY YOU WANT.**

3. If you haven't already done so, start a program to evaluate and measure in your company the processes you want to benchmark.

This will allow you to compare yourself to others in a like manner. It will also teach you which questions to ask and what information to obtain from the companies you will be visiting.

For example, some processes are easy to quantify: products produced per employee, errors per product, and transactions per person. Others are not so easy to quantify and you may have to estimate.

* **COMPETITIVE INTELLIGENCE METHODS CAN HELP YOU MEASURE YOUR COMPANY'S PROCESSES.**

4. Measure the performance of others.

This is the part of the project where you collect and analyze benchmarking information. This requires a large investment in preparation so you don't engage in what some people call "organized tourism." When you benchmark, you must not ask vague questions or ask for wide swaths of information. Your inquiries must be precise and focused.

One of the prime mistakes made during benchmarking projects is lack of preparation. Before you set foot in the other company's door you must do your homework. You must have collected information from external sources such as magazines, newspapers, and annual reports. You must know everything about your target company that's available, including doing reverse engineering on its products. Remember, fishing expeditions are met with coolness. You are expected to know everything but the intimate details before you benchmark. This is not simply a matter of courtesy.

A common error in benchmarking is overlooking the real reason why a company is doing better than you. They may be doing so well because they have benchmarked with the best-in-class. Or they may have gained expertise by merging with or working with a best-in-class company. If so, you should be benchmarking the primary company instead. Competitive intelligence methods will show you the true source of brilliance of the company with which you have benchmarked.

* A WELL-FOCUSED COMPETITIVE INTELLIGENCE PROJECT WILL PREPARE YOU TO ASK THE RIGHT QUESTIONS. IT WILL SAVE TIME AND MAKE YOU A WELCOME GUEST AT THE HOST COMPANY. COMPETITIVE INTELLIGENCE WILL ALSO REVEAL THE TRUE REASON FOR SOMEONE ELSE'S SUCCESS.

5. Use the information you learn to improve your performance.

The idea of benchmarking is not to see how you measure up against your competitors or how much better they do things. The purpose of benchmarking is to improve your performance. Unless you implement what you learn, you're wasting your time benchmarking.

Also, benchmarking is not a one-time event. It should be part of an ongoing program of learning and improvement. Xerox, for instance, has hundreds of ongoing benchmarking programs in progress at any one time.

You should establish a competitive intelligence program to continuously monitor data from companies with whom you have benchmarked against. This is especially true of competitors. Suppose a pricing gap between you and a competitor was 10 percent, and you decided to close that gap within two years by improving 5 percent annually. By the time you reach your goal your competitor may have cut its costs, and you would still be behind. You must keep tabs on the competition.

It should be emphasized that benchmarking is not mimicry. The idea is to learn from the best and adapt their ideas to your own company where applicable. Not everything you learn will work for your company. On the other hand, ideas that may not seem useful at first blush may turn out to be valuable after some thought and fine-tuning.

If you have already set up a system that allows you to use information you've collected from competitive intelligence excursions, you can use that system for implementing what you've learned from benchmarking.

* **THE SYSTEM THAT ALREADY CONNECTS COMPETITIVE INTELLIGENCE AND STRATEGIC PLANNING SHOULD BE USED TO LINK BENCHMARKING AND STRATEGIC PLANNING.**

A funny note: As mentioned, companies like L.L. Bean, American Express, and Domino's Pizza are inundated by those who want to benchmark against their best-in-class processes. Interestingly enough, Xerox now finds itself receiving many requests from companies that want to *benchmark their benchmarking processes.*.

Ethics in Benchmarking

Benchmarking brings a unique set of legal and ethical challenges.

First, the legal considerations. Companies engaging in benchmarking should be aware of potential antitrust violations. The Sherman Act prohibits companies from engaging in any agreements, either expressed or implied, that unreasonably restrict competition and affect interstate commerce. Some of the more obvious and common violations would be price fixing and concentration of power in the hands of a few companies with the intention of forcing smaller companies out of business.

When exchanging information with your benchmarking partners

you should be aware of antitrust considerations. Consult your company attorney for guidance if you're unsure about any facet of the benchmarking project.

The following conditions should raise red flags. It doesn't mean that you can't benchmark, but you should take some precautions.

- If you and your partner together hold the majority share of a market.
- Exchanging general information about processes and procedures is generally safe. Areas of concern include pricing, costs, and strategic planning. Immediately, cut off any discussions that imply restraint of trade.

The general rule is that your benchmarking activities should not lead anyone to believe that you and another company are engaging in anticompetitive behavior. In fact, everything you do should be in support of the benchmarking project—to increase the efficiency and competitiveness of all players—and information that doesn't support this goal should never be exchanged or discussed.

Many benchmarkers routinely bring in an independent third party to collect sensitive information from a group of competitors. The information is packaged and sanitized in such a way that all participants receive the exact same data and nobody knows whose data is whose except for their own.

The ethical considerations of benchmarking are important as well.

The Golden Rule in benchmarking is only to ask for information that you are willing to give yourself. If you are uncomfortable revealing a piece of information, don't ask your partner for it.

Make sure that all partners understand what information will be collected, when it will be delivered, and in what form. This ensures that everyone feels they are receiving as much as they are giving.

Use the same contact people for all inquiries. Don't go outside the people involved in the benchmarking project.

All information you receive should remain confidential and kept internal to the benchmarking project. Never offer benchmarking data you received from one company to another company without the first company's permission. Never reveal to anyone else the companies with whom you've benchmarked without their permission.

Information obtained through benchmarking should only be used for benchmarking purposes. It shouldn't be used for marketing, advertising, or selling your products or services.

The International Benchmarking Clearinghouse and the Strategic Planning Institute Council on Benchmarking have adopted the following code of conduct. Your company should abide by these rules, but you may want to expand upon certain areas that are important to your culture. Most important, all benchmarking partners should agree on the ethical standards under which they will exchange information.

BENCHMARKING CODE OF CONDUCT*

1. Principle of *Legality.*
    1.1 If there is any potential question on the legality of an activity, don't do it.
    1.2 Avoid discussions or actions that could lead to or imply an interest in restraint of trade, market and/or customer allocation schemes, price fixing, dealing arrangements, bid rigging, or bribery. Don't discuss costs with competitors if costs are an element of pricing.
    1.3 Refrain from the acquisition of trade secrets from any means that could be interpreted as improper, including the breach or inducement of a breach of any duty to maintain secrecy. Do not disclose or use any trade secret that may have been obtained through improper means or that was disclosed by another in violation of a duty to maintain its secrecy or limit its use.
    1.4 Do not, as a consultant or client, extend one benchmarking study's findings to another company without first obtaining the permission of the parties to the first study.

2. Principle of *Exchange.*
    2.1 Be willing to provide the same type and level of information that you request from your benchmarking partner to your benchmarking partner.
    2.2 Communicate fully and early in the relationship to clarify expectations, avoid misunderstanding, and establish mutual interest in the benchmarking exchange.

*Reprinted with permission of the International Benchmarking Clearinghouse, a service of the American Productivity and Quality Center

2.3 Be honest and complete.

3. Principle of *Confidentiality*.
   3.1 Treat benchmarking interchange as confidential to the individuals and companies involved. Information must not be communicated outside the partnering organizations without the prior consent of the benchmarking partner who shared in the information.
   3.2 A company's participation in a study is confidential and should not be communicated externally without their prior permission.

4. Principle of *Use*.
   4.1 Use information obtained through benchmarking only for purposes of formulating improvement of operations or processes within the companies participating in the benchmarking study.
   4.2 The use or communication of a benchmarking partner's name with the data obtained or practices observed requires the prior permission of that partner.
   4.3 Do not use benchmarking information or any information resulting from a benchmarking exchange or benchmarking-related networking as a means to market or sell.
   4.4 Contact lists or other contact information provided by the International Benchmarking Clearinghouse in any form may not be used for marketing in any way.

5. Principle of *First Party Contact*.
   5.1 Initiate benchmarking contacts, whenever possible, through a benchmarking contact designated by the partner company.
   5.2 Respect the corporate culture of partner companies and work through mutually agreed procedures.
   5.3 Obtain mutual agreement with the designated benchmarking contact on any handoff of communication or responsibility to other parties.

6. Principle of *Third Party Contact*.
   6.1 Obtain an individual's permission before providing his or her name in response to a contact request.

    6.2   Avoid communicating a contact's name in an open forum without the contact's prior permission.

7.   Principle of *Preparation.*
    7.1   Demonstrate commitment to the efficiency and effectiveness of benchmarking by being prepared prior to making an initial benchmarking contact.
    7.2   Make the most of your benchmarking partner's time by being fully prepared for each exchange.
    7.3   Help your benchmarking partners prepare by providing them with a questionnaire and agenda prior to each benchmarking visit.

8.   Principle of *Completion.*
    8.1   Follow through with each commitment made to your benchmarking partner in a timely manner.
    8.2   Complete each benchmarking study to the satisfaction of all benchmarking partners as mutually agreed.

9.   Principle of the *Understanding and Action.*
    9.1   Understand how your benchmarking partner would like to be treated.
    9.2   Treat your benchmarking partner in the way that your benchmarking partner would like to be treated.
    9.3   Understand how your benchmarking partner would like to have the information her or she provides handled and used, and handle and use it in that manner.

Competitive Intelligence Lessons from the Malcolm Baldrige Award

No one will ever agree on what constitutes the best competitive intelligence or benchmarking practices. It varies from company to company, but we are starting to see some recognized criteria from an acclaimed source.

The most prestigious business award in the United States is the

Malcolm Baldrige National Quality Award. First given in 1988, the award's goals are to promote awareness of quality excellence, to recognize quality achievements of U.S. companies, and to publicize successful strategies.

One of the main categories upon which companies are judged is *Information and Analysis*—how well the company handles information and how it uses it to support all other facets of the business. In the words of the award criteria, this category *examines the scope, management and use of data and information to maintain a customer focus, to drive quality excellence and to improve operational and competitive performance.*

The other categories are: Leadership, Strategic Planning, Human Resource Development and Management, Process Management, Business Results, and Customer Focus and Satisfaction.

Performance must be measured in all categories. Entrants must describe in detail how they have improved performance quality in each category and how that has contributed to the company's overall success.

Each year, there are three awards: for manufacturing companies, service companies, and small businesses (under five hundred employees).

The award is not just symbolic. The criteria involved in choosing the

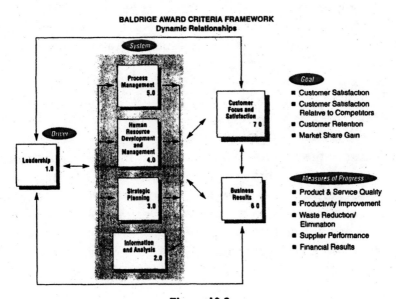

Figure 10-2

winning companies and giving feedback to entrants have important roles in raising the competitiveness of U.S. firms. While the information in the applications is kept confidential, winners are encouraged and expected to share nonproprietary information about their successful quality strategies with other companies. Also, the examiners show entrants where improvements can be made and how they measure up against other companies.

Because of the coveted nature of the Baldrige award, the criteria for the Information and Analysis category give a good indication of what is expected of the best companies in the United States when it comes to competitive intelligence. It also shows what level of results you should strive for from your own competitive intelligence efforts.

Competitive intelligence *must* be part of a quality company's total fabric. It is an integral part of everything it does and, according to the award, if you aren't engaging in competitive intelligence you can't hope to be the best.

The Information and Analysis category is divided into three sections. Here are some highlights of the criteria:

1. Scope and Management of Quality Performance, Data, and Information.

The company must describe how it selects information and the role of information in improving quality and operational performance. Emphasis is on the adequacy of the information to drive process improvement.

The Award recognizes that while cost and financial data provide useful support, process improvement is driven through nonfinancial indicators which are linked to requirements from customers and the company's overall performance.

Applicants must address how information is reliably, consistently, and rapidly available throughout the company and how accuracy is checked. They must also show how the company is shortening the cycle from data collection to access, broadening the access to everyone who needs it, and, most important, how information is linked to process improvement plans and needs.

2. Competitive Comparisons and Benchmarking.

This category looks at how companies compare themselves to others—where they stand relative to competitors and best-in-class practices. Here it is emphasized that benchmarking others can lead to improvements within the company and sometimes be the impetus for significant breakthroughs.

Companies are asked to describe how benchmarking is used to improve their own processes and how the company has used benchmarking to set stretch targets for itself.

3. Analysis and Uses of Company-Level Data.

One of the overall themes of quality, according to the award criteria, is "management by fact," that is, statistics, facts, and figures must be employed to guide a company's actions toward success.

However, this section recognizes that facts are sometimes not enough and that action depends upon "understanding cause/effect connections among processes and between processes and results." The criteria description continues: "Given that resources for improvement are limited and cause/effect connections are often unclear, there is a critical need to provide sound analytical basis for decisions."

The key here is "linkage." Information and analysis act as a link among all "customer-related" sources of information such as Customer Focus and Satisfaction (7.0), Quality and Operational Results (6.0), and Process Management (5.0) in Figure 10-2.

Companies must show how they have turned customer-related information into usable results.

The company must detail "how analysis strengthens the integration of overall data use for improved decision making and planning."

All categories have a scoring system with three potential responses: Approach—how the applicant addresses the requirement; Deployment—the extent to which the applicant's approaches are applied; and Results—what has been achieved.

Interestingly, the Information and Analysis category only requires companies to discuss Approach and Deployment but not Results. Results items are dependent upon data, according to the award criteria, and not having to offer results shows an understanding of the difficulty in quantifying the effects of competitive intelligence.

However, the award criteria also note that if approach and deployment are employed in competitive intelligence, then the subsequent results for the company will be widespread and, in the big picture, quantifiable.

If you look at some of the winners of this quality award you will, not surprisingly, see companies that have well-established competitive intelligence units, including AT&T, IBM, Federal Express, Motorola, Texas Instruments, and Xerox.

CHAPTER ELEVEN

How the Japanese Perform Competitive Intelligence

"Information is the lifeblood of the company."
—Motto of Mitsui Corporation

U.S. corporate managers often wonder how the Japanese economy, devastated by World War II, has grown to be the world's second largest economic power. They lament unfair trade practices, illegal dumping of goods, and the ever present and "unfair" cooperation between government and private industry.

They wonder why it is that although the Japanese used to be outspent in R&D their products are first-rate and technologically superior. They produce one-third of the world's cars, steel, and ships and two-thirds of the world's computer chips. They wonder how a country with few natural resources produces nearly 18 percent of the world's Gross Domestic Product and how it could have doubled its economy between 1973 and 1989. Half of the world's top twenty banks are in Japan.

Then managers say it's because the Japanese don't spend money on defense like the United States. They can spend their money more wisely on industry. What else? Japanese managers don't have to worry about the stock market, satisfying the short-term-minded Street and thus can think long-term. And one more thing: Japanese workers are more committed and more loyal to their company and to their work.

Although all this may be true, it doesn't tell the whole story about "The Japanese Miracle." Our managers overlook the one thread that weaves through all of these items—the one factor that underpins all of these issues—and goes to the heart of why Japanese businesses have been so successful in such a short time.

It is their absolute and unbending belief in competitive intelligence as a strategic corporate tool to make the best decisions possible.

This, more than anything else, separates the Japanese business mind-set from that of their counterparts in other countries. It is the secret of their continued success.

While consulting gurus to American industries tend to look at all of these issues, they very rarely look at competitive intelligence. Why? Because it's not something that's done by many U.S. companies. It's not taught in colleges. And, if it's not done here, it's not worth looking at.

When Japan's economy started to skyrocket in the late 1950s and early 1960s—when Japan's GDP first surpassed the United States's—many Westerners used to say that Japanese companies weren't capable of producing anything of their own. "They are just copycats" was an often-heard phrase. Had American managers been more astute they would have seen beyond the catchall phrase and seen what the Japanese were really practicing: prudent use of competitive intelligence. Information learned from the United States and other economically successful countries was being applied in Japan and integrated into their corporate structures. When you're learning about manufacturing, technology, and management techniques from the best business minds in the world, how can you fail?

How Americans (not just corporate Americans) feel and treat information compared to the Japanese is at the heart of the matter. There is a lot of lip service paid to the information age and how Americans embrace the idea of information and such conduits as the information superhighway. Unfortunately, it is often just talk.

In Japanese, the word *jobo* means two things: information and intelligence. This says right off the bat that information is worthwhile. It has value. In English, information doesn't become intelligence unless something is done to it.

To an American, a scrap of information may not mean anything, but to a Japanese businessperson it has value. Maybe not earth-shattering worth but it means something to someone. Information is revered and coveted. Information is highly valued especially (and sometimes only) when viewed within a context. Why a specific piece of information is needed may not be clear at the time it's collected, but it may come in handy later on.

In Japan, information is a commodity with an intrinsic worth. To an American, it may be like the cardboard box you keep in the attic because it's sturdy and you never know when you may need it. It's only a cardboard box, hardly worth a dollar, but it's perceived as potentially useful enough to keep.

Because so much of the U.S. culture is open and free and information is pervasive, Americans tend to think of information as cheap. The expression "talk is cheap" is a perfect example of an American attitude. To the Japanese, everything someone says has some meaning. You may not have the correct context to exploit it, but it has worth.

To the Japanese, gathering information is a noble calling. It is a worthwhile activity and one that pays dividends.

Information collection is an ongoing part of the Japanese business culture and complements the idea of *kaizen*, which means constant and continuous improvement. As you know, Japanese business horizons are long, very long, as long as a century from now. Every piece of information that's sucked up by the great Japanese information vacuum cleaner becomes part of someone's long-term strategic plan.

Lest you think that I put too fine a point on this, recall the last trade show you attended. Did you notice any Japanese businesspeople taking photos like film was free and collecting brochures like they contained discount coupons? Or perhaps your own company has hosted Japanese visitors who accepted handouts and pamphlets from you with the respect and reverence deserving a precious gift. Ask your public relations office for its list of companies who receive press releases and financial information available to the public. Chances are they contain Japanese companies.

What you see in these instances is typical competitive intelligence gathering. Chances are also good that you may have snickered at these people's zeal and great interest in the smallest detail of some product to which you didn't even pay attention. Well, whatever they gathered will probably find its way back to Tokyo or other cities in Japan to be disseminated to those who can use it. It's an extraordinary worldwide system that boggles the mind of most Westerners, but to the Japanese it's just everyday business.

Why the Japanese Love Information—And Why They're Willing to Share It with One Another

You must know some Japanese culture and history to understand why information gathering and competitive intelligence are so important to them. Herein is a quick and somewhat simplistic history.

For centuries, the Japanese lived in what has been described as a rice-bowl culture. Farming families lived together in groups, and each family was responsible for its own rice paddy. Water was scarce and irrigation was used to ensure nourishment for crops. As a result, it behooved each family to take care of the water supply not only for its own sake but for that of its neighbors. Each family relied on the other. If one failed, the whole group might perish.

This, many Japan scholars say, was the beginning of the Japanese group behavior where everyone helps one another for the common good. Some people call it a sharing culture where even enemies help each other in order to survive. It also helps to explain why Japanese people, in general, feel that they are one part of a larger community where what they do is important to everyone.

This is different from American culture where individual accomplishments are often stressed over group or team efforts. In modern-day Japan, group learning as opposed to individual learning is standard.

For many centuries, Japan was isolated from the outside world by warlords and shoguns who wanted to maintain complete control over the country.

This isolation was broken in 1853 when Admiral Matthew Perry visited Japan in a now classic case of gunboat diplomacy. The Department of the Navy dispatched Perry to Japan with the purpose of getting the emperor to sign a treaty ensuring the protection of shipwrecked American seamen. Perry presented a letter from President Millard Fillmore after making a massive show of naval strength in Tokyo Bay. The emperor, humbled and somewhat humiliated by the American naval might, signed an agreement to protect shipwrecked sailors but also agreed to sell coal to U.S. ships and open ports to American merchants. Subsequently, the fifteenth and last Tokugawa shogun was overthrown by lords who saw the family as weak and its power compromised by the Americans who had forced the end of the country's self-imposed isolation.

Emperor Meiji was amazed how its isolation had left Japan behind the rest of the world—almost hopelessly behind—and he set programs in place to catch up by soaking up everything he could about Western culture, business and economics. His goal was to thrust Japan into the nineteenth century as fast as possible.

One of the sayings popular at the time was *"Wakon yosai"*—"Japanese spirit and Western knowledge." And nowhere was this more succinctly put then in one of the five tenets of the Meiji Charter Oath of 1868:

"Knowledge shall be sought all over the world, and the foundations of imperial rule shall be strengthened."

More than any other person, Meiji set the stage for Japan's insatiable quest for outside intelligence for both industrial and military purposes. Meiji-era leaders sent people out in droves to many countries to study and learn Western culture, industry, and military. They reported back regularly and the information was evaluated and the government copied what they could in order to catch up with the West.

One thing the Meiji leaders learned was the industrial and financial power in the West was concentrated in the hands of a few families like the Rockefellers, Rothschilds, and Morgans. The only problem was that Japan didn't have such families. The government took it upon itself to build crucial industries such as shipbuilding, which they knew would be important for naval might. It also established coal mines, steel factories, and mills. However, these enterprises didn't do well and the government was forced to sell them at bargain-basement prices to family businesses that then blossomed into the *zaibatsu*, which were highly diversified companies owned by a single family or group.

The four major zaibatsu are names you will recognize: Mitsui, Mitsubishi, Sumitomo, and Yasuda.

These zaibatsu thrived and grew monstrously large, especially during World War I when they sold munitions and other war matériel to the Allies. They reached their peak in the 1930s supplying the war effort against China. Later, they were instrumental during World War II building all of the aircraft, ships, and arms used against the Allies. The business of war and industry was inextricably intertwined in Japan until after World War II. Then the zaibatsu were disbanded under the auspices of General Douglas MacArthur, who, like many people, blamed the families for instigating war for the purpose of making money and extending the reach of Japan's influence.

However, the scheme didn't work as MacArthur and his group had planned. Although the zaibatsu were broken up and some directors removed, Japan's postwar minister Shigeru Yoshida kept most of the powerful, forward-thinking directors in place. Also left alone by the Allied commander were two important bureaucracies, the Ministry of Finance and what was to become the Ministry of International Trade and Industry (MITI). MITI is the group that many scholars agree was the driving force behind Japan's dynamic growth after the war.

Old habits die hard and even though the zaibatsu were broken up into smaller companies, most of the senior managers of the individual firms continued to work together, informally, with their old colleagues. By the 1950s—after U.S. occupation was just a memory—these companies banded together once again into new business structures called *keiretsu,* which remain today.

The notion of keiretsu is difficult for Westerners to understand because there is no equivalent in our culture. They are not conglomerates in the Western sense, nor are they simply holding companies.

A keiretsu is a group of individual companies united by the exchange and sharing among them of personnel, money, goods, and, of course, information. The sharing culture of Japan is seen here in all its glory. Cross-directorships are a major feature as well.

There are six major horizontal keiretsus and several huge vertical ones. The large vertical ones are in autos and electronics, and companies can be members of both a horizontal and vertical keiretsu.

The Trading Companies

At the heart of each keiretsu is a trading company or *sogo shosha.* There is no Western version of such an entity either and their mission is, by American business terms, rather vague and nebulous. These trading companies are responsible for coordinating and guiding the group through all areas of commerce. Although trading companies stick mainly to the usual commodities of rice, sugar, steel, and so on,

Mitsubishi Keiretsu

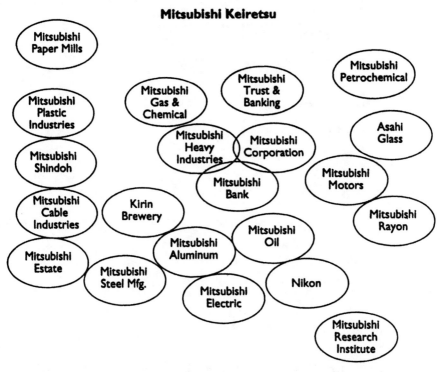

Figure 11-1

they will buy and sell such items as jet fighters and naval warships. They will provide financing, marketing, management services, consulting services, and generally deal in anything as long as they can make money on it.

One of their overall tasks is to smooth the way for their affiliated companies to do business in the domestic and global marketplace. Trading companies do not produce equipment or machinery. Instead, they are defined by ideas, intellectual property, and information. Ironically, when MacArthur and his occupation force dismantled the Japanese military many of its intelligence experts were placed in sogo shoshas. Competitive intelligence comes naturally to these trading companies.

How big are these trading companies?

The nine biggest trading companies have combined sales of almost a trillion dollars, and they handle more than 60 percent of Japan's imports and 50 percent of its exports. Mitsubishi, for instance, imports almost 20 percent of Japan's coal for steel and its machinery group handles 40 percent of the country's machine tool exports. It also acts

JAPANESE TRADING COMPANIES

(Sogo Shoshas)

Major—"Big Six"

Mitsubishi Corporation

Sumitomo Corporation

C. Itoh & Company

Mitsui & Company

Marubeni Corporation

Nissho Iwai

Minor

Tomen

Kanematsu Gosho

Nichimen Corporation

Figure 11-2

as export agent for Mitsubishi Motors, the country's third largest automaker.

Margins are low on these transactions, so many of the trading companies have been moving into more aggressive areas where they actually have an equity position in the transactions themselves.

Mitsui, for example, has established about a hundred joint ventures and subsidiaries to cash in on the growing telecommunications industry. C. Itoh has paired with Hughes Aircraft to form a satellite company. Mitsubishi has a 48 percent stake in Kentucky Fried Chicken Japan, a company with more than nine hundred outlets. The 1993 annual report lists almost 150 subsidiaries and affiliated companies.

Trading companies keep a low profile even though they have field offices in more than two hundred cities worldwide—even in the most remote areas.

On a daily basis, a typical Big Six trading company, or sogo shosha, collects about 100,000 pieces of information from its 10,000 employees in about 180 offices worldwide. In addition, each trading company spends about $60 million annually maintaining their information collection infrastructure.

Mitsubishi, for example, has more than thirteen thousand employees in more than two hundred offices worldwide. They send in more than thirty thousand pieces of information *daily*.

This large web is especially important to a trading company's commodity trading deals, where instant information about a crisis from a faraway place can have a profound and immediate effect on commodity prices.

But the information these trading companies glean is also important to the long-term health and development of their affiliated companies. Collected information is funneled into Japan from points all over the world, around the clock, where it is selected, dissected, analyzed, and disseminated to the affiliated companies.

This is where the previously mentioned sharing culture comes into play. To the Japanese mind, information has value and thus it is important to share it with others so they may prosper along with you. All the companies in a keiretsu share information with one another. Information is even shared with competitors in another keiretsu to get a leg up on a bigger, common competitor, very often an American company. You have to remember that many of the people who manage keiretsus have family members who were in zaibatsus generations ago. To say that Japan's major industries are run by an old-boy's network is quite the understatement.

On the other hand, there is great rivalry among Japanese companies and they can be fiercely competitive.

Who else uses the trading companies as their eyes and ears? It's not uncommon for a Japanese ambassador in a foreign country to ask an office of a trading company in that city for help on a research project.

The government used trading companies during World War II. Mitsui's extensive network was called on to gather intelligence for Japan's war effort. In 1991, Japan's Ministry of Foreign Affairs used Mitsui's network to keep informed about the attempted coup that summer against Mikhail Gorbachev.

It's no surprise that Mitsui's motto is: "Information is the lifeblood of the company."

The Companies

An interesting phenomenon occurred in the 1960s. Large companies in keiretsus established their own competitive intelligence divisions to supplement and in many cases give more value to what is supplied by their sogo shosha.

Some of the best competitive intelligence divisions are located at companies like Canon, NEC, Toshiba, and Toyota.

John Quinn is a former U.S. intelligence officer who was stationed in Japan for twenty years. He is now a private competitive intelligence consultant and tells the following story about visiting Toshiba on behalf of a client. "I wanted to talk to them about video conferencing for a client who was interested in a strategic alliance. I sent them a fax confirming that I would see them on Thursday at eleven o'clock. Usual procedure. When I got there I saw my fax with notes on the top that said, 'This guy's been in Japan a long time, speaks fluent Japanese, his wife is Japanese, and he attended such and such university.' I didn't give them that information. These people are very good."

This is a telling example of how Japanese businesses give themselves a subtle but useful edge over their competitors in negotiations.

The commitment to competitive intelligence by companies is strong. For example, Nissan Motor Company established a Nissan Business Research Library at corporate headquarters and has among its five libraries more than 100,000 books, documents, and reports for use by everyone in the company. The system is used extensively by employees, who have on-line access.

Let's look again at Toshiba. The Toshiba Research and Development Library has more than forty thousand volumes. Its internal network called TOSFILE delivers information from the library, wire services, newspapers, and other news sources to more than five hundred decision makers daily. Worldwide distribution via satellite is being tested. The company has almost twenty competitive intelligence professionals who handle this flow of information.

Information is everyone's job. It is not uncommon to see a district manager in the United States for a Japanese company clipping local newspaper articles and faxing them to the home office in Japan.

In fact, almost all employees stationed outside Japan are required to submit regular—usually weekly or monthly—reports to the company's competitive intelligence unit. From there it is sorted and distributed throughout the company. With urgent or critical information, employees are expected to send it—by fax or phone—to the appropriate person for a rapid response.

Typically, a company has ten to twenty people dedicated to competitive intelligence duties at the home office. They are usually located in the strategic planning or research department.

Where do these practitioners come from?

Some are from government training facilities. In the 1960s, the Japanese government established the Institute for Industrial Protection. Although you might think that with the name *industrial protection* the emphasis was on security, this was only partly the case. Many of the graduates of the four-month course found themselves engaging in collection and analysis of business information once they entered corporate life.

Some corporations are so large and have such complex competitive intelligence needs that they have established separate research institutes or think tanks that employ hundreds of people for the sole purpose of collecting, analyzing, and distributing information. Mitsubishi, Daiwa, and Nomura are examples of companies that have done so. In addition, these think tanks often act as consultancies for other companies.

It's important to remember that competitive intelligence is not a secret in Japan. In fact, a publication in 1993 called *Kigyo Gaiko* was a guide to 1,300 Japanese corporations operating in New York, Chicago, and Atlanta. In it was each company's profile, location, number of employees, and their activities.

The Government

What the trading companies and individual companies collect and pass on is only part of the picture. The government plays a vital role in the operation of the huge Japanese information behemoth.

When we talk about the relationship between big business and government in Japan, we're often talking about the connection between the Ministry of International Trade and Industry, MITI, and the keiretsu.

MITI is responsible for establishing government policies to promote industrial development. MITI sets Japan's business game plan; in essence deciding which areas will receive special emphasis, research money, tax incentives, legislation, and protection in the form of tariffs and so forth to aid the country's goal of market domination in these sectors. (MITI has also set production quotas for some companies but as the keiretsu grow larger and more powerful they have defied MITI's wishes.)

In recent years, MITI has singled out industries such as computers (especially software development), biotechnology, robotics, and semiconductors as areas in which it wants the nation's businesses to lead the world, and it has helped them accordingly.

One of the main ways that MITI helps Japan's industries succeed is through the collection and distribution of competitive intelligence. In that regard, it employs JETRO, the Japanese External Trade Organization.

Formed in 1958, JETRO is a quasi-government organization whose official mission is to support trade between Japan and other countries. Although it does this, JETRO's major role is to act as a source of competitive intelligence for Japan's sogo shoshas and individual companies. The E in JETRO originally stood for *export* but was changed to *external* during the 1980s when Japan first experienced a massive trade surplus.

In fact, JETRO's chairman, Toru Toyoshima, mentions in their latest brochure that "JETRO has a long history of quantifying and analyzing the global economy and international trade. Efforts in this field have already been much acclaimed around the world. JETRO is now upgrading these capabilities to become one of the world's leading data banks for economic information on Japan and other countries."

He is talking about competitive intelligence. Plain and simple.

In fact, JETRO is the only true, large-scale, government-sponsored competitive intelligence agency in the world.

JETRO publishes a massive amount of information and most of it is available to anyone who is willing to take the time and effort to seek it. The bulk of it is in Japanese, but English translations are becoming more common, especially in JETRO centers in the United States. However, not reading Japanese is an impediment to fully utilizing JETRO's resources.

Headquartered in Tokyo, JETRO maintains thirty-two offices in Japan and seventy-nine offices overseas in fifty-seven countries. In addition, JETRO has placed twenty senior trade advisors in various U.S. states. Worldwide staff totals 1,300 people (figures 11-3 and 11-4).

Interestingly, there is no office in Washington, D.C., because the embassy takes up the slack. It is common practice for JETRO personnel

THE LOCATION OF OVERSEAS OFFICES (as of July 1, 1995)

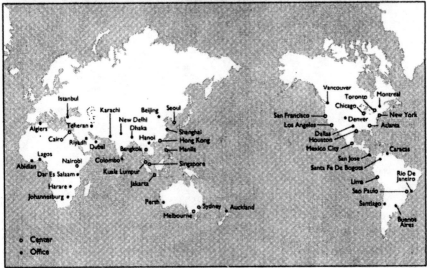

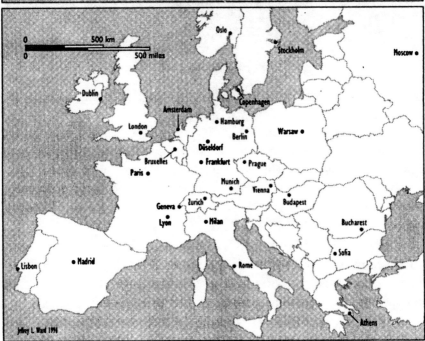

Figure 11-3

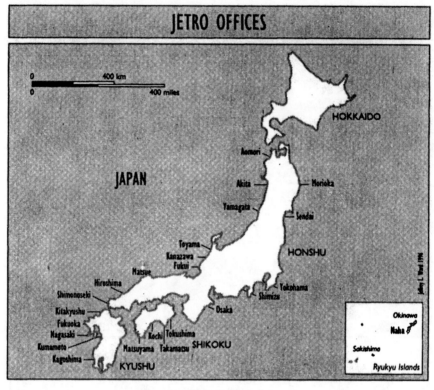

Figure 11-4

to use several attaché posts that have been assigned by the embassy for MITI people.

To understand the depth of JETRO's information, walk into its Tokyo library. Its shelves contain almost every telephone book from almost every city in the United States and the rest of the world. Try to find that in any U.S. library. In JETRO's Japanese offices you'll regularly find people studying mounds of data, piles of charts, and reams of papers with numbers and figures.

Much of JETRO's information is distributed publicly through its own publications such as *New Technology Japan*, a monthly magazine about Japan's industrial and technological world, and *Focus Japan*, a monthly newsletter about economic, trade, and industrial trends in Japan.

JETRO even publishes a bimonthly *China Newsletter* about economic and trading trends in China—the world's largest potential market.

Although the bulk of JETRO's work is public (for about $50 you can buy MITI's directory, which tells where Japan is targeting its high-tech research), there's also a private side. JETRO handles what it calls "custom reports" for Japanese clients. This information is not available to the general public.

JETRO also puts out classified reports on specific topics. To obtain one, you must work for a trading company or otherwise be intimately involved in Japan's business world. Basically, you must be a Japanese citizen. This information is not intended for foreign competitors. The classified reports are often produced by JETRO's so-called area specialists, people who are experts on certain business sectors such as semiconductors or petroleum.

Although it's easier for most of us to understand the Japanese information machine by looking at the three major components separately, we must remember that Japan's culture is one of sharing, and information flows freely among all three collectors and their recipients. It's important to think of these three entities as part of one large competitive intelligence operation all working toward a common goal.

Sources of Intelligence

There is nothing mysterious about how the Japanese collect business information. The great majority of it comes from public sources such as publications, trade shows, and company annual reports. However, the Japanese also employ some sources that are unique to their business system.

First, let's start with the news media.

**Competitive Information/Intelligence
Flows in Japan**

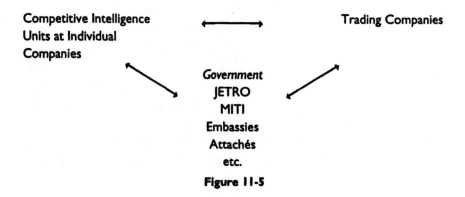

Competitive Intelligence Units at Individual Companies ⟷ Trading Companies

Government
JETRO
MITI
Embassies
Attachés
etc.

Figure 11-5

MEDIA

The Japanese media, although independent, is part of the great information-collection machine. The Japanese business media serves its information-hungry clients like no other media in any other country.

A recent survey by the Japan Development Bank shows that newspapers are the most important source of competitive intelligence for Japanese companies. A survey by the Tokyo Chamber of Commerce reported the same finding.

There are four major business newspaper groups. The competition is so fierce for readers that it's standard fare for them to try to out-publish each other by including more and more statistics, charts, graphs, tables, and lists within their publications.

It's not uncommon to see giant compilations of figures having to do with companies' R&D expenditures, number of employees, sales, and so on. These lists are also turned into directories that are briskly devoured.

The largest business media group is the Nikkei Business Press. Americans read the *Wall Street Journal* or the business pages of the *New York Times* and consider themselves well informed on recent happenings. The Japanese businessperson would consider that inadequate. In its role of working toward the larger goal of the country, Nikkei feeds vast amounts of data into the great Japanese information machine as well as the rest of the world.

Nikkei has twenty-two Japanese and five overseas printing facilities. It has a worldwide staff of 1,400 people sending economic information to Japan twenty-four hours a day, seven days a week.

Nikkei boasts that it is the world's largest economic data bank and that claim is hard to dispute. Nikkei newspapers are distributed through seven thousand outlets in Japan. *Nikkei—The Japan Economic Journal*—is the flagship and the largest economic newspaper in the world, with more than three million readers. In addition to Nikkei, it also produces *Nikkei Sangyou Shimbun—The Japan Business and Industry Journal; Nikkei Ryutu—The Japan Marketing and Distribution Journal; Nikkei Kinyu—The Japan Finance and Banking Journal,* and *The Nikkei Weekly,* which is in English.

Nikkei also delivers news, economic information, and competitive intelligence through a fax service, a satellite TV system, and through on-line computer networks.

SOME JAPANESE PRESS CLUBS AND WHAT THEY COVER

Press Club	Area of Specialty
Bank of Japan	Finances, Bank of Japan
Science and Technology Agency Press Club	High-technology activities of companies
MITI Press Club	MITI and related industries
Heavy Industries Press Club	Aerospace, Machinery, Chemicals, Steel
Automobile Manufacturers Association	Automobiles

Figure 11-6

The press club system in Japan also supports and encourages in-depth coverage of companies and economic conditions. Press clubs are divided into special-interest groups such as the Automobile Manufacturers Association, the Bank of Japan, the Ministry of Health and Welfare Press, the Science and Technology Agency Press Club, and others. Members of each press club are given the right to attend press conferences held by the associated industry group on behalf of companies. Moreover, reporters are given a desk within the club from which they may cover the industry. Clubs are located in every government ministry and large corporation.

A typical business newspaper will send reporters to at least seventy-five clubs while some will send even more. Some clubs rate more than one reporter.

Reporters who are immersed in covering one industry tend to become very close associates of those in the industry and they usually receive good access to the companies they cover. Often, public affairs departments will hold briefings, almost like classroom sessions, with club members to help them understand technical material. (There have been instances of reporters becoming too close to the entity they cover and suppressing embarrassing stories. However, that is changing as more and more foreign reporters are covering Japan and running objective stories. Japanese reporters are being forced to compete with the outsiders.)

Japanese newspapers contain a wealth of information about companies, technology, and investments, but most of it stays out of reach of most foreigners simply because of the language barrier.

"For about 100 yen [75 cents] I can pick up a Japanese newspaper and get more information on Japanese investment in the U.S. than the U.S. Treasury Department has," John Stern of the American Electronics Association told *Fortune* magazine in a 1991 article.

None of this is meant to imply that U.S. newspapers don't have important information as well—if you take the time to read them.

U.S. competitive intelligence experts like to tell the story of a large U.S. medical supply manufacturer who was caught off guard by increased production at the Kokuku Rubber Industry's plant in Kentucky. The U.S. medical supply firm had to scramble to cut prices in an effort to keep from losing market share to its Japanese competitor. The American firm shouldn't have been surprised. Details of the new plant's construction, capacity, employees, and product lines were in an article in the *Lexington Herald Leader* in 1987, three years before the plant went on line. Had management read the article they could've taken action and they wouldn't have had a crisis on their hands.

PERSONAL CONTACTS

Who you know is as important in Japan as it is everywhere else. However, in Japan your personal network becomes a well-used tool for competitive intelligence.

American business people are often taken aback by the great interest their Japanese counterparts have in business card exchange. Because of Japan's vertical society, personal contacts become paramount. As mentioned earlier, calling someone cold and introducing yourself and suggesting lunch as is done in the United States just doesn't occur in Japan. So the business card becomes part of a manager's information network.

In another example, university cliques (*gakubatsu*) are composed of people who attended the same university. These cliques become of great use to someone seeking competitive intelligence. Again, they are methods to meet people who are unknown to you.

There's another university connection that's worth mentioning. Japanese companies often fund students for study in the United States. While these students are not trained competitive intelligence experts, they may be called upon from time to time to answer a question or find a certain piece of information requested by the sponsoring corporation. Students are often in excellent positions to observe advanced research projects at their university.

OBSERVATIONS

Japanese visitors to American factories, plants, and facilities are always gathering competitive intelligence for their companies. It's expected that courtesy tours will yield useful information. Indeed, Japanese are perfectly willing to reciprocate with a tour of their facilities; however, many American firms don't take advantage of that invitation.

In fact, some American firms have recently closed their plants to foreign visitors as they believe they're not getting enough information in return—partly because they don't take up the invitation—but also because they believe that the Japanese are lagging behind. This is shortsighted because even if a competitor is behind in general, it doesn't mean they are behind in all processes, some of which may be helpful to you.

A good example of this thinking was what happened to Burgmaster in the 1970s. The company's Japanese partner, Yamazaki Machinery, sent waves of visitors to Burgmaster's factories to observe. Burgmaster showed the Japanese everything they wanted to see. The feeling at Burgmaster was that there was nothing to worry about and there was nothing to learn from Yamazaki. The Japanese can mimic but they can't innovate, American managers believed.

After several years of observation, Yamazaki discovered that it could do better than Burgmaster, and in 1974 it became the first Japanese machine tool builder to open a facility in the United States. In many cases they improved on Burgmaster's designs and engineering.

A few American aerospace firms have closed their plants to Japanese visitors after discovering that guests were purposely wearing soft rubber-soled shoes on the production floor to catch the shavings of special metal alloys that they would later analyze. These kinds of covert tactics are infrequent but they do happen.

Many American firms don't realize that they are welcome to exchange personnel with some Japanese research laboratories for an extended visit. According to the National Science Foundation, some of the companies that welcome U.S. researchers are Minolta Camera,

NTT, Hitachi, and Fujitsu. While many Japanese companies take advantage of this opportunity, few American companies do. Why? Language is a factor but also American firms don't see it as beneficial to make such a commitment.

Again, it's a mistake to think you can't learn something from someone in the same business.

Trade shows are considered major sources of information for the Japanese. While Japanese businesspeople are seen swarming around U.S. trade shows, Westerners are not often observed with the same verve at Japanese trade shows.

Very often, Japanese companies send teams to cover trade shows so they can save time and be more efficient in their gathering. A team may consist of a marketing person, an engineer, a research person, and a development person. Each team member is responsible for collecting different kinds of information.

It bears repeating that there is no magic to any of these generations-old methods of information collection. No special tricks. It's all a matter of getting information to where it is needed in the least amount of time. If there is anything amazing about the Japanese process it's the amount of information handled each day. Some experts estimate that Japan produces two million pieces of information daily. As we'll see later on, the Japanese competitive intelligence machine does have some trouble analyzing this overwhelming amount of material. How have they chosen to solve this problem?

With competitive intelligence. Stay tuned.

Classic Case Studies from Japan

While Westerners often hide their competitive intelligence activities, companies in Japan are less inhibited about telling stories—both positive and negative. Following are some classic case studies about Japanese competitive intelligence.

TOSHIBA AND THE QUEST FOR THE DRAM MARKET

Toshiba Corporation was doing pretty well in the DRAM business in the early 1980s. DRAM means dynamic random access memory and is, simply, a chip that holds information. It is a building block of personal computers.

The company was doing well in the 16 kilobyte (16K) DRAM but was not being taken seriously in the 64K DRAM business because its products simply weren't competitive.

In 1982, a major industrial newspaper in Japan reported that Toshiba was dropping out of the DRAM business, and everyone believed it. After all, the world was moving to more and more memory on a single chip and Toshiba's 16K was minor-league compared to 64K chips and the next step, 256 kilobyte chips.

It turns out that the newspaper article was wrong. Three years later in 1985 Toshiba bypassed the 256 kilobyte market and introduced a 1 megabyte chip and was producing them at twice the yield ratio of its nearest competitors. It dominated the market and then went on to become a major force in the 4 megabyte DRAM market.

How could Toshiba's competitors have been fooled?

It was a failure of competitive intelligence. All the signs were there, but the competitors didn't notice.

For example, in 1982 Toshiba engineers delivered papers at conferences about developments in 256K technology. It was pretty clear that they were jumping ahead. In addition, a close reading of the papers showed that the processes they were experimenting with were much more sophisticated than were needed for the 256K chips. Other competitors, like NEC, were planning on using older 64K technology and adapting it to the newer 256K product.

There were other clues. NEC and Hitachi announced large investments in current-technology DRAM factories while Toshiba did not. Instead, they announced large expenditures earmarked for ultra-large scale integration, or ULSI, chip development. ULSI is overkill for 256K products but necessary for larger memory chips.

There was one more clue to Toshiba's plans, albeit subtle. According to public financial statements, Toshiba hired 1,200 engineers and was planning on making a 250 billion yen investment from 1983 to 1985 for semiconductor development. Along with the hiring and investment went an organizational change that called for a 256K engineering group, a semiconductor R&D group and a basic research group for future products. As the months progressed, personnel were moved up the ladder from the less-sophisticated engineering tasks of the 256K group to the research group as the industry itself moved from 64K to 256K technology.

The analysis, which its competitors missed, was that Toshiba was not only changing the structure of its DRAM departments but that it was making a huge wager—of money and personnel—on a product that would pay off big in the future—the 1M DRAM chip—and this turned out to be the case.

THE VIDEOTAPE WARS

During the 1970s and early 1980s, 3M dominated the videotape business worldwide. Japanese competitors could not make a dent in their market share.

However, while 3M was basking in the glow of its success, Japanese competitors were gathering information about the industry in an attempt to find a way inside.

Japanese tape makers, namely Fuji, Sony, TDK, and Maxell, looked at market surveys whicn showed that consumers wanted longer taping sessions, and this would be a criterion for buying future VCRs. They also found that VCR makers were already responding to this trend and were giving their suppliers specifications for machines designed for longer tapes.

But there was a problem. The tapes they currently produced could not support longer taping times because the plastic base film was too thick. The tape manufacturers bought the films from outside suppliers, then placed the magnetic particles necessary for taping on the film—monitoring these filmmakers' progress in thinning the material. An important obstacle was that thin tape must also be as strong as thicker tape. (Another problem with thin tape is a phenomenon known as "bleed through," where magnetic particles on one tape layer mix with magnetic particles on another layer.)

The Japanese tape makers noticed two things. Three huge companies—ICI, DuPont, and Hoechst—were fulfilling the current needs of the tape market but because of large R&D expenditures didn't seem to want to advance technology for thinning the films. The tape makers also noticed that two smaller Japanese companies, Teijin and Toray Industries, were losing market share to the larger companies who had superior technology and more efficient production.

In 1980, Toray bought a very expensive coating machine, which signaled to the tape makers that the film producer was embarking on research to produce the next-generation (thinner) tape, which would also be strong.

As a result, each of the tape makers joined forces with the filmmakers to develop long-duration tapes that would be strong and give good-quality images and sound.

The result of this joint partnership was that in the 1980s longer-playing tape was introduced into the marketplace by Japanese manufacturers, catching 3M by surprise. 3M was still buying thick film, which was no longer on the cutting edge of consumer interest.

PRICING BY COMPETITIVE INTELLIGENCE

This example is not quite a war story but in general shows how competitive intelligence plays a critical role in Japanese pricing policies. Ask any U.S. automaker and he'll tell you that price is what got Japanese autos a foothold in the U.S. market. Quality, better gas mileage, yes. But consumers perceived Japanese cars as giving good value, the mental equation we all make when we buy something. Value, to most retailers and consumers, is a mixture of price, quality, and ease of purchase.

Ask anybody who buys consumer electronics and he'll tell you about how Japanese prices on goods always "seem to be just right." That is, consumer goods are sold at a price point that consumers are willing to pay. Ask retailers and they voice the same thing: Japanese consumer products seem to be priced at what consumers are willing to pay.

None of this is by accident. None of this is done by guessing. Competitive intelligence is the key to the magic touch that Japanese manufacturers have employed successfully to gain market share and, in some cases, dominate markets.

Typically, American companies design a product, then calculate the cost (using historical data) to produce it. If the price is too high the company either sends it back for redesign, decides not to make it, or it accepts a lower profit margin.

Japanese companies, on the other hand, start with a target price in mind—based on what consumers will accept—and then design and engineer the product to fit that price.

Put another way, American companies determine what a product will cost, then see if they can sell it for that cost. Japanese manufacturers on the other hand set a price, then work backward to reach that price.

More importantly, Japanese companies also set a target price based on future price—six months or a year from now—not just today's market price. This allows them to compete a little longer on price when a competitor lowers its prices in the future. It also allows a Japanese company to withstand the shock of market changes beyond their control. For example, an American tractor maker using historical data to price his product would not be able to lower it in the future without losing profit. This could happen if crop prices went into a skid and farmers cut back on equipment purchases. However, a Japanese manufacturer of tractors might have anticipated the drop in agricultural prices by studying farming, weather, and other data and planned now to drop prices later.

Clearly, the Japanese manufacturer has an advantage over his American counterpart in that the keiretsu system allows him to obtain information about his suppliers' cost and production data. By sharing information among companies affiliated in the keiretsu setting a target price becomes easier.

Could an American firm do something like this with its suppliers? Perhaps, but it would mean sharing intimate and closely held information, and that is something many companies are reluctant to do even with noncompetitors.

There's something else at play here. Large Japanese firms often browbeat their suppliers to get a lower price on materials and insinuate their own ideas for cutting costs. The tactic is called *tataku*—to beat down—and the close relationship allows the larger firm to intimidate the smaller firms.

In the United States, however, you could make the point that intense competition for customers can often take the place of, and perhaps be more of an incentive, than any browbeating practices.

As for the other part of the equation: what consumers want beyond the target price. There is much more that American manufacturers could be doing that their Japanese competitors already do regularly.

Take the case of Texas Instruments and Casio. TI became the industry leader in electronic watches and pocket calculators 'by paying attention to consumer price points. However, they subsequently lost ground to Casio when the Japanese company did its competitive intelligence homework on what new features consumers wanted in their watches, i.e., waterproof electronic watches with built-in calculators.

So, as technology advances made low-price chips available to all competitors, Casio soared ahead of TI when it offered the features that consumers desired.

Do the Japanese Really Need This Much Information?

By now you have a good idea of the massive efforts at information collection put forth by Japanese businesses and the government. It's a team effort, everyone's involved, and it's ongoing. Clearly, this strategy works but you might ask: Do they really need this much information? Could they get by with less?

The answer may astound you. Yes, they do need all this information, because they're not good at handling it.

Come again?

Although Japanese are experts at gathering intelligence, they fall short in the area of analysis. Therefore, they need to gather much more information than if their analytical skills were state-of-the-art.

In fact, this lack of analytical skills has not only forced Japanese businesses to collect large amounts of information but has also led them, in some instances, into industrial espionage in order to get information they deemed necessary.

Part of the reason they have fallen behind the curve in analysis is that their culture doesn't emphasize linear, left brain thinking, which is an important part of business-intelligence analysis. While the Japanese cultural bias is toward seeing patterns, it sometimes doesn't stress logical progression of facts from A, to B, to C. Although this kind of thinking has many advantages, it also has its drawbacks. (The American is often the opposite. Americans often think too logically, too "inside the box.")

Another reason is that computer software and hardware systems are behind those of Western countries and computers are being used more and more in the West for complex competitive intelligence analysis.

For example, in the United States many offices are already linked with local area networks or LANs, which allow sharing of information among personal computers. This is a direct result of decentralization and the increased use of personal computers. However, in Japan PC usage is behind that in Western nations, especially the United States. In Japan LAN usage is minimal.

In addition, the Japanese language, with its vast number of characters, does not lend itself to computer software. As a result, there is less software available in Japanese compared to other languages. That's also why so many Japanese companies use software in English. The main reason, though, for the lag is that Japanese software programmers are behind U.S. programmers in new techniques and methods.

As the world generates more and more information that must be analyzed, Japanese businesses realize that they are falling behind. They have embarked on a campaign to learn as much as they can about systems for analyzing huge amounts of data, especially by computers.

One of the latest trends is an interest in organizations like the Society of Competitive Intelligence Professionals by Japanese businesses because they perceive SCIP members in the United States and elsewhere as being on the cutting edge of analysis—which they are.

The irony is that Japanese companies are beginning to use competitive intelligence techniques to learn about competitive intelligence methods that they need.

It is probable that Japanese companies will adopt competitive intelligence techniques pioneered by U.S. firms, enhance them, and use them to their competitive advantage.

Let me summarize the tenets of competitive intelligence in Japan:

1. Information is highly valued for its intrinsic and practical worth. This is a cultural trait.
2. Information gathering is an ongoing, concentrated, in-depth process that ties into the notion of kaizen, step-by-step improvement.
3. Information is shared extensively even with competitors.
4. Although all companies have competitive intelligence divisions, the government also plays a crucial role in collecting and distributing information to companies.
5. Gathering information is everyone's job. Even management reads and studies.
6. The cost of gathering competitive intelligence is never questioned. There is no need to justify the practice.
7. The vast majority of information is from public-domain sources, mainly documents, but gathering information from personal contacts and observation plays a vital role as well.

8. Massive amounts of information are collected to ensure thoroughness but also because Japanese companies' skills in analysis are lagging.
9. There is a strong link between competitive intelligence and strategic planning. Management trusts the information that is collected and uses it in decision making.

CHAPTER TWELVE

Competitive Intelligence in Other Countries

"The countries that have been militarily defeated are the countries that now have an acute understanding of the importance of competitive intelligence. If you can't play a military role or a geopolitical role anymore, the only way to remain independent is to be economically successful."
—Jean-Marie Bonthous, President, JMB International

In order to compete against foreign competitors, on their home turf or elsewhere, you must know what drives their competitive intelligence programs.

Each company's competitive intelligence program reflects its individual culture, government involvement, and corporate idiosyncrasies.

You've already seen how the Japanese view information and intelligence and how different it is compared to the American view. So it is with other countries. Culture plays a large role in how competitive intelligence is practiced. This is true not only in how companies view intelligence, but how they use it and what aspects they see as important. Culture affects how they collect it and, indeed, what they collect.

In addition, while government plays virtually no part in U.S. competitive intelligence (except for data collection used for government activities that is then made available to everyone) this is not the case in other countries.

Before we discuss how culture, history, and behavior affect how competitive intelligence is collected and analyzed outside the United States, let's first review how it's done here. This will give you a frame of reference against which you can understand other countries.

The United States

In the United States there is a great emphasis on short-term approaches to problems. Despite lip service, not many American firms have long-term plans. Often, competitive intelligence programs reflect this short-term approach. Clearly, this attitude affects how information is collected, analyzed, and used.

There is also a tendency toward ethnocentricity, that is, that the United States is the best at everything. Our language is the best and so is our system of government. Information from other countries is often discounted or not considered as important as information obtained from U.S. sources. Sometimes it's difficult for American managers to believe that better practices can be found elsewhere.

Americans also like secrets; we like to keep them from others. We think that information becomes more valuable if fewer people have it. Companies, even those that are not competitors, are often considered enemies and little sharing takes place. Americans think of themselves as tough individuals who can get by on brains and courage.

There is a distrust of government by companies, and there is also a belief that government should keep of out business affairs. American businesses desire a limited relationship with government entities, and any relationship that exists is often adversarial.

The most important cultural aspect that affects competitive intelligence is the overwhelming reliance on logical, left-brain thinking. Americans are extremely logical, step-by-step thinkers. There is almost no belief *in business* for a holistic approach to problem solving that would include emotions and instinct.

Sweden

Stevan Dedijer, considered one of the frontiersman of competitive intelligence, summed up Swedish competitive intelligence this way: "It's a small country. Everybody knows everybody."

Indeed, about 90 percent of all new products and services coming from Sweden are produced by a handful of large companies: Volvo, Saab, Electrolux, Ericsson, ABB, Gambro, Nobel Industries, Astra, Skandia Group, SCA, Nokia, and Televerket. Most large Swedish companies do 80 percent of their business out of the country.

And yes, these companies talk to one another and exchange information for the good of the country's common economic position. This is not say that there is collusion or price fixing, but these companies are considered the driving force behind Swedish economic power and they believe it right to work together for a common goal.

Swedes have a sense that their political and economic security are always in jeopardy. It almost borders on paranoia, and one way to keep the country secure is to employ intelligence. During the Cold War, Sweden was concerned about the Soviet threat, and intelligence experts monitored the Soviets for any warning signs of aggression.

This may sound odd to the American mind, but Swedes see competitive intelligence as a humanitarian (read: nonmilitary) way to ensure national peace and tranquillity. Intelligence is a national imperative.

Intelligence is also well respected. If you look at the elite in Sweden you'll see the military, the financial community, and the intelligence community at the country's top social stratum.

Because hardly anyone outside Sweden speaks Swedish, there is a high degree of fluency in foreign languages, especially English and French. To further internationalize themselves, many Swedish companies have located their headquarters outside their country: EKI to Denmark, Scientific Processing to Germany, and SKS Specialty Bearings to the United States.

Most large Swedish companies have very advanced competitive intelligence systems although they are different in structure. Electrolux and Skandia have competitive intelligence units placed at the corporate group level while others like Ericsson and Nobel Industries place it at the business unit level. Still others, like Astra and Volvo, place it in the market and planning department.

ABB, a $40 billion Swedish company headquartered in Switzerland, is composed of more than a thousand subsidiaries and companies in 140 countries. They jettisoned the planning department and replaced it with a competitive intelligence and analysis department (Competitive Intelligence Network) that answers to the CEO and COO. Its job is to study general economics, competitive positions, customers, legal and regulatory issues, and technology. It's also responsible for training managers in intelligence, and generally to stimulate the thinking processes of those in the company.

The Swedish banking community plays a large role in competitive intelligence. In fact, during the 1970s, banks formed Upplysnigs Centralen, a competitive intelligence research company. It provided databases, including information from overseas banking branches. It also has thousands of agents all over the world available for information collection for a fee.

The Swedish government supports competitive intelligence practices, and embassies around the world regularly report on economic and political trends for use by companies. During the past few years, the emphasis has shifted from political information to economic information.

The National Swedish Board for Technical Development also acts as a conduit, feeding public information to private companies.

What's so different in Sweden than anywhere else in the world is the relationship between academia and industry. Dedijer, an OSS officer during World War II, took his military intelligence experience and developed a competitive intelligence program at the School of Economics and Management at Lund University in Stockholm. It is the only college in the world that offers master's and doctoral degrees in competitive intelligence.

Graduates of this program fan out among Swedish companies spreading the ideas of competitive intelligence that Dedijer (who has since retired and moved to Dubrovnik, in Croatia) has expounded. In fact, Dedijer may have built the world's largest personal library collection of competitive intelligence topics.

Unlike American firms, Swedish companies are not shy about reporting some of their competitive intelligence successes.

For example, the market intelligence department at Skandia Group learned that Njord Insurance was running into financial trouble. After further data collection and analysis, all Skandia offices and subsidiaries were notified not to do business with Njord.

By the time Njord's financial problems became noticeable and hit the news media, Skandia had already backed off from some of its deals and relationships, thus minimizing their exposure.

Not so lucky, or well informed, was Sparbanken Kronan, which is said to have lost about 263 million Krona (more than $1.5 billion) because it didn't know in advance about Njord's shaky financial situation.

In another instance, Glaxo, the major player among pharmaceutical companies in the areas of asthma relief products, announced that it was marketing a bronchodilator that also had an anti-inflammatory component. It was clearly a breakthrough product.

Glaxo's competitor, Swedish pharmaceutical company Astra, was concerned that this announcement would preempt their efforts in coming out with their own product, which was not as far along.

Astra researchers studied Glaxo's clinical tests and learned that the anti-inflammatory effect only worked on animals and not humans as had been thought. Using this information, Astra scientists were able to quell the industry excitement about Glaxo's so-called breakthrough product and also buy time for its own clinical trials and efforts. In addition, Astra researchers were able to use data from Glaxo's clinical trials to advance the development of its own products.

France

When the subject of competitive intelligence comes up in relation to France, there is a tendency to think in terms of industrial espionage instead.

The French government works closely with corporations to collect information and sometimes they do so illegally.

(The word "illegally" is used from an American point of view. In France, as in some other countries, almost any method used to collect information is considered moral and ethical by their standards. A good example is bribery. In some countries, bribing company officials to receive contracts is considered a standard way of doing business. It is not the American way, however.)

Competitive intelligence professionals say that France is more interested in obtaining trade secrets than collecting business information and turning it into intelligence.

When Charles DeGaulle returned to power in 1958 he directed the Service for External Documentation and Counterespionage, or SDECE, to obtain information about technology from the United States and other Western countries.

Later, between 1987 and 1989, a twenty-person branch of the Direction Générale de la Sécurité Extérieure (DGSE), France's equivalent of the American CIA, spied on companies like IBM and Texas Instruments and turned information over to their French competitors.

It's also been alleged that French government officials obtained sensitive information by bugging seats or overhearing conversations taking place on Air France jets.

The U.S. Central Intelligence Agency reports that French intelligence agents routinely travel throughout the United States looking for business information, especially in the areas of technology and science. The French embassy in Washington acts as a conduit for information flowing to French scientists and engineers. It's also been alleged that French operatives buy information from American sources.

In fact, a French company can hire government operatives to do competitive intelligence for them.

In 1993, the CIA obtained a twenty-one-page document from the Exploitation-Implementation Office of France's Department of Economics, Science and Technology that targeted dozens of U.S. defense companies. The companies and their products were rated on an interest level scale of 1 to 3.

After the CIA informed the targeted companies, several pulled out of the next scheduled Paris Air Show, including GM's Hughes Aircraft subsidiary.

What is so alarming to American businesses is that these aren't simply cases of company against company but government against company.

This attitude stems from the French belief that they must preserve, protect, and enhance their national economic security. (The country, you may remember, was invaded three times in a 150-year period.) Economic spying can be linked to serving the interests of all French people.

This idea is summed up by the former head of the French spy agency, DGSE, Pierre Marion. He put it this way in a 1991 television interview: "It would not be normal that we spy on the United States in political matters or in military matters. We are allied, but in the economic competition, in the technological competition, we are competitors. We are not allied."

From a behavioral point of view, competitive intelligence units in French companies analyze material more by recognizing patterns as opposed to their American counterparts who rely more on facts and logical analytical techniques. Analysis tends to be qualitative, humanistic, and holistic compared to American competitive intelligence practitioners.

"A typical large French company like Alcatel [the telecommunications company] with thousands of people may have only two or three people who actually have the words 'competitive intelligence' on their business card, but everyone in the company is part of the competitive intelligence infrastructure," notes Jean-Marie Bonthous of JMB International. These marketing or sales specialists are well trained in competitive intelligence and may be paid on commission for finding businesses to enter and also for learning how to defeat competitors. While they may not be thought of as competitive intelligence practitioners in an American sense—because they don't have the title—that is their main job.

Germany

German companies have a long history of competitive intelligence. In the fifteenth century, the House of Fugger bank collected information and published an intelligence newsletter for its sales force throughout Europe. Later, the pharmaceutical company Bayer Corporation systematically analyzed patents of their competitors as early as 1886, nine years after the German Patent Office was established.

However, in modern-day Germany the discipline of competitive intelligence is being accepted more slowly by industry than in other European countries because of the stigma of intelligence being equated with spying. Translation of the English word *intelligence* implies spying.

Like Japan, Germany used competitive intelligence as a way to reconstruct its economy after the country's devastation from World War II.

The United States Congress, believing that Germany should never be able to wage war again, moved the country back to prewar, pretechnology status. The Allies confiscated hundreds of thousands of patents, closed research centers, had the most brilliant scientists emigrate to the United States (especially space and rocket experts), broke down the bank cartels, and scattered the largest chemical company, Spekegigfargen.

Most important, the Allies limited the country's factory capacity and production. To make sure these limits were kept tight, the Soviet KGB posted large contingents in the corporate world to keep watch. In turn, the German authorities formed the Bundesnachrichtendienst, or BND, in 1945 as a sort of economic police to watch the Russians and make certain that factories were allowed to reach their limits as allowed by law. (Politically, the Germans wanted to keep watch on the Soviets as well.)

In 1957, production limitations were lifted and within a few years the country merged some of the conglomerates that had been torn apart. In 1968, BND, which had since grown large and powerful, was transformed into a competitive intelligence force.

This well-trained group exists today and is funded by companies through foundations. The foundations give an arm's length look to the arrangement.

Banks, which are state-run, play a large role in running German businesses and therefore play a large role in competitive intelligence collection and dissemination. Unlike the United States where shareholders control companies, German banks hold shares of corporations. In fact, three banks control 75 percent of all company proxies.

Most companies have a management board and supervisory board with the latter setting policy. The banks control these supervisory boards. These boards (and by association, the banks and the government) control the country's trade associations, which set national economic policy.

Information and intelligence flows back and forth from the BND and the banks to the companies and trade associations.

Because of these huge efforts by the banks and the BND, there are very few independent competitive intelligence professionals in Germany. When someone needs information, he will often call the bank with whom his company is associated.

In Germany, competitive intelligence reports are huge, exhaustive, and in great detail. Because the companies themselves are so rigid with strict procedures to follow, it often becomes difficult to incorporate competitive intelligence analysis that contains radical ideas or concepts into strategic plans. This also means that German companies are poor at seeing early warnings.

In addition, because of the bureaucracy, it may take a long time for information to flow within some companies and the data may become outdated by the time it reaches decision makers.

German competitive intelligence practitioners are always interested in a competitor's historical record. They often focus on how a company makes decisions and what they've done in the past. This is an important factor in their information-gathering and analysis.

Australia

Competitive intelligence in Australia is in an embryonic stage. Compared to other industrialized countries, Australian businesses lag behind.

Part of the reason for this is that the country has been slow to understand or appreciate the effects of globalization. Due to its geographic isolation and high trade barriers, it has been largely protected from global competition.

The country had also focused on serving the domestic market with Australian goods and services with little exportation except for agricultural products and minerals.

Then there is the uniquely Australian factor of "widespread comfort." Melbourne-based Vernon Prior, managing director, Pacific Rim, for Kirk Tyson International, a competitive intelligence consultancy, notes: "We have been a lucky country. With little or no competition to worry about, and without working that hard the average family could have a comfortable lifestyle."

Prior and others agree that the comfort situation is changing as the country breaks out of its economic cocoon. Trade barriers are eroding and subsequent imports from foreign companies are competing against domestic producers.

Agricultural product and mineral exports are declining, but new exports are starting to grow, including pharmaceuticals, medical and scientific instruments, and processed foods.

Like many American CEOs, Australian managers liken competitive intelligence to spying. It is considered unethical behavior. It is also thought of as too costly.

But things are changing. Prior adds: "I've had more interest in the past year then I've had in the previous four years."

The United Kingdom

The situation in England and the rest of the United Kingdom is much like that of the United States. Only a few large companies, mainly blue chips involved in international commerce, engage in competitive intelligence to any degree.

But the field is growing and we're seeing a large increase in the number of independent consultancies who are touting competitive intelligence as a way to understand trading partners and competitors within the European Union.

On the technical side, there has been strong growth in the number of databases and other electronic information sources that are used for competitive intelligence information. Because of the common language, many British firms regularly tap into data banks located in the United States.

There is increased privatization of companies in Britain. This has fueled interest in competitive intelligence as a way to take up the slack left by government. Still, in Britain as in the rest of Europe, there is not as much concern over relationships between the government and businesses as in the United States.

Because of the stock market and pension fund ownership of company shares, there is less worry on the part of banks over companies' health. So, while banks in Sweden or Germany play a large role in protecting their investments by sharing competitive intelligence with companies, you don't find that situation in the United Kingdom.

As far as analysis is concerned, competitive intelligence professionals in Britain are left-brain thinkers like their American counterparts.

It should be interesting to see what influences European Union neighbors like France will bring to British competitive intelligence practices.

The Netherlands

Acceptance of competitive intelligence has been strong because of the country's history of being an open-trading nation. Holland is very export-oriented. It's also the home of powerful multinational companies that see competitive intelligence as a tool to increase exports. Unilever, DSM, and Royal Dutch Shell all employ competitive intelligence methods.

Key companies in the Netherlands have established competitive intelligence units that report to top management. Many engage in competitive intelligence practices in their business units as well.

Switzerland

Like the Netherlands, Switzerland is also export-oriented. There has been growing interest among companies about competitive intelligence strategies.

Because Switzerland is not a member of the European Union, competitive intelligence will become more important as a method to get past any EU trading barriers.

Swiss pharmaceutical companies are big users of competitive intelligence.

Russia

With the collapse of the Soviet Union, the Soviet-Russian foreign intelligence services have changed their priorities from collecting political and military information to economic information.

The economic situation is so dismal in Russia and other former Soviet republics that there is no time or resources for building an industrial infrastructure that will be competitive in world markets.

As a result, the External Intelligence Service of Russia, (EISAR), formerly the KGB's First Chief Directorate, has gained wide support among Russian officials as the agency that will help bring prosperity and hard currency into the country by stealing business information and technology. In fact, one section of the EISR, called Service T, concentrates its efforts on high-technology intelligence.

According to Stansilav Levchenko, a former KGB intelligence officer and defector to the United States, Service T has three branches. The operational branch dispatches intelligence officers to foreign stations and also to work undercover within Russia. The analytical branch coordinates worldwide collection efforts and issues a shopping list of foreign companies and their products. The research institute sorts out the collected information and sends it to the appropriate ministries and research facilities of the Russian Academy of Sciences.

During part of his career, Levchenko was stationed in Japan and his cover was as the Tokyo bureau chief of *New Times*, a Soviet magazine. "One reason why the Soviets were very active in Japan is that they could acquire intelligence on U.S. technology through Japanese companies that were engaged in joint research with them," he testified before Congress in 1992. "The other reason is that some of the Japanese companies had extensive knowledge of U.S. companies."

EISR operations concerning competitive intelligence—really industrial espionage—might begin with a Russian entrepreneur trying to start a joint venture with a U.S. company. He gets the runaround from the Russian bureaucracy and agrees to assistance from a "government insider" if the entrepreneur will hire someone to establish contacts with foreign firms. The person will then supply the EISR with information on foreign competitors, products, and research.

The actions are very subtle and, in many cases, according to Levchenko, U.S. citizens are employed with the belief that they are helping other U.S. companies get a foothold in the burgeoning Russian market. All the time, however, information is being funneled back to the EISR in Russia.

"In some cases, Russian intelligence will establish joint ventures and separate firms exclusively employing its officers for the purpose of collecting corporate intelligence."

Levchenko notes that the U.S. authorities have difficulty detecting Russian intelligence agents because so many engineers, scientists, and researchers are leaving Russia hoping to find employment in Western countries.

The latest wrinkle from Russia is the growing market for industrial espionage by former Russian agents for third parties such as former Soviet bloc countries. These small countries, no longer bolstered by the strength of the Soviet Union, are striking out on their own and are gaining economic intelligence in the quickest way—by stealing it from Western countries.

People's Republic of China

Like Japan, to first understand the Chinese approach to competitive intelligence, you must look at the definition and implication of words. The words *qing bao* have the double meaning of information and intelligence (just like the Japanese word *jobo*). The word/concept was probably brought to China from Japan by military students around the turn of the century.

Then, the word had the connotation of spying when it described intelligence used for military, political, and competitive intelligence. However, this was changed when the director of the Chinese Academy of Sciences decided that emphasis should lean more toward that of ethical gathering of information as opposed to unethical spying.

The first government-sponsored intelligence program was begun in 1956 under the auspices of the Academy of Sciences. It was called the Institute of Scientific and Technical Information of China, ISTIC, and within several years there were offices (qing bao offices) of the institute in provinces, in municipalities scattered throughout the country, as well as in government ministries and academies. By the mid-1980s, more than sixty thousand people worked for the system.

The purpose of the institute is to gather and analyze information that helps the country with its program of central planning. The institute's interests are social, political, and economic. All decisions are made centrally in China and intelligence is a crucial factor.

In addition, Chinese leaders looked to intelligence as a way to help end the country's isolation (just like the Japanese did after the forced opening of the country by Admiral Perry), resulting mainly from the Cultural Revolution, during which China rarely looked outside its borders.

While intelligence for central planning was the prime mover behind the program, it has since expanded to help the country's scientific and technological research, commerce, and product development.

The flow of intelligence, therefore, was from the qing bao departments in the government to the factories and other businesses, which were then told to implement procedures. However, according to Qiahao Miao of the Institute of Scientific and Technical Information of Shanghai, the qing bao departments in the government may be playing a lesser role in the future as business enterprises are given more autonomy to run their day-to-day operations. Industrial policy will still be set by the government, and intelligence will still play a role in policy setting, but business entities will begin to make their own decisions and complement the government intelligence with their ·own intelligence services.

According to Qiahao, new intelligence services and awareness have been seen:

1. Foreign companies in China bringing their own intelligence systems and ideas to the country.
2. Growth of consultancies that specialize in competitive intelligence, including some newspaper-clipping services.
3. Private information brokers in industrial areas. They are also found in rural areas that are not served by government intelligence services.

These trends will continue. It is also expected that government-sponsored intelligence services will increase their interest and activities in economic intelligence areas as opposed to political and social interests. It's also clear that more enterprises will establish their own intelligence networks and programs.

Like their neighbors, Chinese competitive intelligence analysis resembles that of Japan. The emphasis is on historical perspectives and right-brain thinking.

Unlike Japan, however, the information infrastructure is undeveloped. There are relatively few publications and databases, and the kind of worldwide network that the Japanese have built does not exist.

Because of this underdevelopment, lack of resources, and the belief that they need to play catch-up, the Chinese, like the Russians, also engage in state-sponsored industrial espionage activities. Many of their targets are high-technology items that are usually bought through a web of companies authorized to buy sensitive devices from the West.

For example, China may set up a holding company in Great Britain to purchase U.S. computer parts that, because of their strategic value, are not permitted to be sold directly to China. The U.S. shipper doesn't know that the company is actually owned by Chinese authorities, as it is hidden behind several other holding companies that appear to be British-owned.

Sometimes an authorized buyer will simply buy critical technology parts and hand them over to Chinese representatives without the seller realizing where they will end up.

There are many variations on this diversionary tactic, but all of them rely on using a seemingly legitimate third party in a country authorized to receive critical technology from the West.

In the United States, China has the largest foreign presence of any country, with more than two thousand diplomats and government officials and more than forty thousand students. Each year, more than twenty-five thousand Chinese businesspeople visit the United States.

Many of these people are engaged in open, legal information collection, driven by the intelligence needs of their country, which is struggling to become an economic power.

According to FBI officials, however, about 150 companies in the United States are owned by China, many for the purposes of importing and exporting goods between the two countries. Along with this task, the companies are used to move business and economic information from the United States to China.

FBI officials also say it is common for Chinese authorities to ingratiate themselves with Chinese nationals working in the United States, especially those scientists and researchers in high-technology areas. They may be offered free trips home to visit family and friends, but in exchange for that gift they are expected to meet with government scientists in China and chat about their work in the States. The United States-based scientists feel obligated to spend time with the Chinese scientists, as the government has paid for their airfare home several times, which is very expensive.

CHAPTER THIRTEEN

Building a Competitive Intelligence System

"The journey of a thousand miles begins with a single step."
—Chinese proverb

Establishing a competitive intelligence system in your company does not take a lot of money, resources, or material. More than anything else it requires a change in your attitude toward information and intelligence. Bits and pieces probably already exist. It may simply be a matter of pulling it all together.

Step one: Select a director of competitive intelligence and put him or her in the right location.

One of the beautiful features of competitive intelligence systems is that they are simple and fit into your current organizational structure. In the old days, when companies were more hierarchial than they are now—to a large extent they were centralized—competitive intelligence flowed to the top and stayed there. Now, with decentralization, competitive intelligence can flow freely and still fulfill its obligation to inform top management.

A competitive intelligence program requires a focal point—the *competitive intelligence unit*. At the head is the *competitive intelligence director*. This is the person who coordinates the information and intelligence flows around the company. Even in cases where there is a separate competitive intelligence unit for each business line, there should be one competitive intelligence director who facilitates the flow.

As I've already mentioned many times, this competitive intelligence unit must be responsible to top management. It must get its operating mandate from top management. Without that support it will perish.

Very often, middle managers try to get a competitive intelligence unit going without support from the top. They hope they will show their worth, get noticed, and then have the unit move up. Sorry, it doesn't happen.

What kind of person makes a good director of intelligence?

In the days when omnipotent kings and queens ruled the world there was a guy on staff called the court jester. Our view of this person has him wearing a multicolored costume, bells jingling, and hat flopping. He danced around the king, sometimes mocking him, sometimes amusing him with jokes. When someone would try to persuade the king to do something, the jester would listen quietly but sometimes he would jump around and poke fun at the person's ideas.

He was the one person in the entire kingdom who could talk back to the king. He had reverence for the king's position but his job was not to be a yes man. In doing his job, he was guaranteed immunity from the king's wrath. Unlike the king's trusted advisors, his head didn't get chopped off when he told the king something His Highness didn't want to hear.

Don't ever forget, though, that the jester was smart. He walked around town and in the country listening to people, learning and understanding what the common people were thinking. He had his own information network. The jester also knew what made the king happy, what made him tick, and what he wanted.

The king knew that in some areas the jester was smarter than he. The king trusted his judgment and even though he didn't always do what he said, he listened and took his counsel to heart the vast majority of the time.

The director of competitive intelligence is somewhat like a court jester. *The director's job is to tell top management the truth even if it goes against the CEO's personal or business beliefs.* I'm not suggesting that he do this based on hunches or guesses, but it is his job to help the CEO break out of his mental models using hard information and strict analysis to back his claims.

Ben Gilad, in his book *Business Blindspots,* calls this kind of person a *china breaker.* It's an apt description, as the china breaker is not afraid to shatter sacred beliefs and models long held by companies if doing so is going to help them succeed.

Some companies like Motorola have chosen former government intelligence analysts to be in charge of their competitive intelligence units.

This made sense in that there was no other large pool from which to choose people who knew about intelligence other than those in government service. The idea was that it was easier to teach someone from the military or political intelligence world about business than teach someone from the business world about intelligence.

In fact, that was true until recently. No one offered courses in analysis except the government. Indeed, no entity collected data in a sustained and controlled manner like government.

Bringing ex-intelligence-service people into the business world has raised many eyebrows among competitive intelligence professionals. It's a bone of contention in the small community. Some believe that former government agents bring an ethic of "anything goes" to their work, while former government analysts sometimes believe that "civilian" intelligence people don't understand the toughness of the real world.

With the ending of the Cold War many government agents are seeking employment in the private sector doing the one thing they know best: intelligence gathering and analysis. So, we're likely to see more former spies working in the competitive intelligence world.

On the other hand, we're beginning to see an interest, albeit small, in colleges and universities to teach competitive intelligence courses and programs. This is still in a nascent stage in the United States, and I'll discuss it later.

Then Kodak CEO Colby Chandler took a different approach when choosing to build an intelligence organization. Believing that Kodak's efforts should be directed at producing intelligence that was focused on market research—and lots of it— he hired someone who had a lot of experience understanding and analyzing large amounts of data, who was familiar with huge data collection and analysis programs. Chandler decided to hire Vince Barabba, who had been director of the U.S. Census Bureau during the 1970 and 1980 census. What better person to handle large amounts of data?

So who is the best person to choose for your company? It's the person who would make the best court jester. Where should the court jester be located on the chart? Next to the king's ear.

The king in this case is the chairman, chief executive officer, division president, operational manager, or whoever else is responsible for making the company's strategic decisions.

Step two: The director should determine who the key intelligence users are and what they will use the intelligence for.

This involves using the procedures detailed in Chapter 5 on planning and direction.

The key intelligence users are the company's decision makers. They can be in the corporate office or they can be in the business units themselves—or both—depending upon your company's structure.

Step three: Perform an intelligence audit of your company.

Jim Seid, a systems analyst for Chevron's technology group, told *Fortune* magazine about trying to collect information in his own company. He interviewed more than a hundred Chevron employees in marketing, distribution, and production to find out where inventory data was held and in what format (computer, files, and so on). "We found that about 85 percent of what we needed was stored somewhere electronically," Seid said. "But this was scattered throughout a number of different databases across different computers all over the continent."

This is a very common condition. Most competitive intelligence professionals estimate that the majority of the data that a company wants to obtain is already in the company. In a computer database, in someone's filing cabinet, in a library, or hidden in a desk drawer.

Workers have been collecting information for years to help them do their job. They don't always share it with others nor do they care how they store it as long as they can access it for their own use.

The job of the director of competitive intelligence is to find this information, unleash it, and share it with those who need it.

Sometimes, all you have to do is ask.

Bonnie Hohhof is director of Intelligent Information, a Glen Ellyn, Illinois, consulting firm. When helping a certain company establish a competitive intelligence system, she built a database of experts within the firm. It included information about their expertise, language skills, background, what projects they had worked on, and also some personal data.

The information was collected by using the company's current e-mail network.

Hohhof discovered that a woman in the purchasing department spoke a certain Chinese dialect and this dovetailed with the company's need for a translator to help negotiate a deal with a Chinese company. The company had a trusted employee, someone who knew the business, and a translator all in one person.

Getting people to give up information isn't easy. Even in this example, many people didn't respond to requests for information about themselves and had to be prodded.

Never overlook the human intelligence angle in the intelligence audit. Learn who knows what in the company.

Part of the director of competitive intelligence's job is to educate those in the company about the importance of competitive intelligence. Raising awareness about competitive intelligence is essential—but it must be backed by the CEO's own message.

A lot depends upon the company's culture. In many companies, unfortunately, people are not encouraged to share their ideas, thoughts, and information with those outside their departments for fear of hurting their own area. That's because departments and divisions often fight other units for resources doled out by top management. The thought is, "Why give another division an advantage over mine?" Indeed, sometimes this competitiveness among divisions is encouraged as a way to increase productivity. When this attitude is prevalent in a company, it's virtually impossible to encourage people to share information.

In other companies, people are not encouraged to share information because they've never been told that the information they have is important, that what they know can help the company as a whole.

Overcoming this resistance isn't easy and education by the director of competitive intelligence is only part of the story. All employees must know that the CEO fully endorses the idea of sharing information among company employees and with the director of competitive intelligence. The CEO must make it known throughout the company that sharing information will help employees move up in their careers, that it helps the company, that he and other top managers are committed to competitive intelligence, and that people's contributions really make a difference.

It's the director of competitive intelligence's job to make sure that management's message is delivered and reinforced.

If it isn't working, he'll know soon enough when he looks at the e-mail contributions and there are only a handful out of a company of thousands of employees.

Company spirit can take you just so far. Workers who contribute must see a direct benefit from the competitive intelligence program.

Another part of the director's job is to reward people for their contributions. Some companies give out awards to those who submit the most useful information. Others give awards to those who use intelligence in the most successful way. The tack the director should take depends upon the company's culture. What rewards have worked in the past and what motivates people? In many companies a letter from the CEO will go a long way to encourage contributions. Some companies use awards or mentions in the company magazine or newsletter. In other companies, cash bonuses work best.

Ultimately, the critical reward for workers is that they receive information that will help them do their jobs better and more efficiently. Once an employee sees that contributing pays off not only for his fellow workers or the company in general but becomes relevant to his own situation, then he will continue to contribute information to the competitive intelligence unit.

Some directors have instituted a policy where you don't receive information unless you contribute information. In one company, everyone who contributes information receives a monthly newsletter containing information bits from around the company and in the industry. Those who don't contribute, don't receive it. This is negative reinforcement and may work in the short term. However, modern psychology tell us that rewards work better than punishment.

Everyone in the company should learn firsthand the power of competitive intelligence even if they don't contribute to the melting pot of information. Eventually, the message will get through. If they don't contribute but only take information and use it, the system has worked at least partly.

The director's job is to follow up on those who don't contribute, and to find out what can be done to help them share their information with others.

We're at a point in our culture where everyone believes that "knowledge is power," and it's never been easy to get people to give up power.

Part of the director's duties includes keeping enthusiasm strong for the program. He must be a cheerleader and ensure that the program receives adequate funding from top management along with a multiyear commitment. It takes about three years for competitive intelligence programs to be accepted companywide. It takes that long, according to a Stanford Research Institute study, to overcome institutional inertia, break down information barriers, and generally educate people about competitive intelligence efforts.

Without the proper funding and commitment, a competitive intelligence program will wither into a high-priced staff function.

Competitive intelligence is a funny thing. Even when people know that it works, it's still one of the first programs to get lopped off when times get bad. Why? Partly because it's new and many people don't understand it enough to defend it. In addition, the contribution it makes to the bottom line is often indirect and that makes it difficult to defend as well.

Step four: Design a network to move information and intelligence around the company using what is already in place.

Most companies already have what they need in the way of an information infrastructure to accommodate a competitive intelligence system. For example, most companies already have a library, e-mail system, personal computers, and a local area network.

The important aspect is to develop a system that will be accepted by the company culture and top management. By changing some of the processes, like how information currently moves around the company, it's possible to turn an existing information network into a competitive intelligence network with few additional resources.

For example, some companies use their existing voice-mail system as a way for salespeople to feed bits of information to the competitive intelligence unit. The startup cost of such a system is zero—it's already installed—and the rewards are enormous. It's especially useful because it's not something that people have to learn to use.

Step five: Establish companywide ethical and legal guidelines for competitive intelligence.

One of the main reasons why top management is afraid of implementing competitive intelligence programs is that it is still thought of as spying. Despite efforts by SCIP and others, the stigma still exists in the minds of managers and others.

To alleviate these concerns, it's vital that the director of competitive intelligence work with management to establish guidelines, especially as regards collection. Collection methods and techniques are areas in which people can too easily stray from the straight and narrow.

Company Profiles

It's pretty clear by now how successful companies use competitive intelligence. I would like to break out a few particular companies, some already mentioned and some new, and highlight special features of their competitive intelligence efforts.

These profiles are not meant to be comprehensive. Instead, these sketches show the unique *personalized* nature of each company's competitive intelligence program.

The common thread among these companies is that competitive intelligence has been shaped to fit their corporate culture and their specific requirements. You will also notice that competitive intelligence was born from a drastic transformation in their environment—new competitors, more aggressive competition, political/regulatory upheavals, changes in strategy—which prompted them to look at competitive intelligence as a way to get back in the game.

▶ The Society of Competitive Intelligence Professionals

From a handful of people in 1986, the Society of Competitive Intelligence Professionals has grown to five thousand members, having doubled its membership in the last five years alone. This rapid growth reflects the increased awareness of competitive intelligence among companies. SCIP has gone through many changes, including expansion overseas and the establishment of regional U.S. chapters.

SCIP's members give us a snapshot of what's going on in competitive intelligence units in America companies.

According to the group's surveys, SCIP members' roles within their organizations are associated with CEOs, R&D, Sales and Marketing (43 percent); market research (23 percent); and planning (21 percent). The rest are from other areas.

Sixty percent of competitive intelligence units are less than three years old; 80 percent are less than five years old. Staff size is one to ten at the corporate level, one to five within each division. Budgets are up to $2 million. Seventy-two percent of people have been in the profession five years or less.

Before we discuss some large companies, let me relate to you the story of a small manufacturer and what they accomplished in their competitive intelligence efforts. Management asked that their real name not be published. We'll just call them . . .

THE CHASSIS COMPANY

Like the Chassis Company, its competitor the Target Company produces metal chassis boxes for use in high electronics gear such as oscilloscopes and meters. Their main market is defense contractors, who use the chassis in aircraft, ships, and at fixed military locations.

With the defense market shrinking, the Chassis Company felt that it needed to be more aggressive in its competitive intelligence program. The CEO mandated and established a competitive intelligence unit.

Here's what they did:

Step 1: Learned what information they had in the company already.

Most companies have a great deal of information inside their own firm about competitors. They don't even know what they have because it's scattered or unclassified. The company had been gathering some newspaper stories and annual reports on the target but hadn't collated it in any organized manner.

An effort was launched to seek out information already collected and then place copies in one department. Information was placed in files and was later transferred to a computer.

Step 2: Because they were not answering a specific intelligence question but building a system, they decided to make a list of all the things they wanted to know in a broad range of topics.

The list had such items such as: number of employees, major customers, sales, market share, financial information, advertising, facilities, costs, organization, R&D expenditures, and strategic plans. They knew they wouldn't get everything they wanted but it didn't matter.

Step 3: A wide net was cast on several databases using the company's name, products, the phrases *metal chassis, electronic chassis,* and similar terms. Many stories were retrieved and they were read and placed into files under the appropriate heading. In most cases, one story was photocopied and placed in several different files.

In addition, information concerning topics of great importance such as contracts, customers, sales, and pricing were copied onto separate sheets and placed into files. Several ads were found in trade magazines as well as a story written by one of the company's engineers.

Step 4: Federal, state, and local government records were gathered. These included building permits, zoning variances, filings with the EPA, Equal Opportunity Commission (EEOC), and the Occupational Health and Safety Administration (OSHA). Because the target is a private company there were no SEC filings but there were incorporation papers filed with the secretary of the state. Researchers found a court case in which an employee sued the company for allegedly having unsafe work areas. Both parties settled out of court but the initial complaint was on record and it contained information about company and employee practices and went into detail about a process that used a chemical bath.

Step 5: Areas that were particularly lacking—in this case there was very little information about strategic plans and pricing strategies—were put on a new list of things to get. An ongoing program was established to pick up these items in a leisurely manner. Also, databases were to be scanned every week for new stories and information. Some different key words and phrases were also going to be tried.

Although the CEO didn't have a specific question to answer, he now feels as though he has a basic understanding of the Target Company. When management wants to know something specifically, the competitive intelligence unit has the confidence that they either have the information or know where to look for it quickly and efficiently.

MOTOROLA

Bob Galvin, the former chairman of Motorola, had served on the President's Foreign Intelligence Advisory Board in the mid-1970s. There, he learned the importance of intelligence services in making strategic decisions.

This experience gave him the vision to see that companies needed competitive intelligence as much as the government. Business leaders needed intelligence to make the proper decisions in a global economy. He also believed that a good strategy could be no better than the information on which it was based.

In the late 1970s, Motorola had tried to establish a competitive intelligence division but it failed. It was considered part of the marketing division and nobody contributed to the effort who wasn't in marketing.

The company tried again in the early 1980s and again it failed. This time it was because Galvin had hired a former government official but he was stationed in Washington, D.C., and the company's headquarters were in Schaumburg, Illinois. He was too far away to be effective.

Finally, in 1983, Galvin tried again. This time he hired Jan Herring, who was an intelligence officer with the CIA. For the last ten years of his career he was more involved with competitive intelligence than national intelligence and it seemed like a good fit. The first time Galvin asked Herring to join the company, he refused. He wasn't ready to move to the private sector. The second time he agreed to join the company and move to Schaumburg.

Galvin's directives were clear: the operation must be legal and ethical; it must serve both corporate and operational managers equally.

Herring set out to learn what internal intelligence networks existed already. This is textbook procedure for intelligence operations. Find out what information is already in the company and how it's shared.

Herring discovered that there were indeed information intelligence networks at Motorola but nobody had linked them together to serve the needs of senior management.

He also learned that while collections were pretty good, there was little in the way of analysis to put together disparate bits of information and turn them into usable conclusions.

He called the group the Corporate Analytical Research Department and fought for the next two years with Galvin about the name. Galvin wanted to use the word *intelligence* while Herring thought that it would sound too much like spying.

Herring remembers: "Bobby Inman [former head of the National Security Agency] and I were talking and he said, 'Jan, don't call it intelligence in the private sector. The public loves spy novels and movies but once you put it in the business community, it becomes industrial espionage.' "

The group, which was under the strategy office, remained the Corporate Analytical Research Department until Herring finally relented. He gave a briefing to the American Marketing Association in Chicago about what Motorola was doing in this then unheard of and seemingly clandestine discipline and he used the term intelligence for the first time. "I gave the speech to get across the idea that what we were doing was legal, ethical, and necessary in the competitive world we're in," says Herring. "Now when I start up 'little Motorolas,' I tell them to call it 'intelligence.' You have to call it what it really is."

At Motorola, the intelligence department was organized into three functions: collection and reporting, information services, and analysis. Each unit had an operational and an intelligence production capability.

Herring learned many valuable lessons establishing the department. For one thing, he discovered that employee education was key to the group's survival. In a moment of fancy, the group's phone extension was 007, but very few people called it with any information. So, Herring sent his collection manager among all the people at Motorola to educate them about the importance of intelligence. "We increased contributions from 2 percent to 20 percent," Herring says. At Motorola, everyone—no matter what their position—is encouraged to contribute information.

By early 1987, the competitive intelligence system had been developed to the point where it was making meaningful contributions to management both strategically and operationally.

In August 1986, another former CIA operative, Tim Stone, joined Herring's group, and he took Herring's position about a year later when Herring left the company. Herring felt he had accomplished his goal, which was to get the intelligence department up and running.

Motorola's failures and successes at developing a competitive intelligence program offer many lessons for others. The program's success can be attributed to these key factors.

- It needs to be CEO-driven. Without long-term interest from top management, competitive intelligence systems ultimately fail.
- The company's existing current intelligence networks, which may be informal, must be scanned. What's already in place must be audited to see if it can be enhanced and built upon.
- All people in the company should be considered sources and everyone needs to be encouraged to contribute and use the services.
- Competitive intelligence divisions should be located at the highest levels of the company.
- Legal and ethical guidelines must be established early in the program's development.

NUTRASWEET

Bob Shapiro, who was chairman of NutraSweet and now is president of parent company Monsanto, began a competitive intelligence program more than nine years ago. His main question was this: "Which companies want to get into the sweetener business?"

According to Faye Brill, then director, Strategic Business Information, the focus of the group was handling requests from top management. "One of our jobs was to limit the number of surprises coming their way."

In the late 1980s, NutraSweet had many potential competitors who knew a great deal about the company. Overseas competitors had done their homework. The firm had high brand awareness worldwide, and it was no secret who they were and who their customers were. All you had to do was look for the logo swirl on the products.

Robert Flynn took over as chairman and CEO from Shapiro and continued the competitive intelligence unit even though he had no experience with the discipline at his former company.

He understood, however, that competitive intelligence was more important now than ever.

In December 1992, the aspartame patent was about to expire. "We might as well have had a bull's-eye painted on our chest," says Flynn. "We figured every chemical company in the world was going to go into the aspartame business. We needed to know who our competitors would be, who would have the money, the skills, the marketing ability, the technology to be a competitor. And, among the likely competitors, what would their costs be, what would be their expected rate of return, and how long would they be willing to put money into their operation without taking money out?"

The company also had the opportunity to expand aspartame outside the diet market. Because aspartame is ounce for ounce sweeter than sugar it is an economic alternative to sugar and high-fructose corn syrup in some countries for certain applications.

However, building manufacturing facilities, especially overseas, is a high-capital-risk venture, about $150 to $300 million per plant.

This high-risk stance was coupled with the company's post-patent objective of establishing a strong competitive position by driving down costs and providing excellent customer service. They wanted to stay the favored supplier to customers around the world and this led Flynn to utilize competitive intelligence practices to their fullest.

"Our intelligence-gathering capability is a major contributor to our competitive advantage in marketing, manufacturing, and looking at the organizational structure and financial backing of our competitors.

"We've challenged our manufacturing people based on findings from competitive intelligence to reduce manufacturing costs by 60 percent by 1996. That figure was from our competitive intelligence assessments as to what we would have to do to compete around the world.

"We use competitive intelligence to look at organizational structures of companies that want to take market share from us. We look at leadership issues. Who their managers are.

"In the financial area we want to know who has the money to compete against us, who has the staying power."

According to Flynn, he demands four things from his company's competitive intelligence efforts: up-to-the-minute information that is easily translated into action; an insurance policy against being blindsided by competitors and the business climate; a source of unfiltered, unbiased information; and the highest legal and ethical standards.

"Competitive intelligence keeps us from acting in a vacuum. It keeps us from sealing ourselves off from the real value of our business interests in the marketplace and the real threats to our success."

The competitive intelligence unit reports directly to Flynn.

AT&T

Before 1984, much of AT&T's business was regulated. Because of that, the company developed technology, like cellular telephones, and was bound to let others exploit it. However, once Ma Bell was divested of its regulated monopolies, the local Bell Telephone Companies, this collegial approach to business ended.

"The idea of intelligence gathering was new to us," notes Burke Stinson, a twenty-five-year company veteran. "But by 1984, we had to play closer attention to our rivals in the long-distance industry."

In the mid- to late 1980s, AT&T began organizing along business units, each responsible for its own profitability. As a result competitive analysis units were established within each and every business unit. "These units know best their own needs and what questions they want answered," says Stinson.

There are thirty different units but most competitive intelligence activity takes place in the following units because they are in the most competitive businesses:

- Multimedia products, which has about 65,000 people and makes everything from telephones to chips. Individual units include AT&T Consumer Products, AT&T Global Business Communications Systems, and AT&T Paradyne, a modem maker.
- Communications Services, with 93,000 people, includes Consumer Communications Services, Universal Credit Card Services, and Transtech, the network services division that runs the company's global network.
- Network Systems, with 64,000 workers, which sells huge telephone network switching machines in the United States and abroad.

In order to remain competitive, AT&T realized in the early 1990s that it had to build alliances in its weakest areas. That shifted the short-term emphasis of competitive intelligence from competitors to finding acquisitions. One example was the giant deal between the company and McCaw Cellular Communications, which gave AT&T a strong footing in the cellular phone business.

Besides the competitive analysis units in each business line, there is a competitive analysis group at the corporate level assigned to the Strategy and Development Office. This group responds to specific requests from top management as well as looking at big-picture societal and business trends.

One of AT&T's greatest competitive intelligence strengths is Access to AT&T Analysts, a computer network and database that allows any employee to search for expertise anywhere in the company. The network is also used to disseminate industry news briefs on a daily basis.

MARION MERRELL DOW

Marion Merrell Dow has a unique structure to its competitive intelligence program. The pharmaceutical company has two highly formalized competitive intelligence units: *business competitive intelligence,* which began in 1982 and *scientific competitive intelligence,* which started in 1990.

Company officials understood the need for competitive intelligence fairly early (1982) compared to most other companies, but then realized that additional emphasis needed to be placed on the scientific aspect. Pharmaceutical firms are not only competing on traditional business levels but on the technical and scientific level as well, and that was becoming increasingly apparent to top management.

There is no centralized competitive intelligence unit, but the business and scientific sides communicate and share information by an e-mail network.

According to Pat Bryant, manager, Global Scientific Competitive Intelligence, the five-person group not only handles specific requests for intelligence but offers other services. "We have a list of key contact people for each product and we let them know anything important that we learn about a competitor," he says.

Bryant understands that competitive intelligence professionals can be put in a tough situation because they often are the messenger who brings bad news. "We have spent a lot of time building rapport so we don't get blamed for bad news," he says. "We work at maintaining these relationships."

One reason for his group's success is that even though they are scientists, they keep their eyes focused on the bottom line. "We are in a profit-making business and everyone in the group appreciates and understands that fact," Bryant says.

CORNING

Corning competes through superior technology. In the mid-1980s, the company realized that relying on technology alone wasn't enough to remain on top in the global marketplace. They needed a concerted effort at worldwide competitive intelligence.

The company has more than sixty thousand products. Of their one hundred major products more than half are competitive outside the United States.

The impetus for increased intelligence awareness came from James Riesbeck, former executive vice president, who was particularly attuned to the company's need for tracking competitors as well as those who would acquire information illegally. Riesbeck testified before Congress about the effect of industrial espionage on his company. He cited one incident in France in which two moles who had stolen company secrets were uncovered.

As an unwritten policy, the company doesn't use the word *intelligence,* believing that it has negative connotations for corporate America. Indeed, their experiences with industrial espionage may be responsible for this attitude. They prefer to use phrases like "market research" to describe their activities.

Nonetheless, Corning has one of the most advanced competitive intelligence programs around. They excel in two areas: First, they have a centralized database *with* local control. Each piece of information on the Business Information Exchange Network remains the property of the person who contributed it although anyone has access to it. The owner can do what he wants with it, including transferring ownership to someone else if he doesn't need it anymore. If he changes jobs, for example.

Information is flagged, which lets the owner know who is interested in the information and how often it has been accessed. This leads to more focused collection and dissemination.

The second area in which Corning does superior work is in tracking competitors who don't seem to be competitors. Corning's core business is glassmaking, and it would make sense that they follow the activities of other glassmakers. However, they also track chemical companies who are trying to make glass-like materials that might turn out competitive products. Corning has a large investment in glassmaking furnaces, which are expensive to build and maintain. Chemical companies for years have been attempting to produce glass without furnaces and undercut Corning's investment. Corning must know everything they can about these potential competitors before they become a real threat.

PROCTER & GAMBLE

Procter & Gamble's Competitive Analysis unit was formally started about ten years ago. Before that, competitive intelligence was handled on an informal basis as part of the finance unit.

What triggered the systematic effort to a more formal system was a change in the company's strategy to *category management* in which the company's highly visible consumer products were managed on a category-by-category basis. "We needed to know much more about our competitors," says Susan Steinhardt, associate director for business information. "We were up against competitors in multiple categories and in multiple geographies."

At P&G, competitive intelligence efforts are fairly centralized, and Steinhardt still reports to the financial organization even though much of her task involves strategic and not financial analysis.

In some areas, though, competitive intelligence is still done on an ad hoc basis. "There are few formal products being produced on a regular basis," says Steinhardt, "but we're working toward that direction." She notes that some inconsistencies exist in collection and analysis because of the current informal nature. "Communication is not as good as we would like, and we're in the process of trying to change that."

Some top managers are avid supporters and users of competitive intelligence and their organizations' success reflect their use of competitive intelligence. According to Steinhardt, "There is not as much support from very senior management as I would like—not that there haven't been requests —but they're not on a systemized basis. Sometimes requests don't get channeled to the competitive analysis people and therefore their expertise doesn't get fully exploited."

Why It Doesn't Work: A Summary

Competitive intelligence programs don't always work. Motorola, for example, had several stumbles before success, and even companies like Procter & Gamble admit they have a way to go before the program is where they would like it to be.

Why do efforts at competitive intelligence fail? Here are the most common problems:

Top management wasn't involved.

This is the single biggest reason cited why competitive intelligence programs fail.

Support for competitive intelligence programs must come from the top, and there must be a multiyear commitment of resources. It takes time for a competitive intelligence program to be developed. A one-shot, have-it-done-by-next-quarter approach does not work.

Moreover, the competitive intelligence unit must be placed in the top ranks of the company. It can't be just another staff function.

Tasks are not focused or issue-oriented.

A scattershot, be-all-things-to-all-people approach spells doom. Competitive intelligence programs must be targeted to answer specific questions or find out about specific areas of interest. Never forget, competitive intelligence is about making better decisions.

Any investigation must be for a purpose. That purpose is usually in support of strategic or tactical planning.

The CEO of a medium-sized service company asked his newly formed competitive intelligence unit, consisting of one former marketing person, to learn everything he could about competitors.

The program failed.

The request was too broad. The CEO ended up learning a little bit about each competitor instead of precise intelligence he could use to his advantage. As a result, the company's efforts were largely wasted.

The problem, in hindsight, was clear. The competitive intelligence practitioner wasn't given a specific task. He didn't target his queries and he failed to pin the CEO down about his specific needs. The CEO was indeed interested in several items, specifically, new competitors and new services, but he didn't relay his wishes to the competitive intelligence person.

Competitive intelligence efforts must be focused. They must be specific.

Put another way, the competitive intelligence unit must be customer-driven. The customer, in this case, was top management. Competitive intelligence tasks should be initiated by decision makers so they can make better decisions, but they must be sharply focused.

Too much emphasis on collection.

Many competitive intelligence professionals fall into the trap of emphasizing the collection aspect because it is often the most doable part of the triad. In fact, there are volumes and volumes of books about how to go about finding certain pieces of information. Gathering techniques often take creativity but sometimes it's just a matter of keeping at it long enough or searching in enough places or even getting lucky. If you're looking for a specific piece of information, you can usually find it given enough time and effort. That's a very satisfying feeling, and many people stop there.

This phenomenon is sometimes called *becoming a library*. That is, simply collecting and warehousing data without adding any value to it.

The second step in the process, analysis, is tougher, and the third step, getting decision makers to use the intelligence, can be tougher still.

Not involving everyone in the company.

While only decision makers should call the shots on what sort of intelligence is required, information gathering should be on everyone's mind.

It's not easy getting people to understand the importance of information, especially if they don't feel that they are benefiting directly from it. Everyone in a company has a vital role to play in competitive intelligence.

A salesperson returning from visiting a critical customer should be debriefed for tidbits of information. Employees who learn something about a competitor through a friend should be encouraged to pass it along to the competitive intelligence unit. Developing sources of human intelligence is crucial.

Not establishing ethical guidelines.

Many people already think that competitive intelligence is the same as spying. After educating them to the contrary, don't let an unethical incident ruin the program.

A good example of this was when a computer service company in an office park came into possession of confidential documents from a competitor. The two companies were preparing to bid against each other in an upcoming contract. The sender dialed the wrong number and reached a fax machine inside the computer service company. The information contained in these papers would have given the company a competitive advantage in the bidding process.

The fax was given to the competitive intelligence unit.

The competitive intelligence person notified his CEO of the nature of the papers but not their specific content. A decision was made to notify the sender of the mistake. Officials of the company to whom the bid was to be offered were also told of the incident.

"I don't think the other bidder believed that our bidding people didn't see their information, but it was true nonetheless," says the competitive intelligence director. "In the end, neither we nor the other company got the job but it helped solidify the competitive intelligence unit's ethical standing with our own people. Looking back, it was definitely the right way to go."

Education—A Missing Link

One of the reasons why competitive intelligence courses haven't caught on at U.S. colleges and universities is because so few companies have full-blown competitive intelligence programs.

One of the reasons why few companies have full-blown competitive intelligence programs is that colleges and universities don't teach it.

Okay, which came first?

Instead of being on the cutting edge of business thoughts and ideas—like competitive intelligence— many business schools reflect traditional, rather old, and often outdated approaches to business.

Harvard Business School is a good example of a facility once on the forefront of new ideas that has fallen in with old-fashioned and comfortable American business ideas.

Instead of introducing new ideas to graduates who then spread out among American industry with bright, innovative ways of doing business, Harvard and other business schools are churning out the same old MBAs steeped in the same old ways of running businesses.

A recent example of this is the subject of entrepreneurship. After years of student demands, business schools are now, finally, teaching about entrepreneurship—how to start a business, secure financing, create new products, and guide the company from start-up to maturation. Business schools and faculty didn't want to touch the topic; they thought it was unacademic and beneath them. Now in response to their customers, the students, entrepreneurship is being taught at Wharton, Babson, USC, and UCLA.

In the schools' defense, CEOs and other people in power at American businesses aren't demanding that colleges teach competitive intelligence courses because they themselves don't know enough about the subject.

Only now are middle managers experiencing competitive intelligence in real life. When they reach management level, colleges will respond to what they see as interest from these enlightened top managers.

So many new ideas in business come from academia that it behooves colleges to start teaching competitive intelligence as part of management curriculum. In other countries, at Sweden's Lund University, for example, students are offered extensive curricula in competitive intelligence. They just graduated their first Ph.D.s in competitive intelligence. In countries like France and Japan, intelligence officers teach college courses in the subject. In the United States only a handful of schools teach any individual classes and none have a degree program aimed at competitive intelligence.

Ideally, competitive intelligence should be taught at all levels in conjunction with companies that use competitive intelligence. The companies would benefit from interaction with the schools and students would benefit from learning about real-life situations. In the long term, of course, companies would benefit from having a pool of available intelligence analysts.

Unfortunately, case studies are very difficult to come by because companies feel the need to keep their competitive intelligence initiatives confidential. To overcome this shortage, students can act as researchers to companies in their competitive intelligence units and learn the discipline firsthand. These kinds of work-study programs are very common in other disciplines.

Despite these obstacles, some schools are taking on the task of bringing competitive intelligence to the academic community, albeit slowly.

Mercyhurst is a college in Erie, Pennsylvania, that offers a four-year program designed for training intelligence analysts. The two-year-old program was started by Robert Heibel, a retired FBI agent who worked as a deputy chief of counterterrorism during the mid-1980s when the bureau was starting to bring analysts on board. "We tried to hire analysts but couldn't find what we wanted so we started to train our own," Heibel says of the FBI.

The goal of the Research/Intelligence Analyst program is to train students who can work as intelligence analysts mainly for government agencies such as the Secret Service, the FBI, and the CIA. Although the program doesn't offer any business courses in conjunction with the program, the course of study will give the graduate the ability to work as an analyst in the private sector. The program requires that students, who receive a BA in history with a special concentration in Research/Intelligence Analysis, work as an intern or in a cooperative program with an agency or company.

At the graduate level, Walter Barndt, at the Hartford Graduate Center School of Management, has been teaching a course titled Competitive Intelligence and the Intelligent Manager since 1983.

"I had been teaching marketing and related courses, then realized that there was nothing around about gathering information on the competition to make market decisions," Barndt says. He notes that the domain of competitive intelligence has not yet been widely established in many companies so it's difficult to know what to teach or what needs to be learned in a course to make training relevant to the private sector.

To that end, Barndt invites many competitive intelligence leaders from industry as guest lecturers to help his students understand how the discipline is practiced at companies.

He also has individual and team assignments that simulate projects like those practiced by competitive intelligence professionals inside companies. One time, the class was organized into two teams, the Blue Team representing the competitive intelligence unit of Southern New England Telephone, and the Gold Team representing the competitive intelligence unit of the *Hartford Courant* newspaper.

The assignment was to prepare a report for senior management outlining the threats posed by your competitor as well as opportunities for joint ventures. Each team was briefed by a company representative. The final results were presented to the senior officials of each company.

Another assignment asked students to select a company and prepare a report on what major moves the company was likely to make and how they would affect its industry. Because many of the students are getting their graduate degrees while they're working for companies, they are encouraged to use a company that is competitor of their own. One of the project goals is to learn if someone in your company is already tracking this competitor either formally or on an informal basis.

Although he doesn't teach it anymore, Liam Fahey taught a competitive intelligence course at Boston University as part of the School of Management's MBA program. The course emphasized four points:

1. Understanding why you were doing it.
2. Kinds of analysis that can be done.
3. Kinds of sources for data collection.
4. Leveraging intelligence that you created to making better decisions.

Even though the competitive intelligence community is small and the procedures not yet codified, Fahey often finds himself at odds with what he sees as practices that are already old-fashioned and too traditional. Mainly, he rails against the emphasis on collection of data and lack of analytical skill.

Fahey's expertise is in strategic management and his course reflected that interest.

Fifty percent of the grade was a true-life assignment in which the student was expected to find a client company and perform an analysis of that company's competitor. Students who were working for companies (usually evening students) were encouraged to use their own firm as a client. Full-time students were to find a client who was willing to take them on.

One of the other pioneers in education about competitive intelligence is John Prescott, associate professor of Business Administration at the Joseph M. Katz Graduate School of Business Administration at the University of Pittsburgh. Prescott has been teaching Competitive Analysis for Strategic Decisions since 1982.

The course, an elective that is taught one semester each year, emphasizes two areas. First, methodology—how information is collected, analyzed, and distributed, and second, management of the competitive intelligence process—how competitive intelligence should be managed as one of many disciplines within a company and how it fits into a company's structure.

The course centers on students conducting a real-life competitive intelligence project with the cooperation of a local company. Prescott chooses companies that will think of the course work as something that will be of value to them when it's completed. He requires that the company give students access to their facilities and people. "It's something we negotiate with the company," says Prescott. When the project is completed, students make a presentation before top management, who grade their work.

Prescott has worked with insurance companies, electric utilities, telecommunications companies, and some diversified companies as well.

"One of the things I try to show students is that competitive intelligence is cross-functional; it's very interdisciplinary."

Prescott hopes that through courses such as his, competitive intelligence will one day become accepted.

PART THREE

Issues, Opportunities, and the Future

CHAPTER FOURTEEN

Justifying the Cost of Competitive Intelligence

"Japanese firms place a tremendous value on information and do not feel the need to justify information management expenditures."
—Ernst & Young report, *Information Management and Japanese Success*, 1991

"Competitive intelligence, in my opinion, is worth about $50 million a year to NutraSweet. That's a combination of revenues gained and those not lost. . . . Fifty is probably a low number."
—Robert Flynn, Chairman, CEO, NutraSweet

There's an old saw that goes something like this: "I know that half of the money I spend on advertising is wasted. I just don't know which half."

Advertising works; that's why companies do it. In fact, without advertising most businesses would fail. The flip side is also true; companies that do superior advertising succeed more often than companies that do poor advertising.

It wasn't always like that.

During the boom years of advertising—radio in the 1940s and television beginning in the 1950s—the practice was looked upon with suspicion in some quarters. Oh sure, companies knew that advertising worked—they had spent money on billboards, magazine and newspaper advertising—but ad agencies often had trouble showing that it was cost-effective. If you spent one dollar for advertising, did you receive at least one dollar in sales?

While ad agencies and the advertisers themselves have gotten more sophisticated about tracking return on investment, there's still an intuitive nature to advertising and its relation to return on investment.

Hence the old saying about half of your ad dollars being wasted.

Take a company like Procter & Gamble, the world's largest advertiser. The company spends more than $1.5 billion annually on all kinds of advertising. Asked if it was worth it, the answer would be "of course" even though company officials cannot correlate a one-to-one (or more than one-to-one) relationship between money spent and revenues received. They are more likely to say that if they didn't advertise, their revenues would certainly suffer. They also know, from studies, that when they increase advertising, their sales also increase. However, the return is never in lockstep to expenditures. (This also doesn't take into account that some ad campaigns flop miserably for reasons that no one understands.)

Look at P&G's success rate: Of the forty or so product categories in which it competes, it holds a number one or number two market share in about thirty of them.

There is a certain amount of faith involved in advertising and a certain acceptance to the belief that doing without it would be disastrous.

It's also accepted on faith that while advertising may not always return money directly to the bottom line, it is part of a chain of actions that companies do that make them successful.

Trying to quantify the direct effect of competitive intelligence is like a city trying to quantify the return it receives on having excellent schools, fire department, police, and trash pickup. We all know that cities with good services attract more residents, indeed, upscale residents who deem it a desirable place to live. Home prices increase from demand and that leads to increased property values and tax revenues for city coffers. This has been shown many times, but you can't directly quantify the effect good schools or other services have on a city's revenues.

So it is with competitive intelligence.

The effects of competitive intelligence are indirect. No simple correlation between revenues and money spent on competitive intelligence exists. Everything works through an intermediary.

Anecdotally, though, we know that competitive intelligence leads to increased quality, better strategic planning, and a greater knowledge of markets, but putting a dollar figure on those facets is difficult if not impossible in most cases.

Looking at it a different way, how much money did your company lose by not having competitive intelligence? For example, how much market share did you lose by not knowing your competitors' activities?

How much did you lose by not getting an important contract? Was it because you didn't have enough information about your competitor?

Gil Press, formerly the manager/corporate market analysis at Digital Equipment Corp., says that part of the problem in quantifying the effects of competitive intelligence is that companies are not used to charting the flow of information and its relative costs.

The U.S. government for many years could not quantify the effects of the service sector on the rest of the country as the nation moved from a manufacturing economy to a service economy. Government accountants had to design a new paradigm for figuring productivity in the services sector. Blue-collar productivity was easy: Just count how many widgets were produced, how many miles of roadway were built, or how many tons of steel were shipped.

No one had ever before tried to quantify the productivity of an office worker, and some people say the economic models are still not quite correct.

Press and others point out that a full-blown competitive intelligence unit doesn't require that many people, only a handful. They also point out that because there probably is already some competitive intelligence activity in your company, albeit disorganized or ad hoc, companies can save money by concentrating the competitive intelligence function in one place. This saves many people from having to gather the same information. "You're already paying for many people to do the same thing, why not just pay for one person to do it," notes Press.

This is one of the most compelling arguments for establishing a complete competitive intelligence program. Your company is already doing competitive intelligence in some way, shape, or form. You already collect information and turn it into intelligence, but you're probably not calling it competitive intelligence, and you're probably not doing it in a systematic, cost-effective manner.

YOUR COMPANY PROBABLY IS DOING SOME TYPE OF AD HOC COMPETITIVE INTELLIGENCE ALREADY. WHY NOT SYSTEMATIZE IT AND REAP THE MOST BENEFITS?

Price Waterhouse Gives It a Shot

Price Waterhouse inadvertently showed that the best companies use competitive intelligence and those that don't, suffer. It's pretty close to a cause and effect as you're likely to get.

A two-year benchmarking study from the consultancy involved twenty-four divisions of aerospace and defense companies. The goal was to discover best-in-class practices. The study, called TQM/100, was completed in 1993 and compared practices among companies who joined this particular benchmarking alliance.

Measurements included how much it cost to win contracts, overall program budget performance, on-time customer deliveries, engineering drawings released on time, and incoming material acceptance rates.

According to Michael O'Guin, who managed the study, one of the important results was the role of competitive intelligence in winning contracts.

"Competitive intelligence played a crucial role in explaining why some companies won 67 percent of the contracts they went after compared to the industry average of 18 percent," O'Guin says.

Competitive intelligence was used by the best-in-class companies as part of their "capture plans." It gave them a way to focus on what it takes to win contracts. Accurate knowledge of customers' and competitors' strategy and position was crucial to setting their own strategy and positioning.

O'Guin notes that companies' "capture teams" received help from the company's competitive intelligence units in collecting the information they needed. The competitive intelligence units also provided direction and analytical help for the teams.

"The key to being successful at the capture process requires you to work at the process before the RFP [request for proposal]," says O'Guin. He notes that the most important contribution from competitive intelligence comes in the "down-select" process, the time when companies decide which contracts to go after and how much money they are willing to spend on it.

Costs for going after contracts can run into the millions of dollars and companies must carefully select which projects they have a chance at capturing and which are better left to competitors. However, the leverage in these contracts is huge. Spending a million dollars could net a contract worth ten or twenty times that amount. The study showed that competitive intelligence played a large role in some 60 to 70 percent of the down-select process alone.

O'Guin was impressed at how the most successful companies' capture teams were focused when it came to their information needs. "They knew exactly what information they needed and how they were going to use it to win contracts."

The study also showed that the most successful company in the alliance had a dedicated competitive intelligence staff with a formalized program. The company, whose identity is kept secret, also kept track of which contracts its competitors won. Even after a contract was lost, the company continued to collect information for future use about the winner's strategy, pricing, strengths, and weaknesses.

NutraSweet: $50 Million a Year

Because only a few companies actually have a fully functioning competitive intelligence unit, CEO testimonials are rare. Even in those companies with programs, CEOs are somewhat reluctant to go public with how competitive intelligence has helped them. (There was a full discussion of NutraSweet earlier.)

Robert Flynn, the chairman and CEO of NutraSweet, is different.

"I'm a firm believer that competitive intelligence has helped us to make more good decisions and far fewer bad ones. I can even place a price on it: Competitive intelligence, in my opinion, is worth about

$50 million a year to NutraSweet. That's a combination of revenues gained and those not lost. . . . Fifty is probably a low number.

"I wouldn't think of sending my people out in the world [to do battle every day] unprepared, and they're not prepared without the best competitive intelligence that we can provide them."

CHAPTER FIFTEEN

Using Competitive Intelligence in the European Union

"Americans look at the European Union and all they see is a market with 350 million people. Numbers don't mean anything."
—Daniel Gautschoux, European Business
Development Alliance

Daniel Gautschoux remembers being in Cairo several years ago and meeting some Japanese businessmen from Nissan and their spouses. They went to a bar, and he learned that the Japanese were in Egypt to learn Arabic. They were planning to stay several years, learn the language and all they could about the culture.

"You don't see any Japanese cars in Egypt, only American or European cars. So what were they doing there?" Gautschoux asked himself. "Then I realized that they were looking way into the future. They were learning the customs, the language, and all they could about the market for the one day when they will try to sell cars here. This is the way competitive intelligence is really done."

Gautschoux says that Americans think they can be competitive in the European Union because they look at some databases, maybe speak the language, and visit a few times a year. That doesn't work, he notes.

Adds his colleague Joseph H. A. M. Rodenburg at the European Business Development Alliance, a Dutch national associated with Adrian H. Koppens Partners: "It's difficult to get information from the European Union compared to the United States. Even when you get the information, how do you know what it means in their context?"

Indeed, the Japanese began their competitive intelligence work in Europe during the 1950s and 1960s, and stepped up the pace in the 1980s when it became clear that a single market would be a reality in the 1990s. Japanese competitive intelligence practices are credited with that country's success in displacing traditional European industries such as camera making, watchmaking, and consumer audio goods. The same intense study that was done on U.S. industries was done on European industries.

While we may be moving in the direction of a single European economy, differences are still great among nations in the European Union. Look at the obvious: There are 15 countries and more than 10 languages.

For an American marketer to think of the countries as one can be shown to be a mistake time and again. For example, life expectancies are very different. In the Netherlands, the average male lives to seventy-four; in Portugal it's seventy-one. The average Dutch citizen has 13.9 years of school while the average German receives 15.2 years. France has the highest use of nuclear-powered electricity with 73 percent while in Italy it's negligible.

The point is that while economically the countries may be linked, doing business in one country does not mean that you can do business the same way in another. The dream of having one big trading partner to deal with—and only one entity to compete with—does not exist.

Another good example is Spain. Government agencies in Spain are reluctant about giving out information. Moreover, if you're trying to do business in Barcelona, speaking Spanish isn't enough. You must speak Catalonian. This is crucial because Spain is a speaking country. People don't like to write reports; they prefer to deal with spoken words. (That's very different from the American way of business.) This makes computer information virtually worthless even when it's available.

On the other hand, databases in Britain, Germany, and France are reliable. They are very good first steps in a systematic competitive intelligence program.

The bottom line is that competitive intelligence must be done on a country-by-country basis.

As the European Union grows and coalesces it will be more and more difficult for American firms to compete there against Japanese businesses.

"We're just beginning to see pressure from the Japanese in Europe, especially in the car industry," says Rodenburg. In addition, countries of the EU are strengthening and growing their own competitive intelligence systems to learn about their trading partners within the union.

The stakes are particularly high for American firms. Right now, U.S. companies have about 25 percent of their foreign investment in Europe. This investment must be protected and enhanced. Unfortunately, many U.S. companies are underrepresented and will pay the price in the future.

Even though Europe is not a single market when it comes to gathering information, it is becoming a single economy in other aspects. Although citizens of each nation will tenaciously hold on to their cultural traits for a long time to come, their economic differences are disappearing.

As the European Union becomes more solidified you will see the following occurring:

- standardization of warranties and trade laws
- pan-European brands and products
- changes in distribution channels
- customers becoming more Europeanized, wanting many of the same products and services even though cultural idiosyncrasies will never fully disappear
- increased commercialization and growth of broadcast outlets such as TV, radio, and cable
- recognition that economies of scale can be reached through pan-European acquisitions and mergers
- a pan-European patent system

The only way for a company to monitor all these changes is by using competitive intelligence methods. Only by establishing an early-warning system can American firms hope to compete in the new Europe.

Clearly, companies like Coca-Cola, Ford, and IBM, which already have wide European exposure and large market recognition, will do well because they are so integrated into Europe that they see the changes every day and can respond. They have their radar up and their competitive intelligence systems operating.

For companies with limited exposure in the single market, competitive intelligence becomes a necessity for survival against the giants who want the market to themselves.

U.S. companies with no European presence will be under intense pressure from new European companies born from the union. Not to monitor their activities in the single market could lead to diminished market share once they enter the United States.

Let's take pharmaceuticals as an example. A unified Europe would bring administrative and some operating costs down for all major European companies. In fact, the European Union estimates that the administrative cost of trade barriers, in other words, the bureaucratic cost of companies doing business across country borders in Europe, exceeds $275 billion. When these costs are eliminated companies will have more money to spend in other areas such as U.S. expansion. How much more powerful will a European competitor be against your company once that money is unleashed? Can your company estimate how much of this $275 billion a competitor will have available?

What U.S. Companies Can Do

U.S. companies should use competitive intelligence on two tracks:

• **Monitor the social, political, and economic changes in the European Union and their effect on the market and your competitors.**

As I've said, collecting information will be done country by country for the foreseeable future. However, learning about big-picture European changes requires a look at information coming from the heart of the European Union.

Many competitive intelligence consultancies have already set up shop in Brussels, Belgium, the EU headquarters. And many large U.S. and Japanese firms have already opened offices in that city hoping to influence policy. They are watching legislation, regulation, standards, certification, and other agreements and decisions.

Even the smallest U.S. firms doing business in Europe are affected. For example, technical standards that are set in the union must be adhered to by all those who want to sell their products there. If you wait until standards are set, will you have the money and time to retool?

One of the positive aspects of the European Union is that information will be easier to obtain as time goes on. In fact, the union has already spawned newsletters, databases, and newspapers containing a great deal of information. This is especially true of information about smaller firms, which, because they seek investment capital from the United States and elsewhere, are making more company data available to the public.

As more harmonization takes place, more and more information will be available through centralized sources. A good example is the newly established European Environmental Agency, which will be a data collection and regulatory point for environmental issues. Some of the information will be private but some will be public-domain.

Another example is the Bank Accounts Directive, which collects data from reporting financial institutions in the EU.

- **Learn what other companies are doing to exploit the single European market.**

It's useful to see how Japanese firms have been positioning themselves for the new Europe and to learn from their experiences. The Japanese have learned that they must welcome European management into their companies and give them autonomy if they are to be suc-

▶ European Union Databases

Eurodicautom—In all EU languages, more than a half million phrases and terms used in the union.

Eurcom—Legal decisions of the EU.

Celex—EU laws, agreements, treaties, and other documents.

SCAD—Hundreds of thousands of citations to articles, periodicals, and documents concerning the EU.

cessful in their expansion plans. However, this has not yet happened to any great extent, and American firms can learn from these mistakes.

Another area in which the Japanese have not yet succeeded is in bringing their workaholic attitudes to Europe. American firms should watch and see how Japanese managers handle this difference in working habits between Japanese and European workers.

CHAPTER SIXTEEN

Ethics

"Try not to become a man of success but rather a man of values."
—Albert Einstein

It all came to light in 1991 after cosmetics giant Avon had for several years successfully thwarted takeover attempts by rival Mary Kay Cosmetics. To learn more about Mary Kay's strategic plans, Avon employed all the standard competitive intelligence methods, but they went one step further. They hired private investigators to collect Mary Kay's garbage and search through it for notes, reports, and memos.

Avon admits they went dumpster diving but did so to prevent Mary Kay from destroying possible evidence in a court case involving the aborted takeovers. Avon officials say they did nothing illegal, because Mary Kay had shredded and thrown out the documents and, most important, the dumpster was on public property. They even shot videotape to support that claim.

Both sides eventually came to an agreement about the garbage. Avon would be free to reassemble the material while Mary Kay would be allowed to be present to see what material they retrieved.

Did Avon do anything illegal? The answer is no, according to the law. Taking trash left out for pickup is perfectly legal. On May 16, 1988, the Supreme Court ruled in the case of *California v. Greenwood* that garbage left in front of Greenwood's house was not in violation of the Fourth Amendment's protection against unlawful search and seizure.

The court said: "Since the respondent voluntarily left their trash for collection in an area particularly suited for public inspection, their claimed expectation of privacy in the inculpatory items they discarded [in this case they were drug-related items] was not objectively reasonable."

This means that once a company or individual places trash out on the sidewalk for collection, it's no longer theirs. Anybody can take it. It's considered abandoned property.

It's important to note that this only holds for trash placed at the curb or some other public area. Trash sitting in your home's backyard or company's parking lot is still private property. Otherwise, the garbage is fair game for anyone who wants to pick it up.

Yes, but is it ethical?

This is one of those questions that haunt competitive intelligence professionals. If a collection method is legal, is it also ethical? The answer you hear sometimes depends upon the background of the competitive intelligence practitioner. Those from government service, such as former CIA operatives, often think in terms of the letter of the law. If something is not over the legal line, it's okay. However, those raised in corporate American culture tend to think in terms of "what would it look like on the front page of the *Wall Street Journal?*"

Most people involved in competitive intelligence would not permit garbage retrieval and search by those in their organization. To them, it smacks of unethical behavior and is simply not done.

What about the following example?

You're trying to collect information about a competitor and decide to call up and request some information from a sales representative. The information is public-domain, perhaps a price chart that they would send to any customers who ask. Do you tell him that you are with a competitor straight away or do you make believe you are a customer? Perhaps you could justify being a customer because in your nonbusiness life you might be interested in the product. Or maybe you don't identify yourself at all and just say you want the information. If he asks why, you skirt the question and just say you want it for reference. What's ethical behavior in this instance?

Before I answer that, try this one.

You're walking in a public parking lot and see an envelope on the pavement. There is no name on it and no return address. You don't know where it came from. Inside are sensitive documents relating to your competitor. In fact, they are confidential (marked as such with a big rubber stamp) internal memos that clearly came from your rival. You could use the information to your advantage. What do you do?

Actually, this kind of predicament happens more often than you may think. Many companies have received letters on their fax machines aimed for someone else. What do you do with information that you've received by mistake or accident?

Let me give you one more to try.

Suppose you're conducting a job interview. The candidate works for a competitor and during your discussions he reveals some confidential information. It's not as if he whispered it into your ear or told you something he thought you would like to know to curry favor even though it was confidential. There was no winking or sly nodding involved. The information just came out during the conversation. Can you use what he told you?

The Problem with Ethics

As more information gathering takes place, ethics will become a larger issue. As pressure increases to obtain information, there are incentives to cut corners and violate ethical restraints. The situation can be exacerbated by management that looks the other way at ethical infractions—or doesn't question how some information was obtained—as long as the job gets done.

Ethical considerations are also increasingly important as companies do more and more business globally. Legal standards differ from country to country. For example, it's perfectly legal to discriminate in hiring based on sex in some countries. It's not legal in the United States. In some countries, public servants expect a tip when giving you public documents. It's not how we do business in the United States.

Because of these international differences, companies need their own set of ethics that should be higher than the legal standards they encounter.

On October 11, 1996, President Clinton signed into law The Economic Espionage Act of 1996. This makes theft of trade secrets a federal crime.

Until this law was enacted, the prosecution of secret thefts was left to the states. Unfortunately, legal definitions varied among states even for basic concepts such as the phrase "trade secret "

Many, but not all, states had already adopted the Uniform Trade Secrets Act, which defines a trade secret the following way:

"Information, including a formula, pattern, compilation, program, device, method, technique or process that:

(1) derives independent economic value, actual or potential from not being generally known to, and not being readily ascertainable by proper means by other persons who can obtain economic value from its disclosure or use, and

(2) is the subject of efforts that are reasonable under the circumstance to maintain its secrecy."

The new federal law follows closely the UTSA but expands it to include all forms and types of information including financial, business, scientific, technical, economic, and engineering. It includes plans, formulas, designs, prototypes, methods, techniques, processes, procedures, computer codes, and so on. Most important, it includes them whether they are tangible or intangible.

It includes any kind of storage technique including material that is written, memorialized, electronically, graphically, or photographically stored.

For something to be a trade secret the owner must have taken reasonable measures to keep it a secret and the information must have economic value—actual or potential—which is derived from its not being generally known to, and not being readily available through proper means, by the public.

Penalties for breaking the law can be severe. A person who commits an offense in violation of the law can be imprisoned up to 10 years and fined up to $500,000. A corporation or other organization can be fined up to $5 million.

Penalties are higher if the offense benefits a foreign government or foreign entity. An individual can be imprisoned up to 15 years and fined $500,000 while a corporation can be fined up to $10 million.

In some instances, the Act applies to trade secret thefts committed outside the United States. This is a crucial part of prosecuting cases that may involve transmitting trade secrets over the Internet.

It's important to note that obtaining stolen property that you didn't know was stolen or possessing information that you didn't know was secret, is not against the law. Not returning it, however, is against the law.

It's also important to know that while it is against the law to have another company's trade secrets in your possession, it has been argued in many courthouses that companies have lost the right to call something a trade secret by their own actions.

The best example is reverse engineering. Once a company puts a product on the market, it has no control over whether or not others take it apart to learn about it.

In another instance, a grommet maker lost the legal right to say that the way it made grommets was protected as a trade secret because it failed to put a barrier around the production area or inform employees and others that anything confidential was going on in the plant. Any visitor to the plant was able to view the production area with ease.

The legal stuff is easy, now let's look at the squishy areas.

What Are Good Ethics?

Ethical behavior is hard to define. Webster's defines ethics as *a discipline dealing with good and evil and with moral duty*. For most of us a practical, everyday application is more useful. For example, how would we feel seeing the activity on the front page of the newspaper? How we would feel if this activity were done to us? Would we feel wronged or deceived?

These are the principles that should guide your information collection activities.

While many companies give their employees ethical guidance, such as in their mission statement or in an employee handbook, the principles are not always brought home. In fact, in the day-to-day race for revenue, ethics can get lost.

While many managers pay lip service to ethics, they are also under enormous pressure not to limit the ability of their competitive intelligence units to collect information even it means engaging in marginal behavior. What we find are many companies rewarding competitive intelligence units for doing their jobs but not rewarding them for doing it ethically.

One of the arguments on management's side for not enforcing ethical behavior is that, "The competition is doing it. Why shouldn't we do it, too?" Studies have shown that one of the reasons some college students cheat on tests is because they believe that others are cheating. If they don't cheat, they believe they will fall behind. The same is true of managers. When asked about certain activities, such as posing as a graduate student doing a term paper in order to obtain information, many managers believe that because their competition would do it, they would be crazy not to do it as well.

This is one of the most difficult arguments to counter, because ethics do change as society changes. Perhaps cheating is becoming part of our culture. On the other hand, do we encourage poor ethics by condoning the activity and considering it normal?

One of the toughest parts about monitoring ethics is that you almost have to go inside the head of the person under scrutiny. For example, while all people agree that hiring someone from a competitor just to obtain trade secrets from them is unethical, it's also possible that you hired that person because he is the best qualified of all candidiates. In most businesses, people travel from company to company searching for new opportunities within the industry and it is almost impossible to prove otherwise.

Good Ethics Pays

Adhering to good ethics is not only the right thing to do, it pays dividends.

Probably the most important reason for good behavior is to keep your company out of court, avoiding legal entanglements and costs. The case with Avon and Mary Kay is a good example.

Another reason to subscribe to good ethical conduct is that it makes life easier and less stressful for employees. With a strict code of ethics, people know exactly what they are permitted to do and not do. No problematic decisions are necessary.

A third reason is company credibility and public profile.

Marriott's image was tarnished when it hired an executive search firm to help it collect information about the economy hotel business. The headhunter held interviews with managers of some of these companies. Although the headhunter didn't lie and say that jobs were available at that time, he noted that jobs may be available in the future. In fact, Marriott did indeed hire some of these people. However, the interviewer obtained information about hotels in the economy end of the business that he might not have obtained otherwise. Clearly, telling someone that a job may be in the offing encourages participation beyond what they might reveal under different circumstances. Again, it's impossible to get inside the head of the interviewer as to his true motives and method, but the incident seemed suspect to many observers.

Because so many managers think that competitive intelligence is "sleazy" anyway, it's absolutely crucial that the director of competitive intelligence present to management a code of ethics that encompasses the company's existing code (if there is one), tailoring the competitive intelligence activities to the company's code. In fact, the code should be specific about what information can be collected, what information cannot be collected, and the manner in which collection is to be handled. The code should also include policies on how to handle inadvertent receiving of proscribed information such as confidential memos and personal letters.

Over the long term, ethicists say that unethical business behavior and the lowering of standards can cost a lot of money in security costs. The argument is that if overall ethics standards decline, businesses must pay more to defend against unethical tactics—which could become everyday accepted activities—and these preventive measures can be expensive.

A fitting analogy is the price society pays for not giving children ethical and moral guidance from a young age. It costs more to house a person in prison than send him to college. This is above the damage he or she leaves behind by violent actions and illegal activity.

You can also make the point that if ethics violations escalate within the business community, management will have no choice but to limit how much information each employee can have. This can lead to distrust among workers and also keep them from doing their job more efficiently. Lynn Sharp Paine, associate professor at Harvard Business School, noted in the *Journal of Business Ethics*:

"Avoiding the use of the telephone and restricting access to information to employees who demonstrate a 'need to know' impose obvious impediments to the exchange of information vital to cooperation within the firm. When researchers are denied information about the projects they are working on and about how their work relates to the work of others, they are cut off from stimuli to creativity and useful information."

The last reason for good ethics is the most simple.

It is not necessary to violate codes of ethical behavior to collect the information you need.

Even in this young discipline there are old adages. One is: *"Eighty-five percent of the information you need is out there in the public domain. The other 15 percent you probably don't need."* Some people even put the number as high as 90 percent.

By using ethical practices and expert analysis, competitive intelligence professionals should be able to do their jobs effectively and efficiently.

The following is a code of ethics presented by the Society of Competitive Intelligence Professionals for its members:

CODE OF ETHICS

- To continually strive to increase respect and recognition for the profession on local, state, and national levels.
- To pursue his or her duties with zeal and diligence while maintaining the highest degree of professionalism and avoiding all unethical practices.
- To faithfully adhere to and abide by his or her company's policies, objectives, and guidelines.
- To comply with all applicable laws.
- To accurately disclose all relevant information, including the identity of the professional and his or her organization, prior to all interviews.
- To fully respect all requests for confidentiality of information.
- To promote and encourage full compliance with these ethical stan-

dards within his or her company, with third-party contractors, and within the entire profession.

Individual competitive intelligence unit and consultants should spell out exactly what activities are allowed and which are proscribed.

For example, Fuld & Company has published its own guidelines for ethical behavior called "The Ten Commandments of Legal and Ethical Intelligence Gathering":

1. Thou shalt not lie when representing thyself.
2. Thou shalt observe thy company's legal guidelines as set forth by the Legal Department.
3. Thou shalt not tape-record a conversation.
4. Thou shalt not bribe.
5. Thou shalt not plant eavesdropping devices.
6. Thou shalt not deliberately mislead anyone in an interview.
7. Thou shalt neither obtain from nor give to thy competitor any price information.
8. Thou shalt not swap misinformation.
9. Thou shalt not steal a trade secret (or steal employees away in hopes of learning a trade secret).
10. Thou shalt not knowingly press someone for information if it may jeopardize that person's job or reputation.

In the end, it is top management's responsibility to see that his or her company abides by ethical standards not only in competitive intelligence but throughout the company.

CHAPTER SEVENTEEN

The New
Gatekeepers

"The smart eagle does not show his talons."
—Japanese proverb

Because the United States is an open society with a great deal of information available in the public domain, competitive intelligence professionals don't have to resort to illegal or unethical methods to get what they need. It's the 85/15 rule.

However, this is true only for skilled practitioners. Collection and analysis takes time and brainpower, and there will always be people who will try to find shortcuts, who don't want to play by the rules, and who don't want to do the work.

In the real world, companies must protect themselves against those who will try for the other 15 percent and use illegal or unethical means to get it. Moreover, as we have seen, the ethical standards practiced by most competitive intelligence professionals are not shared worldwide.

Although competitive intelligence is a positive step in that it eventually leads to increased competition and better products and services, nothing says that you have to make information collection easy for your competitor. It behooves all companies to maintain an air of secrecy surrounding their information, even that information which they must give up to the public domain. It becomes even more important for companies to protect information that is proprietary—like a trade secret—and information that could give their competitors a large advantage.

The Cost of Lost Information

Companies wrestle with figuring the costs involved in information loss or theft. It's kind of the opposite of trying to calculate how much you gain by using information.

In an attempt to discover the cost of such losses, the American Society of Industrial Security (ASIS) in 1992 sent surveys to five thousand of the group's members asking for information in this area. Although responses were double-enveloped for anonymity, only 246 companies responded, which may imply how sensitive the issue is to companies.

Of the 246 companies, there were 589 instances of reported illegal activities against U.S. technology, trade secrets, and business plans. Of the thirty-two companies actually reporting figures, the loss was estimated at $1.8 billion.

The study showed some surprising trends:

- Thefts rose 260 percent since 1985.
- Customer lists were the most frequently reported target.
- Pricing data was considered the most financially damaging loss.
- Current or former employees were responsible for 58 percent of all incidents.
- About 30 percent of incidents were from foreign entities, up fourfold from 1985.
- About 21 percent of incidents occurred overseas; foreign nationals were included in 37 percent of these cases.
- Of 817 methods of loss, 33 percent involved actual theft; unauthorized reproduction accounted for 43 percent. Bribery occurred in less than 8 percent of cases.

An important factor to consider is that these companies knew that a loss had occurred. More than forty respondents said their companies had no mechanism to learn if a loss had taken place, which indicates that companies reporting "no losses" may not know about it. In addition, even those companies reporting a loss may have other losses of which they aren't aware.

When asked to quantify the loss, more than half of those companies reporting losses said they had difficulty assessing the actual costs. However, the impact of the losses was seen in increased costs in the following sectors: administration, loss of market share, increased legal activities, increased security, and embarrassment to the company.

The loss of market share and profits to legal and ethical competitive intelligence methods has never been surveyed in this manner. However, companies should apply the same thought on information in the public domain and what it would cost them if other competitors were to collect, analyze, and use it.

You may know what value you place on certain information in your own company; this will give you an idea as to what it's worth to your competitors.

Protecting Information—Old and New Ways

Before the days of competitive intelligence, information was locked up in vaults, kept behind closed doors, and every bit of paper shredded. This method is expensive and usually unnecessary.

Moreover, this level of security curtails the free flow of information among employees and forces them to live in an atmosphere of distrust and secrecy that is unnecessary and demoralizing. Also, by considering all information as top secret, employees tend to become desensitized to legitimate security concerns over time because they are always in a high-alert mode.

A new method called OPSEC, or Operations Security, is making its way from the military to the private sector. OPSEC is a tactic that protects both public-domain and proprietary information with efficiency, low cost, and without the drawbacks just mentioned. OPSEC can put available resources where they can do the most good in a rational, thoughtful way. The idea is to identify the relative importance of a piece of information and take appropriate measures for its protection.

OPSEC weighs the importance of information and looks at how a competitor could obtain that information and use it against its owner. OPSEC offers a mechanism to justify the expense of protecting information but also looks at the cost of losing it.

If done correctly, OPSEC saves money because it eliminates unnecessary security expenses. And, if information is lost, it allows you to factor that loss qualitatively into your strategic plans.

Unlike traditional methods of security that try to avoid risk at all costs, OPSEC techniques help you manage risk in a reasonable, analytical, and cost-effective manner.

Another way to look at it is that all companies have vulnerabilities but not all of them are worth protecting.

This is a vast difference from how most companies secure information. Indeed, until the 1970s, it was how the military and defense community secured information. The framework of OPSEC was developed during the Vietnam War as a way to secure information about air strikes from North Vietnamese spies. As the war progressed, it was clear that North Vietnam had prior knowledge about many U.S. attacks. Although previous bombing runs and reconnaissance flights confirmed that soldiers and matériel were present at certain bases, when the U.S. bombers arrived, the areas had been evacuated.

At first, U.S. intelligence officers thought there were spies feeding information to the enemy. However, they later realized that the Vietcong were watching the activities of Strategic Air Command personnel and matériel at certain bases, thereby guessing at the targets.

The problem for the U.S. forces was how to continue moving troops and machinery without tipping off the enemy. They developed OPSEC, which allowed routine and other activities to continue but in such a way as *not* to give the enemy too many pieces of the puzzle. For example, many different air bases would receive shipments at the same time so one base would not stand out from the others. Another ploy was to slowly move troops around, making it look like routine deployments and not a massing action.

After the war, the OPSEC concept continued to be honed and was adopted by the executive branch of the federal government in 1988.

The official definition comes from the National Operations Security

Doctrine: "OPSEC involves the application of a systematic analytical process to determine how adversaries derive critical information in time to be of value to them."

In the corporate world, competitive intelligence professionals are in a unique position to implement OPSEC. Because they know how to collect and analyze information, competitive intelligence practitioners should also handle OPSEC matters. They know which puzzle pieces are crucial and which are not.

OPSEC consists of a five-step process:

1. *Identification of critical information.* This is what your competitor needs to gain advantage over your company. In most cases, it's the same information you would like to obtain from your competitors, such as pricing. Critical information can also be items like formulas, trade secrets, pending acquisitions, and strategic plans.

2. *Analysis of the threat.* This includes identifying competitors and what they're able to accomplish with their competitive intelligence units. Simply, what are their capabilities? Do they have access to the databases that you do? Do they know what to look for about your company? What do you think they know? How does their top management view competitive intelligence?

3. *Vulnerability analysis.* Where is your company vulnerable to information leakage? Do your employees understand the problem? Is too much information needlessly being let out when it should be kept confidential?

4. *Risk assessment.* What might happen versus what could happen. What are the effects of your competitor getting certain information? Would you lose market share, customers, technological superiority? What are likely scenarios if these losses occur? How long should certain information be kept confidential?

5. *Implementing countermeasures.* Unlike traditional security measures, OPSEC countermeasures change the way people do their jobs, the way they think about their jobs, and the way management thinks about information. It takes a strong-willed person to help a company break down long-standing and archaic barriers, to challenge the status quo and help the organization think in new and different ways.

Like competitive intelligence, OPSEC is an ongoing process and changes as the industry and competitive climate changes. These changes should be reflected in OPSEC practices.

The parallels between OPSEC and competitive intelligence are striking. Both require a total commitment from top management and both need the participation of everyone in the company.

For companies that handle a lot of government work, OPSEC may already be part of their culture. For others, it can be expanded from the competitive intelligence unit, and the two functions should become integrated.

Robert Margulies, of McDonnel Douglas, Herb Clough, a former FBI agent, and others have been promoting an approach called the *competitive intelligence/counterintelligence team,* which fosters a symbiotic relationship between the two groups.

They see it as an offense/defense type of activity with a common goal of achieving and sustaining a competitive advantage in the global marketplace.

"Who other than the competitive intelligence people know the importance of each piece of information," says Margulies. "And who knows better than the counterintelligence people how best to limit the competition from getting that information. That's why you need a team approach."

Preventing Leaks

Whenever a business transaction takes place, information is generated. Preventing every single leak is impossible and not cost-effective.

A good example of this is the White House and Domino's Pizza deliveries. Several days prior to the Gulf War, some reporters noticed that Domino's pizzas were being delivered frequently to the White House and Pentagon during evening hours. It was clear that people were staying late; something was in the works.

However, did it matter? Should the White House and Pentagon have stopped ordering pizzas? No, although outsiders knew something was up—tensions in the Gulf were building and it was certain that a conflict was imminent—the amount of information they obtained from counting the pizza deliveries was negligible. Not only that, they could have learned people were working late by seeing how many cars were in the parking lots anyway.

Now, whenever lots of pizzas are delivered to the White House, people know something important is afoot but so what? If other safeguards are in place, they don't know what it is.

Companies should use the pizza analogy when they reveal information. What is the relative cost of letting information out versus the cost of protecting it?

The following are areas to watch:

Press releases. Sensitive press releases should be checked by the competitive intelligence/OPSEC people before going out. Is the information being let out worth the cost of having the competition know it? In some cases, a little pruning may be necessary.

Public filings. The same goes for public filings with federal, state, and local agencies. It's illegal not to provide the requested information, but the form should be checked to make sure you haven't "overfiled," given more information than necessary. Indeed, the information that is left out should be noted so that the competitive intelligence unit knows what puzzle pieces are out there and available to the competition. While the competition may have some information about you, the idea is to keep them from having all the pieces needed to make a strong analysis. Keeping them from having that critical mass of information takes skill and experience.

For example, on blueprints submitted for a city building permit, are machinery positions required to be included? What's the least amount of information you can supply about the machine's description?

Technical papers. One of the main leaks from companies is through technical papers delivered at conferences by engineers and researchers. While a free exchange of ideas benefits everyone, the papers should be examined to make sure that strategic plans or other confidential information isn't being broadcast inadvertently.

Speeches and presentations. The same holds true for speeches by the CEO or other top managers. While no one will purposely give away confidential information, it's important to check speeches for certain pieces of information that could help a competitor analyze something and give them a competitive advantage.

Plant tours. Using the old methods of security, all plant tours would be considered off limits. OPSEC allows companies to fulfill civic duties or business obligations by allowing visitors in their facilities. However, visitors should be kept to areas with little strategic value to competitors. They should be escorted and not allowed to roam free.

Nonemployees. Suppliers, distributors, mailers, printers, bankers, and others are privy to some of your confidential information. Although you may want some of them to sign nondisclosure agreements, it's more important that they all understand the importance of keeping your secrets to themselves. A package delivery service, for example, might not understand the importance of not telling others that you're giving them a lot of business lately. To them it's something to be proud of. To your competitor, it could be an indication of increased sales and so something that needs to be kept quiet.

Employees. Some Apple Computer's conference rooms signs read: "Spies have booked this room after you. Please erase the board and dispose of any confidential paper into a confidential bin."

While Apple's admonition is somewhat tongue-in-cheek, it serves as a reminder to all employees how simple it is to protect information and how devastating some leaks could become.

Employees should never discuss confidential information in public places. In Japan, it is common for people to purposely sit next to a competitor's employees on commuter trains to pick up tidbits of information. During the go-go years of Silicon Valley, it was common for Soviet spies to sit in bars frequented by high-tech engineers and just listen to them unwinding after a creative day.

Open discussions about private information should never take place in elevators, airplanes, hotel lobbies, trade shows, or cocktail parties.

Documents. Sensitive documents should be kept secure. Instead of disposing of them in the trash, they should be pulverized or made into confetti so that reassembly is impossible. Companies should use OPSEC to analyze the cost/security expenses to decide which documents should be destroyed and which can be simply thrown in the trash.

Companies should also be aware of recycling programs that encourage people not to destroy documents. They should also be aware of nefarious recyclers who go through clients' trash and sell information to competitors.

All companies should institute a rating system for security such as *private* (for only one person), *confidential* (not to be publicized openly), or *restricted* (open to some people). Each carries a different meaning and indicates exactly which people with whom they may share the document's information.

The situation has reached critical mass in some companies. Hewlett-Packard, for example, has limited distribution of its company phone books because phony job interviewers were calling key researchers, enticing them with nonexistent high-paying jobs, and pumping them for information about their projects.

Help wanted ads. All help wanted ads should be screened for information. Decide if what they say is important enough to keep confidential. It might be worth placing a blind ad instead or working through a headhunter.

Computer data. Many people don't know it, but just because you erase a file, it doesn't mean that the information can't be brought out again. In fact, several companies have reported the loss of critical information through rental laptops whose hard disk files were erased yet the information was un-erased by the next renter.

Truly critical information should be kept in a secure computer or kept on floppy disks and the disks should then be kept in a secure place. When disks are thrown out, they should be degaussed, a simple process involving a strong magnet to remove information from the disk. Even so, the National Security Agency and the Department of Defense have developed techniques for retrieving information that has been degaussed. The process uses state-of-the-art, sophisticated equipment not generally available to the private sector. OPSEC procedures would tell us that the risk of degaussed material being read by a competitor is low, so degaussing would be sufficient. If the risk is still too high, you might want to shred the disks.

Litigation. Lawsuits are increasing. With these lawsuits often comes disclosure of information that might give your competitors an advantage. It's incumbent upon companies to factor in the loss of information involved in suing someone or being sued. Although courts can be sensitive to keeping private information confidential, the potential loss of information may force you to settle out of court even though other legal considerations weigh heavily toward continuing the litigation.

Misinformation

Dial and Save, a small long-distance company in Chantilly, Virginia, found themselves $2 million in the hole and their reputation sullied because someone spread the rumor that they were giving away free calls to Cuba. Like other upstart telecommunications companies, Dial and Save leases long-distance lines in bulk hoping to sell telephone time to consumers for a few cents less than larger competitors like MCI, Sprint, and AT&T.

Dialers use an access code, then call a phone number, and the charge is billed by their local phone company. Unfortunately, callers believed the calls were free as part of a promotion. Some consumers received bills as high as $10,000.

In an effort to quiet angry customers, Dial and Save had to hire extra staff, including twenty Spanish-speaking operators.

Nobody knows who was behind this campaign of deliberate misinformation, but it demonstrates how powerful false information can be to a company.

While all competitive intelligence professionals agree that deliberately putting out false information about another company, or even yourselves in some cases, is unethical, concealing what you're doing with other information-based actions is perfectly acceptable.

For instance, if a company is working on two projects, it may purposely overpublicize one over the other to distract competitors' attention away from the more important and more secretive project.

It's also acceptable for a company that may be looking into acquisitions in several cities to allow the CEO to give a public speech in Denver where one of the companies is located but not in other cities where acquisitions could take place. The idea is to make the competition think, Why did he do it in Denver? Was it because the deal will happen in Denver or is the CEO doing it as a diversion? Knowing how your competitors analyze information is crucial to your own counterintelligence plans.

CHAPTER EIGHTEEN

Why the U.S. Government Must Get Involved in Competitive Intelligence

"In a world that increasingly measures national security in economic terms as well as military terms, many foreign intelligence services around the world are shifting their emphasis to targeting American technology. . . . Nearly twenty governments overall are involved in intelligence collection activities that are detrimental to our economic interests on some level."
> —CIA Director Robert M. Gates before the Judiciary
> Committee, House of Representatives, April 29, 1992

"The resources of a corporation—even a large one such as Corning—are no match for foreign espionage activities that are sanctioned and supported by foreign governments."
> —James E. Riesbeck, Executive Vice President, Corning
> Inc., before the Judiciary Committee, House of
> Representatives, April 29, 1992

"I'm willing to die for my country, but not for General Motors."
> —Anonymous CIA agent to Director Robert Gates

The Western view of the world as one controlled by military power is over. It is being replaced by a model that can best be described as *comprehensive national strength.*

Contributing to comprehensive national strength are factors such as economic power, science and technology, education, culture, and, to some degree, military affairs. The emphasis, however, is increasingly on economic strength.

Even those in the U.S. government are starting to realize this change. While the old model of foreign diplomacy involved the secretary of state, the new model displaces him or at least merges him with the secretary of the treasury. Just before he left Washington, Treasury Secretary Lloyd Bentsen noted: "Everyone's been saying for a long time that foreign policy is becoming economic, but like everything else it's taken a while for the message to sink in."

Indeed, foreign policy is now more in the realm of the U.S. trade representative, the Department of Commerce, and other economic bodies rather than political bodies like the Congress. Even the lingo has changed as we talk about a *trade war* with Japan. Moreover, in dealings with China, the administration has often used threats of economic sanctions to help promote the policy of human rights compliance.

It's obvious that countries such as Japan, Germany, and France are already pursuing economic priorities as if they were fighting a world war. They and others have realized that the true war for global supremacy is not based on military might but economic power. To that end, they have justified using military spies to steal trade secrets from other countries, mainly the United States. The pursuit of economic power is thought so important that behavior deemed unethical to U.S. minds is employed without reservation by other countries.

In addition, many countries encourage other interactions between government and business that bolster the country's industrial policies, such as the competitive intelligence activity of JETRO in Japan and INTELCO in France.

Senior National Security Council advisor Kenneth deGraffenreid, who served in the Reagan administration, called this movement *neomercantilism* and noted that foreign countries are willing to use all their policy tools toward helping their national economies.

Whenever the discussion of economic strength takes place in the United States, the Central Intelligence Agency is mentioned. While it has been shown that other countries use their government-run intelligence agencies to collect economic information, the CIA has not played a significant role in helping the United States increase its economic power.

With the ending of the Cold War, however, talk of CIA involvement in economic intelligence has been gaining. Part of the discussion is in response to such ideas as, "What do these spies do now?" and, "Other countries do it, why not us?"

This talk reached new heights during the early 1990s, when former CIA Director Stansfield Turner advocated that the agency gather economic information for American companies. Underscoring the belief that military strength was out and economic strength was in, Turner tried to include economic intelligence gathering as part of the CIA's mission because economics was a matter of national security as much as a well-armed military. He wrote in the Fall 1991 issue of *Foreign Affairs* magazine:

"We must, then, redefine 'national security' by assigning economic strength greater prominence. This means that we need better economic intelligence.... Economic intelligence can range from the broad trends that foreign businesses are pursuing, all the way to what individual foreign competitors are bidding against U.S. corporations on specific overseas contracts. Some argue that when it comes to specific data such as competitive bids, the government should not become a partner of business and distort the free enterprise system. The United States, however, would have no compunction about stealing military secrets to help it manufacture better weapons."

Turner was unsuccessful at turning the CIA into the country's lead business-information-gathering entity and in fact his beliefs were in direct opposition to director Robert Gates, who said that the CIA should not be in the business of spying for American firms. He said it was the job of companies to gather their own information. Period.

The current discussion rests in the middle, with some in Congress advocating that the CIA gather information for companies to bolster U.S. economic strength but stop short of engaging in industrial espionage like some of its foreign counterparts.

This plan has merit but suffers from the most basic and unique characteristics of Americans—a distrust of government involvement in our business and personal affairs. While citizens in other countries may distrust their government's actions from time to time and certainly may not agree with all of its decisions, nowhere is cynicism about government assistance more pronounced in a free market nation than in the United States.

Unless Americans are willing to change this deep-seated notion, the idea of the CIA or any other government agency engaging in competitive intelligence activities for corporations will never be accepted.

While supporters of this idea say that Americans can learn to overcome this cynicism about government once shown that a system could work, there are other concerns about and barriers to this scenario.

For one thing, there is the retraining of agents from the military-political sector to the commercial sector. While many retired agents have successfully made the move, it's problematic whether it can be made on a large scale. In addition, the agency must itself overcome agents' own moral dilemmas regarding whether or not they agree with the notion that what's good for business is good for the nation. The idea of dying for General Motors, as one agent put it, is a large obstacle.

Agents are used to doing what's expected of them, and that includes covert and illegal activity. Some agents may feel hamstrung by more rigorous and stringent rules.

There's also the problem of changing an agency whose culture has been one of silence to one of being open and telling what it learns to many people. Even after many years of promising to publish classified documents—most so old that they have no strategic value—the CIA still has not opened millions of pages of files from decades ago.

Probably the biggest obstacle to CIA involvement is deciding what information to collect and how to disseminate it to companies equitably. While other countries sometimes have their intelligence agencies perform services for a fee, that sort of arrangement would be unworkable in the United States. In addition, just having the CIA collect basic or large-scale information for companies about foreign competitors would not serve corporations' interests for specific items.

All of these obstacles can be overcome, though, once people in and out of government understand that economic security and power are becoming more important than military security and power. It's a concept that many U.S. citizens have not yet grasped—nor do they want to admit it.

Unfortunately, Americans feel much too comfortable with the notion of military power as a tool for world power. After all, the United

States is the world's largest weapons maker and merchant and the greatest military power. Many Americans feel proudest and most patriotic when the country is at war. This military notion feels secure and safe. For Americans to feel comfortable with the shift from military to economic power would take an unwavering and absolute belief that American industry is globally competitive.

Americans don't yet feel that is true.

The Sematech Experience

One possible role for government is that of competitive intelligence supporter and facilitator in a manner similar to that of the Sematech program, which focused on the nation's waning semiconductor industry.

In 1975, the United States' share of the world's semiconductor market had dropped from 100 percent to 65 percent. Japan had garnered only 20 percent.

However, by the middle of 1985, the two countries each held about 45 percent of the market, and Japan's share was growing while the U.S. share was shrinking.

The U.S. free fall seemed to have no end in sight until 1987 when several U.S. agencies, including the Departments of Defense and Commerce, and industry leaders got together and formed an alliance known as Sematech.

The purpose was to rejuvenate an industry begun by U.S. companies but lost to Japanese competitors who were backed by their government's initiatives. It took an act of Congress and funding from industry and government to get Sematech rolling. By 1989, the United States semiconductor industry had stopped its free fall. Market share began to increase at the expense of Japanese market share, and by 1993 the two nations were once again matched, each holding about 42 percent of the market.

This time, however, U.S. share is still on the uptrend while Japan is moving lower.

Without any doubt, Sematech proved that a government-industry research and development consortium can improve U.S. economic positioning in a strategic sector.

Sematech proved something else. It showed that U.S. companies within an industry could pool their competitive intelligence expertise and beat the best competitive intelligence machine in the world—that of the Japanese.

Sematech's Competitive Analysis Group (CAG) collected, analyzed, and disseminated intelligence about competitors and the market in general to its member companies. That intelligence effort helped individual member companies collectively wrest back market share from their prime Japanese competitors.

Compared to their Japanese counterparts who receive government intelligence assistance, individual American firms are at a terrible disadvantage. Yet, a consortium such as Sematech showed that they could level the playing field with government funding and industry cooperation.

CAG's mission statement was the guiding light:

> The Competitive Analysis Group contributes timely communications from analysis of data that provies intelligence about semiconductor industry equipment, technology, manufacturing, and business trends to create strategic plans to guide programs and projects at SEMATECH, and to support member company understanding of the requirement to be world class competitors.

The CAG staff hovers between nine and eleven people, most of whom rotate on a two-year basis from member companies. They are paid directly by their companies.

The group's accomplishments include a project that analyzed leading competitors' costs. They looked at costs involved in factory setups, equipment and performance, staffing, commercial space, and R&D. The group projected costs for each foreign competitor down to the smallest detail. This not only gave the first in-depth view of these competitors but also allowed individual members of Sematech to benchmark their operations against them process by process.

In June 1993, representatives of Sematech took a five-week "low-cost producer" trip to Japan and Korea. They learned many nitty-gritty details about chip production from the lowest cost producer that they then added to knowledge they already had obtained from *construction analysis*—a program where they cut up chips to see how they were fabricated—and other projects.

CAG officials learned about competitors' strategies, including Korean companies that have set their sights on "owning" DRAM technology, that 256 megabyte chips are critical for their industry's survival, and that twelve-inch-sized wafers are not a priority until they reach 1 gigabyte of memory.

The group also put together a chart of alliances among Japanese chip makers showing interlocking relationships, including some with Western manufacturers for patent sharing. This kind of big-picture analysis is crucial when studying where competitors get their expertise and strength.

There was one more important thing that U.S. chip makers hadn't learned until SEMATECH was formed. Japanese companies control 98 percent of the world market in special high-purity resins, which are crucial in chip packaging. The lesson is that U.S. makers need to focus on this vital ingredient.

One of the most gratifying discoveries was how Sematech was perceived by Japanese competitors. At various trade shows, Sematech representatives found that they had better access to people and information when they wore a badge with their own company name instead of a badge that read Sematech.

Sematech was considered a potent enemy especially when its representatives were collecting information about foreign competitors. Competitors were less wary of individual U.S. firms.

Sematech is planning to go on its own by 1997 without any government funding. They believe the group can survive on monies from members only.

Interestingly enough, Sematech may spring an information leak. The group consists of the following members: Advanced Micro Devices (AMD), the Advanced Research Projects Agency (ARPA, a Defense Department branch that handles government grants), AT&T, Digital Equipment Corp., Hewlett-Packard, IBM, Intel, Motorola, National Semiconductor, NCR, Rockwell, and Texas Instruments. In 1991, NCR was bought by AT&T, which then called it AT&T Global Information. AT&T has given notice that it may leave the group in two years. It has sold the old NCR company to Hyundai, a Korean firm, and under the rules they can take with them all the intelligence they've gathered over the years.

This intelligence could give the Korean semiconductor makers a good look at what their Western competitors know about them in addition to what they know about Japanese chip makers.

Korean chip makers are growing fast and control 24 percent of the world market. In DRAMs, in which they excel, the three major memory makers—Hyundai Electronics Industries, Goldstar Electronics, and Samsung Electronics—had 29 percent of the world market in 1994, up from 19.6 percent the year before.

A New Intelligence Model for the United States

Sematech proves that government-funded consortia can work and reap large benefits for industry sectors. These consortia are also the closest thing to an industrial policy program that we're likely to see, considering our antitrust laws and the atmosphere of distrust that often permeates dealings among American companies.

However well these consortia might work, they are only part of an overall business industrial policy for the United States.

Any policy must embrace the nation's intelligence community as well.

The U.S. intelligence agencies are, by many accounts, the best in the world. Not perfect, but excellent. Not to use their expertise in analysis and collection would be a waste of America's resources.

With that in mind, we should find another model for the government-industry competitive intelligence relationship that will utilize what the government does best—including the CIA—and is the most palatable to industry and the American culture.

The first area of improvement is for the federal government to provide easy access to the information it already collects from foreign sources. This data is collected to help run the country.

This information should be packaged, marketed, and distributed to interested parties by a new government entity—the U.S. Government Information Clearinghouse. That entity can be newly formed or be in an existing agency (figure 18-1). The Department of Commerce is a logical choice because this information will be used to increase commerce and trade, both within the purview of the department.

Today, the government produces incredible amounts of information but it is spread among hundreds of agencies and bureaus some so

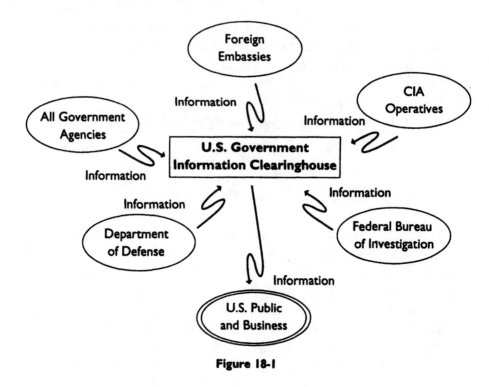

Figure 18-1

obscure that they can't be found by even the most studious information gatherer. This web is so tangled that many consultants make their
living by finding nearly hidden government information, and repack-
aging it and selling it to users.

Agencies such as the Department of Energy produce some of the
best foreign-energy-related data anywhere. Likewise, the Food and
Drug Administration, in its mission to protect the American market
from unsafe drugs, collects large amounts of information from overseas sources about pharmaceuticals and pharmaceutical companies.
Even business sections of embassies generate information that can be
useful to U.S. companies.

While much of this information is made public directly by the gathering agency, some of it is disseminated to other agencies, who may or
may not decide to pass it along to competitive intelligence users.

Let's be clear about this: *What is needed is one central distribution
point for all government information and analysis.* This is not unlike
JETRO, which makes almost all of its information available to anyone
who asks—providing he reads Japanese—and is willing to travel to a
JETRO office in Japan.

The Role of the U.S. Intelligence Community

Not only doesn't the CIA want to spy for U.S. businesses, it's clear that American businesses don't want the CIA involved in collecting explicit information just for them.

However, with the notion that national security relies on economic security, shouldn't the CIA have a commercial intelligence role?

Let's also consider that other countries use their intelligence agencies to collect information, and the United States would be foolish not to follow suit, albeit in a way that fits with our culture and view of government.

The first role that the CIA and other intelligence agencies can play is in corporate education. As we have seen, while competitive intelligence is starting to be taught at the graduate level in some U.S. colleges it is still very rare. Why not take up the slack with current intelligence officers who have the necessary expertise?

Indeed, here lies the largest, best-trained pool of intelligence collectors and analysts in the world. Not to exploit them would be a waste of resources.

There is precedent for government teaching industry. The Small Business Administration, for example, provides education, funding, mentor programs, research, and so forth to help small businesses prosper. They don't run the businesses but business owners can avail themselves of the SBA's resources. In the same way, government intelligence services should be available to teach corporations how to build, develop, and run their competitive intelligence units.

The Department of Agriculture is another example. Staffers don't plant crops, but they educate farmers on how to plant crops and farm efficiently. On the local level, cooperative extension services help farmers and consumers with agriculture-related projects. Because the United States is becoming a nation of less farmland but higher yields by large agribusiness farmers, there is talk of phasing out the Department of Agriculture. As farmers need less help this makes sense, but it also makes sense to put government support behind technology and research efforts to help different industry sectors.

The KGB and other Soviet intelligence services have in the past trained other countries to spy. These countries are now setting their sights on U.S. competitive intelligence. According to former CIA Director Gates: "A number of Third World intelligence services—fifty in fact—have profited from training they received in the past from East Bloc services, and they are now more able to act unilaterally." Education of American businesses by the CIA can help level the playing field in this area.

The CIA should continue and, in fact, increase its efforts to collect general business information from foreign sources and make that available through one government information entity along with information collected by other government agencies.

Agents should be encouraged to pass along *legally* obtained business information to CIA headquarters for dissemination. Because this information is in the public domain, there is no reason to stall it anywhere along its route.

A good example of what the CIA already publishes from openly available source material is the *World Factbook*. These books provide in-depth profiles both politically and economically for every country in the world. The information and analysis are from public-domain data as well as firsthand knowledge collected by operatives in their respective countries.

There has never been an outcry against this sort of information being collected and distributed, and the CIA should do more of it.

The CIA should also step up its efforts in thwarting illegal intelligence efforts by foreign companies and governments.

According to Gates, foreign intelligence services are more inclined to operate against American targets outside the United States.

"They know there is a greater chance that American officials will detect an operation taking place on our own territory, and a greater likelihood of serious repercussions once the operation is detected," he told Congress in 1992. "Most services are consequently more aggressive inside their own countries where they can control the operating environment better and the legal environment is benign."

However, the CIA has pinpointed six patterns of competitive intelligence activities that are most likely to be promulgated by foreign government agencies against U.S. economic interests. Often, several actions coexist at the same time.

By learning which patterns are more likely to be perpetrated by certain countries the CIA can more efficiently allocate its resources. In addition, corporations themselves should be aware which patterns to expect in countries in which they operate.

It's important to remember that these are government-sanctioned activities that, because of their illegality, would.be unavailable to the U.S. intelligence community.

1. Classic espionage, in which foreign governments recruit agents to work for U.S. companies as moles. Their job is to remain undercover and send back to their intelligence agency information that could not have been obtained in a legal manner. Other activities might include setting up phony businesses to collect information.

In a high-profile case still under investigation, French intelligence placed agents inside French offices of IBM and Texas Instruments during the 1970s through late 1980s. The agents stole trade secrets and passed them along to French competitors.

2. Instead of outright recruitment, a foreign intelligence agency would subtly use foreign nationals living and working in the United States and visiting tourists to obtain information. Many of these people see this activity as a patriotic duty to help their country.

Several years ago, the U.S. Customs Service stopped an Egyptian C-130 plane ready to take off from Baltimore-Washington Airport. The plane contained missile components taken by an Egyptian national working in Sacramento.

3. The foreign intelligence agency itself engages in stealing information from visiting businesspeople. They may bug hotel rooms, search briefcases, and steal laptop computers.

The French intelligence agency DGSE has been accused by U.S. officials of these activities.

4. The foreign intelligence agency operates through trade associations, embassies, and other groups in the United States to systematically collect information mainly from publicly available sources. While this information may be public domain, their methods of collecting it—using phony credentials for example—are illegal.

The scientific section of the French embassy in Washington regularly collects large amounts of technical data for use by French firms. It hires people who often pose as academics doing research.

5. A foreign government targets specific weapons or other sensitive technology and uses special intelligence agencies reporting directly to top leaders to buy these items through front groups or military channels.

6. A relatively new pattern has emerged where freelance intelligence operatives sell their services to the highest bidder. The people

are often former government intelligence officers but may be well-connected nongovernment entrepreneurs.

In 1992, former Argentine intelligence officers were accused of planting more than five hundred wiretaps in offices of foreign companies and selling the information to local companies.

While I'm not suggesting that the CIA or any other agency inhibit legal and ethical collection by anyone, including foreign intelligence services, *the CIA should be vigilant in keeping track of the activities of foreign intelligence services outside the United States.*

Because the CIA is prohibited from operating within the United States, the FBI should also continue counterespionage efforts within our borders. In addition, the CIA should bolster its cooperation with the FBI to exchange information about illegal foreign activities within the United States. Although the two agencies try to work together in this area, in some cases their exchange of information has been less than adequate or cordial.

The CIA should also alter the way it provides information about industrial espionage activities.

Currently, the CIA disseminates information in four ways.

First, it provides information to the Congress and the president. Second, the CIA holds briefings for government contractors working on classified projects. Third, it works with the FBI to inform specific companies that they have been targeted by foreign agents. Fourth, the CIA informs other government agencies if a U.S. company has been the object of illegal intelligence operations. It is then up to that agency to inform the company so it can take appropriate measures to protect itself. If necessary, the CIA may contact the State Department if diplomatic responses are deemed necessary.

Currently, the CIA focuses on espionage and illegal activities directed against defense contractors and other related industries. There are few if any cases of the CIA informing companies in other industries about foreign activities directed against them.

In order to protect all U.S. industries from unfair and illegal intelligence gathering, the agency should look at all industries, not just those that support defense and weaponry or are considered critical. After all, the entertainment business is one of the United States' largest exports. Yet it isn't considered critical like the computer or aerospace industry; that should change.

Again, the CIA needs to move away from a military mentality when thinking about the effects of economic espionage.

In addition, the CIA, perhaps in cooperation with the FBI, should issue public bulletins about activities trends against U.S. companies that threaten American competitiveness.

Their approach to information should be open and timely, sanitized if necessary for legal considerations, but keeping this information hushed defeats the mission of keeping U.S. companies competitive.

The FBI's Development of Espionage and Counterintelligence Awareness Program (DECA), started in the late 1980s, is a good example of an organization that has taken on an educational role concerning U.S. businesses and espionage. The FBI operates DECA out of its existing field offices. At first the job of the DECA coordinator in each office was to visit companies that have received classified government contracts and keep them abreast of foreign intelligence threats. However, that job has been expanded to visits to companies not only engaged in classified contract work for the government but to companies involved in work that could make them targets of foreign espionage. Anyone can call the FBI and receive information about counterintelligence procedures for their company.

The latest FBI program, implemented in 1992, is called the National Security Threat List, which divides such threats into two categories:

Category A: A list of activities that, if confucted by a foreign power, would trigger a response from the FBI.

The activities that would trigger a response are:

1. Clandestine foreign intelligence activity in the United States.
2. Foreign intelligence activities involving the targeting of U.S. intelligence and foreign affairs information and U.S. government officials.
3. Foreign intelligence activity directed at the collection of information relating to defense establishments and related activities of foreign preparedness.
4. Foreign intelligence activities involved in the proliferation of special weapons of mass destruction, including chemical, biological, nuclear weapons, and delivery systems of those weapons of mass destruction.
5. Foreign intelligence activities directed at U.S. critical technologies as identified by the National Critical Technologies Panel. (These

critical technologies are within six categories: materials, manufacturing, information and communications, biotechnology and life sciences, aeronautics and surface transportation, and energy and environment.)

6. Foreign intelligence activities directed at the collection of U.S. industrial proprietary economic information and technology, the loss of which would undermine the U.S. strategic industrial position.

7. Foreign intelligence activities involving perception management and active measures activities.

This last one is fascinating because it shows the new interest by government in the power of information from foreign entities on the fabric of American life. *Perception management and active measures activities* are governmentese for secret operations that are designed to alter the perception of the public or U.S. officials of U.S. policies. These actions go beyond acceptable lobbying efforts by diplomats and others advocating their own country's position. To put it even more simply, we're talking about misinformation and propaganda campaigns.

Lest you think countries don't engage in misinformation campaigns in order to gain economic advantage, think again.

Several years ago a film showing deformed American babies allegedly injured by eating tainted U.S. food products was being shown throughout Japan in an effort to lower Japanese interest in buying American food. The film was produced by Japanese business groups linked to the Agricultural Ministry. Exporting American-produced food to Japan has always been difficult and government-supported propaganda programs make it harder.

From time to time, the Japanese government also supports misinformation campaigns aimed at discrediting United States–produced microchips and airplanes.

These seven criteria are rather broad, and allow the FBI to get involved in many cases of espionage or illegal information collection even in instances where the military or national defense, in the traditional sense, are not being compromised. The key to most of their involvement is the first criterion having to do with "clandestine foreign intelligence." This allows foreign governments to collect information legally and ethically in an open manner but not clandestinely.

Category B: A list of foreign powers whose activities have been deemed so hostile to U.S. national interests that they are actively monitored by the FBI.

This list is classified, but it's not difficult to guess which countries are on it based on current and past activities.

A Glimmer of Hope

When it comes to information flow, the U.S. government should resemble corporate America's best-in-class intelligence-gathering units. All foreign agencies, no matter what their purpose or mission, should be responsible for sending to Washington regular dispatches about business, industry, and general economic trends they have gleaned from publicly available sources. As mentioned, this information should then be available for dissemination in a timely manner to anyone who wants it. The same should be the case for domestic agencies as well.

We're beginning to see some movement in this area.

When President Clinton took office he made it clear that the CIA was to expand its role in economic intelligence, but, for the reasons already mentioned, this movement has been slow. However, we're starting to see some changes.

The newly formed Department of Commerce's Advocacy Center is helping U.S. companies cement huge deals overseas. By employing all the resources it has, and working with other agencies including the CIA, the center can aid companies in securing financing and sending government personnel to foreign countries as their representatives.

One project where agencies came together concerned a deal in 1995. A consortium of American firms including Enron, General Electric, and Bechtel was bidding on a billion-dollar power plant project near Bombay, India. The CIA was used to collect information about the risks of such big projects and also to look at what the competition was bringing to the table. Thanks to government help, the consortium won the contract.

What the government team did in this case was not unlike the intelligence efforts of many other countries.

In another instance, the CIA's expertise in counterintelligence helped seal a deal.

Raytheon and French Thomson were both bidding on a $1.5 billion project to establish an electronic surveillance system for monitoring environmental conditions in the Amazon rain forest. The equipment would detect poachers, illegal mining operations, and drug activities by using a network of radar and satellites.

The CIA learned that French officials were offering bribes to Brazilian officials to help curry favor and win the project.

U.S. officials exposed the French activity and matched the French financing terms. They won the contract. What worked here was exposing the illegal activity. It also gave notice to other countries that the CIA will be watching other large deals and that illegal intelligence will not be tolerated.

The U.S. government owes it to its citizenry that, as it has done in the past militarily, it will make certain that the country becomes the premier global economic power. Only through this economic power can the country not only be physically secure but also prosperous enough to reach its social goals both at home and abroad. Information and intelligence are the foundation of this economic strength.

CHAPTER NINETEEN

Competitive Intelligence— The Next Generation

"Think of the challenge this way: In a competitive world whose companies have access to the same data, who will excel at turning data into information and then analyzing the information quickly and intelligently enough to generate superior knowledge?"
    —former American Airlines chairman Max Hopper

"And all the future lies beneath your hat."
    —John Oldham, essayist, author

While managers at most American companies are still wondering what the heck competitive intelligence is all about—and if it's worth the investment—companies in Japan are already in the next generation.

The world's largest telecommunications/computer network for a single (non-telecommuncations) company was installed by 7-Eleven, Japan. The system connects more than four thousand stores, including their point-of-sale equipment—which were upgraded to meet the network's standards. The system, which began operation more than a decade ago, not only allows management to know instantly what product is selling where, the state of inventory at any moment, it also allows each store to collect and transmit business information and intelligence to top management so they can make better decisions.

Other Japanese companies have installed similar equipment. Toyota and Sony have connected factories with their administrative and sales offices around the world. This lets each facility act as a data-gathering unit, sending business and political information and intelligence to top management.

In all fairness, it should be noted that many U.S. firms use their existing e-mail systems to move information around and some even use their point-of-sale information to automatically gauge shipments to stores. However none use their networks to routinely and extensively move information and intelligence to top decision makers for strategic reasons.

Clearly, these large-scale networks are the future of competitive intelligence, but they will eventually play another role. *These competitive intelligence networks will one day be part of an overall social intelligence network that all countries must build in order to remain prosperous and compete for the world's resources.*

In the same way that business leaders need intelligence to make decisions, the same is true of social leaders.

In international affairs, for example, the president of the United States has relied on the CIA and others in the intelligence community to collect and analyze information, and offer courses of action. During wartime, the military relies on their intelligence apparatus to do the same. The Gulf War was won by United States–led forces, according to Commanding General Norman Schwarzkopf, because of their supreme intelligence. Or, as he also put it, because the Iraqis had very poor intelligence about their enemies' strengths and capabilities.

Let's take this a step further. Not only do political and business leaders need intelligence to do their jobs effectively, so do the citizenry and their institutions.

This free flow of intelligence will eventually take place when all facets of a society are interconnected and everyone acts as a collector of information, and everyone uses the intelligence that comes from that data.

We're not talking about domestic spying nor are we talking about a Big Brother–type scenario where the state spies on citizens to keep them in line.

What we're talking about is a national intelligence infrastructure that serves the interests of its citizens by supplying local, state, and national leaders as well as everyone else with the intelligence they need to make informed decisions.

Therefore, it behooves all companies to build their competitive intelligence programs so that they can become a part—a crucial part—of their country's overall intelligence network.

This national intelligence community consists of many parts, including government, companies, social groups and associations, media, schools, health care institutions, individuals, and labor unions.

The basic philosophy is to trade ideas, reading materials, concepts that can enrich everyone. Don't forget; we're not talking about trading secret information. We all have a basic right to keep information to ourselves, our families, and our institutions. We're talking about open-source information—data that is not hidden, not confidential, and not personally sensitive.

The intelligence community should become international in scope

The National Intelligence Community

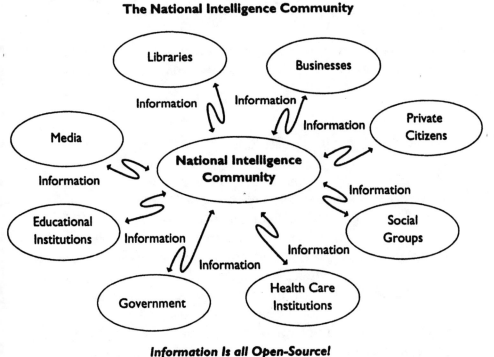

Information Is all Open-Source!

Figure 19-1

with countries' intelligence communities sharing and trading intelligence to benefit everyone.

The winners in tomorrow's world will not be those with the most information. They will be those with the most intelligence. As Max Hopper noted, those who can turn information into intelligence will be the ultimate winners.

There is a lot of talk these days about the information haves and have-nots. Social scientists estimate that many countries, the United States included, are already divided along financial lines with very rich and very poor people separated by huge gaps. The fear is that this gap will extend to information and intelligence as well. The belief is that we will again place poor people into a disadvantaged predicament unless we do things like put computers into all schools no matter how poor the neighborhood.

Everyone needs to learn how to use computers and everyone should be able to access as much information in as many channels as possible. However, more than 85 percent of the world's information is still available on hard copy (often *only* on hard copy), including books, magazines, newspapers, microfilm, and so on. While computers are excellent sources of information, they are not crucial to being an information have.

What's more important is that people have the skill to take information and turn it into usable intelligence; that innate ability has little to do with a person's social status.

Open-Source Information

One of the most exciting trends to come along in the world of intelligence is something called *open-source information.*

Simply put, open-source information is data that is available to anyone. Open-source information is another name for public-domain information. It's not classified, secret, or otherwise restricted and, if handled properly, can fulfill virtually all intelligence needs.

Even the world's political and military intelligence communities are moving toward open-source material—information that is available to everyone equally and openly. It's a name that is catching on among political intelligence agencies as well as among competitive intelligence practitioners.

Robert Steele, a former intelligence officer and founder of Open ' Source Solutions, a nonprofit educational association, is one of several proponents of open-source information. He claims that compared with information gained through special agents or extraordinary means, open-source information is not only cheaper but more than adequate for most anyone's needs. Use of open-source information eliminates much of the danger and compromising activities involved in traditional spying with little loss of information.

Open-source information proponents tend to divide information into four categories along with their corresponding expenses:

- Open Source (information that is available to anyone): Eighty percent of what is needed for sound decision making at 20 percent of the cost of using clandestinely obtained information.
- Open Proprietary (information you obtain legally through concentrated measures): This yields only 5 percent of what you need for an additional 10 percent of cost.
- Closed Proprietary (information you obtain through industrial espionage or clandestine technical operations such as wiretapping): This yields only 5 percent of what is needed for an additional 20 percent of cost.
- Classified (information that is closely held, perceived to be of great strategic value, and only gotten through clandestine human or technical operations such as spy satellites): Ten percent of what is required for an additional 50 percent cost increment.

Clearly, open-source material is the best value for the money. However, money is not the only cost savings.

As mentioned, information collectors pay another price for operating clandestine operations. First there is the cost of human life. Spies can be killed in the line of duty by those who don't want their secret information taken.

A second cost is the toll secret operations take on those who collect and analyze secretly obtained information. There is the personal stress of working with secret information, of analyzing it in private, restricting access, and not even being able to tell family or friends what they do every day. There is as well the added psychic cost of knowing that the enemy is trying to take your information away.

Countries pay a price in prestige and image when they spy. Since the end of World War II, many countries, especially the United States, have been embarrassed by the operations of their clandestine agencies. Time and again, nations have come to the brink of war, trust has been broken over incidents of espionage and secret operations that have gotten out of hand. It is not naive to think that even the most important intelligence could be derived from open-source material if we are smart enough to interpret and analyze what is already out there.

Those who advocate open-source information for everything—including political and military needs—say that we could eliminate many problems by only using open-source material.

We would eliminate not only the regular out-of-pocket costs but also the psychic costs that I've just outlined. Could we ever eliminate all political or military clandestine operations? Maybe not, but we could come so close that expensive intelligence operations could have their budgets slashed and that money put to better use.

Then, of course, it's proper to ask: "How do I get an advantage over my competitor if we all have the same information?"

With open-source material, the great advantage must be obtained from speed and human interpretation skills.

During a lecture at the Army War College in Washington, D.C., a navy wing commander commented on spying and information this way: "If it is 85 percent accurate, on time, and I can share it, that information is a lot more useful to me than a compendium of top secret codeword information that is too much, too late, and requires a safe and three security officers to move it around the battlefield."

As we learned in the section on OPSEC, old methods of security can slow down the intelligence process.

The competitive advantage in open-source information comes to those who can obtain information the quickest, analyze it fastest, and exploit it before their competition.

To gain a competitive advantage you must know information before it becomes a secret, to learn something before your competitor knows that the information is valuable and keeps it a secret.

If you read something in the newspaper and act on the information before your competitors, that is tantamount to that information being secret, isn't it?

This technique requires computers and telecommunications capability, something we already have in most cases. More important, it requires that everyone become a collector of information. Information collection and dissemination must become decentralized and open to everyone.

A vision of the future that I share is one of open sources in which all citizens become part of the information collection process, that information easily moves around, and that each person, government, or business uses the information in its own way for its own purposes.

Despite what you might think, this doesn't lead to a national or global "dumbing down" where, because we all have access to the same information, we all come to the same conclusions and therefore nothing progresses. On the contrary, each of us has different needs and different purposes for information. What I need in my business may not be important to your company. This holds for countries as well.

What will happen instead, I suggest, is that we will learn how to exploit the same information in unique ways. We will learn new ways of thinking and analyzing that can be passed on to others. Just like benchmarking eventually leads to better products and services, sharing information leads to more social progress.

In the future, information will become cheap and accessible to even the poorest people, but they can become prosperous if they can turn it into intelligence that they can exploit.

In the future, everyone will be a *collector of information* and everyone will be a *consumer of intelligence*.

Glossary of Competitive Intelligence

Analysis The process of taking information—often seemingly unconnected information—and turning it into intelligence.

Benchmarking The process of continuously comparing and measuring a company against the best-in-class to gain information that will help the organization improve its performance.

Classified Information Information that is closely held, perceived to be of great strategic value, and gotten only through clandestine operations.

Closed Proprietary Information Information obtained through industrial espionage or clandestine technical operations such as wiretapping.

Critical Success Factors Those tasks that have to be completed for a company to succeed. Learning a company's CSFs is crucial for understanding its competitive intelligence activities.

Hard Information Information that is quantitative.

Humint Human intelligence, what you learn directly from people as opposed to reading documents.

Information Unfiltered, raw data such as facts, numbers, statistics; scattered bits about people, companies, and industries.

Information Audit Seeking and discovering what information is already in your company and how to retrieve it for use by the competitive intelligence unit and everyone else.

Intelligence Information that has been filtered, distilled, and analyzed. It has been turned into something that can be acted upon.

Intelligence Cycle The four steps in turning information into usable intelligence: 1) planning and direction; 2) collection; 3) analysis; and 4) dissemination.

JETRO Japanese External Trade Organization, part of MITI. Its official mission is to support trade between Japan and other countries. Its major role is to act as a source of competitive intelligence for Japanese industry.

Keiretsu A group of individual Japanese companies united by the exchange and sharing among them of personnel, money, goods, and information.

Mission Statements The operational, ethical, and financial guides of companies. Other names include philosophies, goals, game plan, beliefs, vision, and values. They expound the goals, dreams, behavior, culture, and strategies of companies. Mission statements offer excellent insights into competitors.

MITI Ministry of International Trade and Industry. The Japanese government entity responsible for establishing policies to promote industrial development.

Moment of Change A short time in a company's life in which it is undergoing a massive change or upheaval. During these times the media produces many stories, and the company itself generates large amounts of paperwork resulting in public-domain information.

Open-source Information Another name for public-domain information. It is data that is available to anyone.

Open Proprietary Information Information you obtain legally through concentrated measures.

OPSEC Operational Security. A tactic that protects both public-domain and proprietary information without the unnecessary bother and expense of keeping large amounts of information under lock and key.

Primary Sources Unadulterated facts directly from the source. It could be a company CEO, president, government agency, or someone else who has access to absolute and correct information. It's information that has not been changed, altered, or otherwise tainted by opinion or selection.

Public-domain Information A vast sea of data that is open and available to anyone who seeks it.

Secondary Sources Altered information, but not necessarily inaccurate, such as in newspaper and magazine articles.

Soft Information Information that is qualitative, not just numbers and statistics.

Sogo Shosha Japanese trading company that is at the heart of each keiretsu. They provide financing, marketing, management services, consulting services, and competitive intelligence services.

SWOT Strength, Weaknesses, Opportunities, and Threats. A matrix-type technique for analyzing a competitor.

Trade Secret a) That which is used in one's business and which gives the holder an opportunity to obtain an advantage over competitors who do not know or use it, or, b) A program, device, method, technique, or process that is kept confidential from outsiders. It is not readily obtainable by proper means by other persons who could obtain economic value from its disclosure or use.

War-Gaming Analysis technique in which teams of people take on the persona of their competitors and themselves. In the course of the game, strategies and plans are proposed, acted out, and tested in as real a simulation of business conditions as possible.

Acknowledgments

Many people have helped me to produce this book. Some spent many hours, over many days, sharing their information, intelligence, and expertise. Others spent only a short time with me, enough to answer a quick question or two and get me back on the right track through their insight. I would like to thank the following for their contributions:

Cyndi Allgaier, Prof. Walter Barndt, Philippe Baumard, Alan Bergstrom, Jean-Marie Bonthous, Faye Brili, Pat Bryant, Herb Clough, Prof. Stevan Dedijer, Rich Dooley, Prof. Jeffrey Ellis, Prof. Liam Fahey, Robert Flynn, Leonard Fuld, Dr. Ian Fyfe, Andy Garvin, Daniel Gautschoux, Prof. Ben Gilad, Jan Herring, Dan Himmelfarb, Bonnie Hohhof, George Hosking, Prof. Bernard Jaworski, Pat Jones, Leila Kight, Guy Kolb, Tim Krol, C.J. Kurtz, Reto Lippold, Mark Lowenthal, Robert Margulies, George Marling, Mike Meurisse, Mary Ellen Mogee, Juro Nakagawa, Francis Narin, Michael O'Guin, Cheryl Poirier, Tim Powell, John Prescott, Gil Press, Vernon Prior, John Quinn, Joseph H. A. M. Rodenburg, Gary Rousch, Seena Sharp, Robert Steele, Susan Steinhardt, Burke Stinson, Karen Wolters, and Larry Zilliox, Jr. I would also like to thank the staffs of the Society of Competitive Intelligence Professionals and the American Society for Industrial Security for their assistance.

Most important, I would like to thank my agent, Gordon Kato, and my editor, Bob Asahina, for their support and guidance.

Index

About the Author

Larry Kahaner is an award-winning journalist, author, and licensed private investigator. He is founder and president of Alexandria, Virginia-based KANE Associates International, Inc., a firm that specializes in intelligence matters for corporate clients.

Kahaner has written five books including *Say It and Live It,* which was translated into five languages, and the best-selling *Cults That Kill.* He is a former Washington correspondent for *Business Week* magazine, a founding editor of *Communications Daily* and a reporter for The Columbus, Georgia, *Ledger-Enquirer.* Kahaner has written for many newspapers and magazines including *The Washington Post, The International Herald Tribune, The Christian Science Monitor, Omni* magazine, *Popular Science* and *Wilderness.* He has appeared on CNN's *Larry King Live!,* CNBC's *Management Today, Evening Magazine,* National Public Radio's *All Things Considered, CBS Evening News* and local TV and radio stations throughout North America. He lectures at companies, police academies, and colleges.

He is a member of the Society of Competitive Intelligence Professionals and the American Society for Industrial Security. You can reach him at lkahaner@access.digex.net.

Printed in the United States
103942LV00005B/190-249/P